BROTHERS AND FRIENDS

BROTHERS AND FRIENDS

Kinship in Early America

NATALIE R. INMAN

The University of Georgia Press

ATHENS

Paperback edition, 2020

© 2017 by the University of Georgia Press

Athens, Georgia 30602

www.ugapress.org

Most University of Georgia Press titles are available from popular e- book vendors.

Printed digitally

Library of Congress Cataloging- in- Publication Data

Names: Inman, Natalie Rishay. author.
Title: Brothers and friends : kinship in early America / Natalie R. Inman.
Other titles: Early American places.
Description: Athens, Georgia : The University of Georgia Press, [2017] | Series: Early
    American places | Includes bibliographical references and index.
Identifiers: LCCN 2016055415 | ISBN 9780820351094 (hardback : alk. paper) |
    ISBN 9780820351100 (ebook)
Subjects: LCSH: Kinship—United States—History—18th century. | Kinship—United
    States—History—19th century. | Families—United States—History—18th
    century. | Families—United States—History—19th century. | Cherokee Indians—
    Kinship. | Chickasaw Indians—Kinship. | Donaldson family. | Social networks—
    United States—History.
Classification: LCC HQ535 .I56 2017 | DDC 306.850973—dc23 LC record available at
    https://lccn.loc.gov/2016055415

ISBN 9780820357867 (paperback : alk. paper)

Contents

Introduction: Comparing Families in Cultural and Political Borderlands

In 1853, eighty-year-old Joseph Brown, a resident of Tennessee, gave several interviews telling of his experiences as a teenager. Brown told audiences that he had been traveling with his family on flatboats in 1788 when his boat was boarded by Chickamauga Cherokee Indians, a faction of Cherokees that had declared war on those moving into their hunting grounds in the region that would become Tennessee. During the raid, Brown's father was killed in front of him. He recalled that when a "dirty, black looking Indian" robbing their boat was "about to kill" him, his father saved him, but at the cost of his own life:

> The Indian then let me go, but as soon as my father's back was turned, he struck him with the sword, and cut his head nearly half off. Another Indian then caught my father, and threw him over-board. I saw him go overboard, but did not know that he was struck with the sword; it astonished me, therefore, to see him sink down, as I knew him to be a good swimmer. As this took place in the stern, and my brothers and the other young men were with Vann [the Chickamauga man who translated for the group of Indians] in the bow, I went to them, and told them that an Indian had thrown our father overboard, and he was drowned.[1]

Joseph Brown, then fifteen years old, was led, along with several other children and women, to a nearby village to spend the night. The captive men stayed on board to travel farther downstream to another village. After a few minutes, Brown heard gunfire that signaled to him the end of his older brothers' lives. Brown and his younger siblings were taken into the Chickamauga towns, where they were ritually adopted. Families took them in and treated them as they did other children in the towns. Brown noted that when he came to Nickajack town with his Indian family/captors, he "found there the Indian who had [his] little sister. . . . [T]he old squaw seemed to think as much of her as though she had been her own child."[2] His sister did not want to return to her relatives in the Cumberland settlements. Although his sister had emotionally accepted her adoption while she was at Running Water, Brown did not accept his. Nearly a year later, however, they were returned to their former community as part of a captive exchange. A few years later, in 1794, Joseph Brown would serve as the guide who would help the Cumberland troops find and then decimate the Chickamauga towns.[3]

Joseph Brown's story highlights the ways ideas of family and kinship networks were constructed and reconstructed in the colonial and early republic eras. While Brown's sister accepted the Indian family who adopted her, Brown rejected his, remained loyal to the family of his birth, and vowed to have revenge on his adoptive family. In early America familial relationships were sometimes fluid, flexing with the needs of a family, clan, or tribe. At other times, the cultural constructs of family were rigid and unyielding. Brown had seen his father killed and presumably heard his brothers shot. He would not accept a new family in place of loyalty to his old one. Whereas Cherokees and Chickasaws often incorporated Anglo-Americans into their systems of kinship through adoption and marriage, Anglo-Americans were often less willing to cross cultural boundaries to forge alliances. The definitions of kinship relationships and responsibilities were important to each of these groups during the colonial and early republic eras in American history. They were also, however, culturally defined and representative of divisions as well as commonalities.

Kinship networks facilitated actions and goals for people in early America across cultures, even if the definitions and constructions of family were different in each society. These networks help us to understand why and how the intercultural relations of the colonial and early republic eras happened the way they did. Each of the chapters in this book explains the formation and extension of these networks, their intersection with other types of personal, political, and business networks, their impact upon key events in the history of the eras, and how they changed over time. By following kinship networks in Cherokee, Chickasaw, and Anglo-American societies from 1750 to 1850, this book uses case studies from each society to illustrate how these networks worked at ground level, facilitating and directing the actions of their members as they decided the futures of their people.

In the trans-Appalachian South, familial relationships had profound effects upon the broader course of events during this period of extreme change. Kinship networks helped to further political and economic agendas at both personal and national levels even through wars, revolutions, economic change, and removals. Comparative analysis of family case studies provides a foundation for understanding how the institution of family shaped intercultural negotiations between these three groups, as well as how this interaction changed definitions of family in each of these cultures. This analysis adds new perspectives to the historiography of early America by revealing the connections between the social institution of family, politics, and economies. It also provides historical context for the role of family and kinship networks within colonial and imperial contexts that can be compared to other works within the genre of global imperial and colonial studies.[4]

Historians of the trans-Appalachian South have long recognized the complicated nature of the intercultural negotiation, the push-pull of diplomacy and warfare, and the personal level at which people interacted there. These people and governments operated in a contested borderland, in which they frequently crossed the political and cultural boundaries of the U.S., Cherokee, and Chickasaw polities for travel, trade, and warfare. These relationships must be recognized as a force in U.S. and other national histories.[5] The trans-Appalachian frontier was embroiled in intense competition among native peoples as well as the English, French, Spanish, and Americans for political and economic control of the region. The national, imperial, and Atlantic world contexts that shaped British, Spanish, and French attempts to gain control over the region also came to influence American Indian patterns of war and negotiation that had long shaped regional political boundaries. Kinship networks (forged out of birth, marital, and fictive kinship relationships) shaped their diplomatic and military tactics, as such networks had shaped the politics of native and European competitions for centuries. Understanding the role of kinship networks in these conflicts is central to understanding American history as it provides clear pictures of the motivations and the methods behind the major events of the time.[6]

Historians of the early republic period have for the past two decades challenged the assertion that kinship networking was no longer relevant to Americans after they had shed the husk of British aristocracy and patronage in the Revolution. Lorri Glover, Carolyn Billingsley, and many others have argued that Americans of British descent continued to utilize their familial connections in the early republic era as political and economic networks as well as for social support.[7] The Anglo-American patrilineal kinship system shaped patterns of descent, inheritance, and migration. Patriarchal fathers on the trans-Appalachian frontier, like John Donelson, encouraged their children to engage in specific economic, social, and political ventures as land speculators, lawyers, military officers, and politicians, creating an informal monopoly on land and influence through their kinship ties. Similarly, scholars of American Indian history including Theda Perdue, Andrew Frank, Cynthia Cumfer, and others have argued that kinship networks were foundational to the ways American Indian politics worked, both internally and diplomatically. Clans provided the avenue to political voice, connections between towns, and protection from enemies.[8] Bringing these two trends together creates a more complete understanding of how these interpersonal relationships guided both sides during intercultural negotiation of the early republic era. The importance of kinship networks was not diminished by the American Revolution, nor were kinship networks characteristic of backward, tribal, or monarchical societies. Kinship networking was among the most powerful forces behind early American politics and economics across cultures throughout the long eighteenth century. This book connects American history and American Indian history by recognizing the influence of kinship networking within this highly contested place in early America as illustrated in family case studies relevant to both historical traditions.

This work also builds upon the larger historiographical field of imperial and colonial studies. Beyond the British Atlantic world, these case studies can be compared to other colonial contexts in which the cultures and families of Europeans collided with native peoples in the Americas, Africans, Australia, and other contexts. Anne Hyde, Ann Laura Stoler, and Richard C. Trexler have provided exemplary works on gender, kinship, and colonialism that are part of the global discourse on colonial interpersonal relationships that informs this comparative analysis.[9]

Better understanding of the roles that familial relationships played in intercultural negotiation between American Indians and Anglo-Americans requires the use of shared terms. Humanists and social scientists have often boxed Anglo-American families into nuclear, patrilineal units and American Indians into clan-based kinship systems, neither of which allows for the flexibility and cross-cultural similarities characteristic of the families studied here. Therefore, this book defines the terms "family" and "kinship networks" so that both terms are applicable to the history of native and Anglo-American actors.[10]

American historians in particular have emphasized the "rugged individualism" of individuals and nuclear families rather than recognizing their interconnectedness and interdependence on extended family networks. "Kinship networks," on the other hand, traditionally brings to mind large groups of people or family gatherings in which kin relationships were dictated by tradition and blood relations rather than by personal interaction and affective relationships. "Kinship" has been much more frequently applied to the American Indian context than to that of Anglo-Americans. However, historians can talk about American Indian "families" in addition to "kinship" or "kin groups" and Anglo-American families as kin without limiting the conversation to nuclear households. Challengers to the European nuclear definition of family have argued that terms such as "family" and "friendship" had multiple definitions, even within English society.[11]

Joseph M. Hawes and Elizabeth I. Nybakken argued that the colonial family was "viewed as a little kingdom that produced most of the goods and services required by its members. Providing sustenance, shelter, job training, religious instruction, and care for the young, sick, and elderly was the collective responsibility of each unit . . . [under the direction of the patriarch]."[12] This system, they argue, transitioned with increasing modernization to one focused on the nuclear household in the late eighteenth and early nineteenth centuries. The Anglo-American and American Indian families on the trans-Appalachian frontier, however, did not make such an easy transition. The records left behind by the Donelsons, Colberts, Ridges, and others reflect an ongoing dependence on extended family networks to facilitate success in the competitive environment of the frontier during that time.

Historians' definitions of nuclear households and nuclear families often obscure the interactions within, and between, kinship networks that shaped larger political and economic institutions. Similarly, maintaining the division between extended family and clan-like family types reinforces difference rather than the commonalities that allow for comparison. In this book, "family" refers to the group of individuals and their parents, siblings, grandparents, aunts, uncles, nieces, nephews, and others they deemed kin whether these relationships were natal, marital, or fictive. Households on the trans-Appalachian frontier were not exclusively nuclear but rather maintained a fluidity that reflected the needs of the family as well as the ways that family could benefit from embracing extended family ties, both within and between households. Families chose for practical, traditional, or ambitious reasons to maintain extended familial ties.

Kinship systems analysis has been used in anthropological, sociological, and historical circles since the end of the nineteenth century. While this book draws on their theoretical framework, for the reader's ease and to facilitate cross-cultural analysis I define "kinship networks" as the system or organization of people related through blood, marriage, and adoption extending through the branches of family trees in many directions. We can think of kinship networks as a variation on the concept of a family tree. The branches connect living relatives (members of a family), providing those individuals with access to one another and conveying responsibilities on each to respond to their kin in culturally defined ways. These relationships were binding but also mutable. If a kinship tie was found to be unproductive, the members might choose not to utilize that relationship. Rather than strictly fixed relationships, the political and economic roles of kinship were flexible for both American Indians and Anglo-Americans.[13] Kinship networks knit these family ties together to provide a safety net or a ladder for advancement. Together, these definitions of family and kinship networks provide a common vocabulary with which to compare and contrast native and Anglo-American institutions of family and the functionality of their kinship networks.

Families were culturally constructed groups of related individuals who adhered to culturally specific definitions of familial responsibilities. For example, brothers owed each other a particular kind of loyalty in each of these societies, but the precise responsibilities varied by culture. These variants provided the basis for intercultural communication and miscommunication.

Anglo-American kinship networks were based upon a patrilineal kinship system. Names, inheritances, and reputations were passed down from a father to his children. Men exercised authority over their children's education, discipline, and often their future endeavors. Sons owed obedience to their fathers. Women held significantly less influence within society and the household than did their husbands or grown sons. Therefore, women received minimal exposure in the historical record despite their importance in families and kinship networks. The extended kinship network of the Donelson family operated within this context but also embraced marital and natal kin, ensuring a solid base for economic alliances when opportunities permitted.

Several historians and anthropologists have highlighted the central role of matrilineal kinship in the social organization of Southeastern Indians in the late eighteenth century.[14] While in many ways a nephew's relationship to his uncle in a matrilineal society was characterized by loyalty and obedience similar to that a son owed a father in English society, inheritance of one's position depended upon several factors. One man might have had several sisters and dozens of maternal nieces and nephews, and a child might have had many maternal uncles. Aptitude and capability, however, also played a central role in the selection of how a leader might be trained for his or her future place in this society. James Adair, writing in 1775, noted that "the Indian method of government . . . consists in a federal union of the whole society for mutual safety. . . . The power of their chiefs, is an empty sound. They can only persuade or dissuade the people. . . . It is reputed merit alone, that gives them any titles of distinction above the meanest of the people."[15] Rather than revealing tension between the importance of kinship to Southeastern native societies and their individualistic political systems, the two worked together as within large households aptitude determined which nephew, or even niece, would be trained to take up the mantle of clan or town leadership.[16] Clans were established through the women in this society, and they influenced the tribe accordingly. Anthropologist Charles Hudson described clans as "a category of people who believed themselves to be blood relatives [through the mother's bloodline], but who could not actually trace their relationships to each other through known ancestral links" which encompassed extended family, known and unknown, throughout the town and region.[17]

Both clans and women, however, were often ignored by the Anglo-Americans who wrote the documents at the time. As a result, the treaties and letters that form the archival basis for this study ensure that this is a book largely about men and masculinity. Women in each of the represented societies were central to the functioning of families themselves, but these functions are difficult to glean from diplomatic sources. Women in Anglo-American society were active parties in uniting families in marriage, central to maintaining the households, raising the children, running the home or the family business in the absence of the patriarch, and were active in communicating with family and even business associates to keep the family economies steady or improving. They often voiced their opinions on issues of familial importance, including the induction of new kin through marriage. While they were rarely part of the intercultural negotiation that showed up in the treaties and formal relationships between Anglo and Indian polities, they were just as present as the men, which meant they were physically involved in supporting the men defending their homes, they were among those captured in raids, they were party to business transactions, and they were the ones bearing the children who would be the next generation of diplomats and "Indian fighters." They educated their children and passed on stories that shaped their children's views of themselves and those around them. Much of this action, however, is not included in the sources that provide the foundation of this study.

Cherokee women served as clan leaders and were consulted on matters of great importance. Despite this, few documents recorded their part in diplomatic negotiations. Similarly the Women's Council weighed in on important issues and even issued challenges to the men making decisions that they found counter to the good of the clan, town, or tribe. Some of these were recorded in the early and mid-nineteenth century as they were presented by Nan-ye-hi, or Nancy Ward. The impact of these statements is not clear for historians, although it is clear that Cherokee men and men who married into the Cherokee nation continued to do the things against which Ward and the Women's Council spoke, like selling tribal land. Cherokee women initiated and ended marital alliances, weighed in on decisions regarding diplomacy, land sales, removal, and other subjects, determined the fate of captives, farmed the land belonging to their clan, processed food and clothing, and served in many functions that were not recorded.

Even fewer sources exist on Chickasaw women's roles in family and kinship relations. They had kinship structures within "house groups" as well as within clans and were often involved in plural marriages in which a husband would have more than one wife. They engaged in many of the same activities as the Cherokee women, but even fewer sources referred to specific Chickasaw women and their actions. Those that do mention Chickasaw women hint that they could be quite a force in their own right. From suing their husbands for property in Mississippi's state court system before Mississippi women could legally own property to mitigating the challenges of Indian removal, the stories of Chickasaw women in this book point toward their resourcefulness, determination, and knowledge of the political climate of the time. Although the sources are sparse, they indicate that much more went on behind the scenes than treaty papers and official correspondence indicated.

While Anglo-Americans did stay in touch with extended family through correspondence, they did not have a parallel institution to clans.

However, as they found themselves a minority in native-claimed territory, they began to invoke the racial category of whiteness as a way of creating bonds with other Anglo-Americans in Indian country and as a way to distinguish themselves from their "red" neighbors. The case studies in this book are of families that intersected the cultural and political boundaries of the time. This meant that many of the native families studied left written sources because an Anglo-American married into them. Thus the case studies are less representative and more a study into the families of some of the most influential figures of the time.

Within their democratic systems of government, Chickasaw, Cherokee, and Anglo-American societies created traditions of leadership that grew out of the relationship between kinship networks and politics. Kin-based factions in Chickasaw and Cherokee governments stemmed from the decentralized nature of those governments, allowing these groups additional freedom to negotiate with multiple native and imperial powers but also sometimes straining the relationship between their governments and those with whom they treated. Towns provided the central unit of government for Chickasaws, Cherokees, and other native peoples within the region. The relationship between kinship and government among the Chickasaws had the added complexity of including moieties, or divisions between peace and war clans, which facilitated the emergence of leaders to fulfill particular roles. Connections between kinship and politics within the U.S. political system were deemed nepotism, but they existed nonetheless, entangling the public interest with their town-related and familial goals. Over time, Cherokee and Chickasaw matrilineal kinship systems began to be replaced by a hybrid system born out of Anglo-American pressures on the tribes to "become civilized," or assimilate Anglo-American cultural practices. Comparing these systems and their change over time brings to light parallels between native and Anglo-American uses of kinship networks in politics.

Stories of the Chickasaw Colbert family, the Anglo-American Donelson family, and the Cherokee families of Little Carpenter and Major Ridge illuminate how kinship networks shaped early American politics and economy. Because these families included influential political and military leaders, their use of kinship networks helped to determine policies for each of their governments. I chose these families as case studies because of their influence in the regional and national politics of their people but also because they left sources for investigation of the role of kinship networks in their personal and political decision making. Such networks helped determine the power relations between native and non-native polities in their political contests in the colonial and early republic eras. The conflicts surrounding the Cumberland region borderland illustrates in detail what was at stake in intercultural negotiation, not solely for this region but with consequences in national politics and for the broader history of the interaction between native groups, European empires, and the United States. Family goals remained a central motivating factor for undertaking risky economic and political ventures for the leadership of each of these polities, as well as an important means for achieving success in those endeavors. The actions of each of these families were controversial within their own political contexts.

The sons of Scots trader James Logan Colbert—William, George, Levi, and James—emerged as chiefs of the Chickasaw nation in the 1780s and remained influential representatives of the Chickasaw even after the tribe emigrated to Indian Territory (present-day Oklahoma). From the prominent Incunnomar house,[18] these men utilized their dual heritage as cultural brokers to serve the diplomatic interests of the Chickasaw people. The Colbert kinship network fought against the Cherokees as allies of South Carolina during the Anglo-Cherokee War that broke out during the larger French and Indian War, engaged in military campaigns against Spanish boats on the Mississippi during the American Revolution, and fought alongside the United States in the Northwest Territory wars in the 1790s and again during the Creek War. The Colberts also took advantage of the changing economy. In 1805, the Colberts helped to secure permission for a great road to be built through the Chickasaw nation with the condition that only Chickasaws could own or run taverns on the road to service the travelers. The Colbert family owned most of these establishments and profited from the large number of Anglo-Americans traveling south through Chickasaw territory. William, George, and Levi Colbert also amassed wealth in the form of plantations and slaves, mirroring the practices of the most affluent Anglo-American planters of the time. When the Indian Removal Act of 1830 threatened Chickasaw lands and government, Levi Colbert led negotiations to minimize the cost in lives and financial assets by determining the terms for, and implementation of, Chickasaw removal. The history of the Colbert family provides insight into how political and economic strategies of American Indians could so thoroughly adopt pieces of "Western culture" while retaining Indian identities and sovereignty.

Members of the Donelson family, including Col. John Donelson and Gen. Andrew Jackson, orchestrated plans to elevate their wealth and prestige through creating marital alliances between prominent families, land speculation, and seeking political office. Jackson in particular left records indicating his active efforts to encourage marriages that would add individuals with social or monetary assets to the family. These connections added different varieties of security to the kinship network in an environment of warfare, rapid change, and opportunity. The networking strategies of the Donelson family were typical among families that aspired to capitalize on their existing wealth and increase both their wealth and prestige in the fluid and fertile environment of the land booms of the early republic era. The family of John Donelson emigrated from eastern Virginia to western Virginia, then on to the Watauga Settlements in what would become East Tennessee, and finally helped to lead one of Nashville's founding expeditions. This family capitalized on the booming land market to become upwardly mobile and eventually become part of the local and national political and economic elite. As the new nation continued to grow, this family would become prominent members of North Carolina, Tennessee, Alabama, and Mississippi society. For the Donelson family, kinship networks served as key social networks tying together individuals, including Senator Daniel Smith and future president Andrew Jackson, who could help each other climb professional ladders in law, politics, and business. Analysis of how kinship networks helped to build wealth among elite westerners helps to explain the enormous growth of influence and prestige in the region that swayed Congress and the presidency toward political measures like the Indian Removal Act that profited the western territories during the early republic and antebellum eras.

While the Colbert and Donelson families leave relatively clear genealogical records, records of Cherokee families in the period leave much to be desired. Most often British and American observers left records noting father/son relationships and, more rarely, uncle/nephew relationships, but they rarely noted the names of the wives, mothers, sisters, and aunts upon whom the matrilineal kinship system rested. For this reason, this book looks at two prominent Cherokee families that played important roles in the political and economic negotiation of the Cherokee nation. These Cherokee families represent the movements for and against alliances with the British and the Americans, as well as the variety of methods of political and economic negotiation employed by representatives of the Cherokee nation. As leaders of peace and war factions, the kinship networks they drew upon reflected the centrality of family and clan affiliation to their political and economic strategies. It is for these reasons that this book details the actions of mostly the men in these families. The families were hugely influential rather than representative. This book, therefore, is about familial networking, but mostly as it reflects masculine ideals and ambitions.

The first of these families was led by Attakullakulla, the renowned diplomat also called Little Carpenter. He served as both a war chief and an advocate for peace from the 1730s through 1777. He was among the best-known Cherokees of that time and frequently appeared in the historical record as the main negotiator between the Cherokees and the British. His son and niece both held important political positions in the tribe, shaping the negotiation between the Cherokee nation and their settler neighbors. The lineage from Little Carpenter to his niece Nancy Ward and grand-nieces hints at a tradition of peaceful accommodation and emphasis on trade alliances with the Anglo-Americans. Dragging Canoe, Little Carpenter's son, resisted accommodation and declared war on those who sought to pressure Cherokees into selling their hunting grounds in the Cumberland region. The relationships of these figures illustrate how matrilineal kinship networks guided the reactions of these actors to increasing pressures on Cherokee lands as well as give insight into internal tensions within the Cherokees over how to respond to Anglo-American encroachment.

The second family was led by The Ridge, who fought as an ally of Andrew Jackson in the Creek War of 1813–14 after which he self-identified as Major Ridge. He later became infamous as the leader of the "Treaty Party" that signed the Treaty of New Echota, which ensured removal of the tribe to Indian Territory. The actions of Major Ridge's son John Ridge and nephews Elias Boudinot and Stand Watie showed how both matrilineal and patrilineal influences shaped their lives, including their attitudes toward American culture, Cherokee political sovereignty, and their duties to their family. This family depicts both the changes that kinship underwent in the early nineteenth century and the ways that kinship networks were used to effect both change and continuity in the Cherokee nation.

Together these case studies present kinship networks as a common tool for implementing Chickasaw, Anglo-American, and Cherokee political and economic strategies at the local, regional, and, at times, national levels. They further illustrate that the culturally defined definitions of family and kinship networks created a basis for understanding and misunderstanding one another in intercultural negotiation.

Comparative methodology provides the foundation for the argument that not only were kinship networks central to the societies of the Cherokees and Chickasaws, but they were also central to the economic and even political practices of the early American Anglo-American society. The actions of the Donelson family, which would come to include Andrew Jackson and his descendants, prove that kinship ties played a very strong role in their upward mobility as both individuals and as a family unit. As land speculators, Indian agents, treaty negotiators, and policy makers, the Donelson family created a network resembling a vertical integration business model that facilitated the acquisition and distribution of Indian lands. These lands were transformed into the basis of wealth for the family and the nation. Instead of American dependence upon kinship ties declining with the end of monarchical government, the Donelson family's kinship networking increased following the American Revolution.[19] Kinship networking did not belong primarily to simplistic, clan-based, or monarchical societies in opposition to the modern American nation-state; it retained its importance. While Cherokee and Chickasaw structures of families and uses of kinship networks were much more similar to each other than to those of Anglo-Americans, the similar use of kinship networks in political and economic strategies across all three groups belies that contrasting of native and Euro-American societies.

The importance of interpersonal relationships is key to understanding the roles kinship networks played in the early republic era across cultural and ethnic lines. People chose who they would call upon to fulfill the cultural obligations associated with kinship ties. They decided which of their kin would be good business partners and which proved far greater liabilities than assets. In each of these familial case studies, concepts of family and kinship networks mediated the political and economic decisions of individuals, families, and the nations they represented. Family provided the foundation for reliable alliances within and across ethnic lines. Kinship networks were, of course, not the only set of interpersonal relationships at work. Historians are working to tease out the roles town and community played in each of these societies. Friendship and ideological networks also played important roles in the intercultural negotiation of early America. Histories of nationalism and democratic ideologies have improved our understanding of how political ideas were disseminated, adopted, and made potent. This same historiography has obscured the ways personal networks shaped those ideas and the political process. Due to time and space considerations, this book, however, will address these subjects only as they relate to the function of these familial networks.

Historians must look beyond the local and institutional role of family to see how it fundamentally shaped the thought and behavior of key actors in the national history of the United States, as well as in Cherokee and Chickasaw politics. These personal relationships guided the socioeconomic and political goals of Little Carpenter, Andrew Jackson, Levi Colbert, Major Ridge, and others at crucial moments for their peoples. Family strategies and personal ambitions became possible through the engagement of kinship networks. This cannot be separated from the ways these politicians viewed their political and economic worlds or their responsibilities as influential political leaders. In all three of these societies, family responsibilities were intertwined with all aspects of the personal and political lives of their members.

1 / Founding Networks, 1740–1765

In 1756, Attakullakulla, a Cherokee headman known to the British as "Little Carpenter," described his understanding of the relationship between Anglo-American kinship and the Anglo-Indian trade in his speech to Capt. Raymond Demere, the commanding officer at Fort Prince George near Keowee Town on the border of South Carolina. Little Carpenter argued that a trader named Elliott "imposed upon [the Cherokees] in a most barbarous Manner" and monopolized the trade. He had "heard that Elliott was related to [South Carolina's] Governor [James] Glen and that he was concerned in the Trade with him which has surprised [Little Carpenter] very much."[1] Little Carpenter expected Anglo-American family members to be involved in business dealings with one another, but he also thought that those business relationships obligated Glen to provide oversight ensuring the quality of his relative's relationships with trade partners like Little Carpenter.

Within Cherokee society, individuals were responsible to, and responsible for, their matrilineal clan members. Honor or dishonor and retaliation would accrue to the clan because of the actions of its members. The accountability was so thorough, in fact, that if a kinsman committed a crime that required punishment, he was to be found and delivered for justice by his kinsmen to the wronged party. Failure to hold the guilty party accountable meant that the wronged party could, and would, exact revenge upon one of the other clan members, who would voluntarily or involuntarily be punished in his place.[2]

However, while Anglo-American family members invested in lucrative opportunities together, families like Glen's were less concerned with seeing that the needs of Indians were met than with how their familial networks could provide profits to family members, especially themselves. This contrast between British and Cherokee cultural norms governing familial relationships provided the foundation for economic and political tensions between British and American Indian leaders. Kinship connections, however, also held the key to creating relationships that could cross intercultural divides, decreasing tensions between these governments, especially in times of war. During the 1750s and 1760s, the intersection of kinship and trade fundamentally shaped the relationships of Cherokees and Chickasaws to the British colonies in the midst of Britain's conflict with France known as the French and Indian War.

Cherokees followed a tradition of matrilineal kinship that ensured that a child's maternal relatives, bound together within the same clan, were the most important influences on his or her life. Marriages created an intersection for clans that ensured that the two clans would support one another, but each lineage existed and operated separate from one another. Fathers would bring gifts to their children and encourage them, but the mother, grandmother, and mother's brothers held authority over and the responsibility for the children. Cherokees lived within a society that maintained that family, or clan, responsibilities were primary and central to town governance. James Adair wrote of the Southeastern Indian method of governance: "When any national affair is in debate, you may hear every father [uncle] of a family speaking in his house on the subject, with rapid, bold language, and the utmost freedom that a people can use. Their voices, to a man have due weight in every public affair, as it concerns their welfare alike. Every town is independent of another. Their own friendly compact continues the union."[3] Clan leaders spoke for their families, raised up the next generation of war leaders or diplomats, and ensured their families were provided for with meat and skins, as well as trade goods acquired by giving up surplus skins. Clans also provided the mechanism for facilitating positive relationships and alliances between towns.

Individual actions reflected family identity and responsibility and thus could bring honor or shame on one's kin. In this context, Governor Glen was responsible for his trader kinsman Elliott and should have stopped his "barbarous" treatment or made amends for the sake of the family honor and Glen's relationship with his native allies. By not doing so, Glen allowed the dissension caused by his kin's activities to mar his family's, as well as South Carolina's, trading reputation with the Cherokees.[4]

Forging kinship connections during the 1750s helped individuals and governments pursue the shared goal of establishing profitable trade and military alliances across cultural and political lines. The emphasis, however, of each group on one of these goals to the detriment of the other also caused these governments to clash. The creation of these Cherokee, Chickasaw, Anglo-American, and intercultural familial networks, through intermarriage, ritual adoption, or adoption, mediated these clashes to some degree and paved a way for future interactions between these family networks and governments. The kinship connections of Little Carpenter, of his niece Nan-ye-hi, and of James Logan Colbert, a British trader to the Chickasaws, as well as the language of treaties illuminate both the possibilities and limits of the degree to which kinship could create the basis for peace during and after the French and Indian War.

Using familial relationships as links between communities was not new in the 1750s. By then, both American Indians and Anglo-Americans in the Southeast identified kinship as a way of bonding British people who traveled and lived in native towns to those communities, extended families or clans, and the nations of which they were a part.[5] Traders and officials who married native women gained the protection of their wives' clans, a place to live in the town, and a degree of acceptance there. Children born of that union would be members of their mother's clan.

The language of treaties invoked friendship as well as parental, sibling, or uncle/nephew relationships to define the obligations and rights of the negotiating parties. Kinship relationships required members of a kin group to look out for each other's interests and to support one another in fair trade and warfare against enemies. Failing to live up to this alliance would result in additional negotiations to restore the relationship, but if those negotiations failed, war would follow.

Intermarriage proved a foundation for alliance. British traders and officials recognized the power of native societies to determine the terms of trade by agreeing to native insistence upon intermarriage to unite the interests of traders and Indian agents with those of influential native families. Ritual kinship, often formed through ceremonial smoking of the calumet pipe, sharing of the black drink, and other ceremonies, could provide the basis for a temporary relationship between a stranger and the town with which he wished to trade or create a treaty. Intermarriage relationships created a more permanent bond and also reflected

British traditions in which members of royal families, as well as the merchant class and aristocracy, married to create political alliances and to reinforce their wealth and status. British attitudes toward race, however, kept many from choosing this path as they saw Indians as having materials or land they wanted but not as sharing their own class, status, or "civilized" culture. The most common intercultural alliances in this period involved marriages of traders to native women of powerful clans, the ritual adoption of diplomats forging a fictive kinship, and wartime adoption of captives into native families. These forms of alliances were not mutually exclusive, but rather one could lead to another. The language of treaties reinforced the importance of these bonds.

Kinship relationships had special significance in the aftermath of the Yamasee War. Native and European polities aligned their economic and political interests to compensate for the loss of life incurred both in the war and in the previous slaving wars in the Southeast. Factions among the Cherokees were willing to form trade connections with British or French traders, which created tension between towns and clans over resources and alliances.[6] As competition between the European colonies increased, so did British pressure to bring all of the factions in line to make the trade alliances exclusive and to secure military allies for the conflicts against France. Chickasaws maintained a firm alliance with the British in opposition to their French and Choctaw enemies, who had been waging war against them for decades.

Attakullakulla, or Little Carpenter, had traveled to England in the 1730s as part of a Cherokee delegation to see the king.[7] What he saw there impressed upon him England's capability to be a good trading partner. English goods were abundant, of good quality, and seemed to be endlessly available. As wars between the French and English increased pressure on American Indian allies to take sides, Little Carpenter became an advocate of alliance with the British and launched several forays against French convoys traveling down the Mississippi River. His support, however, did not ensure that all Cherokees backed the British. Old Hop, chief of Chota, an Overhill Cherokee town, was among those maintaining ties to French traders alongside ties to English traders.[8] Lt. Henry Timberlake of Virginia noted in 1761:

> On my arrival in the Cherokee Country, I found the nation much
> attached to the French, who have the prudence . . . to conciliate
> the inclinations of almost all the Indians they are acquainted with,
> while the pride of our officers often disgusts them; nay, they did not

scruple to own to me, that it was the trade alone that induced them to make peace with us and not any preference to the French, whom they loved a great deal better. . . . [Fondness of the French] was not only their general opinion, but the policy of most of their headmen; except Attakullakulla, who conserves his attachment inviolably to the English.[9]

Little Carpenter was prominent within the government of the Cherokee town of Chota, and his opinion was important but contested. Other towns chose alliances with the French to counteract South Carolina's trade monopoly that limited the amount of goods flowing into Cherokee towns.[10]

During the 1740s and 1750s, tensions mounted between British and French colonial authorities over competing claims of jurisdiction. After war was declared in 1754, both sides, short on troops, called upon their native allies to back competing colonial claims militarily. The British government of South Carolina had created relationships, through its traders, with both Cherokees and Chickasaws by the 1730s. Most Cherokees and Chickasaws remained allies with the British and sent warrior bands to support their allies in the Seven Years' War against the French.

Although South Carolina maintained control over a majority of trade with both the Cherokees and Chickasaws, Virginia provided the colony with some competition for the Cherokee trade. By the early 1750s the Cherokees, unhappy with the scarcity and price of goods from Charles Town, sought to break that colony's monopoly on trade. Sending diplomats to Virginia, Georgia, and the French along the Mississippi, Cherokee leaders hoped that soliciting new traders for their towns would fix their problems by providing them with all of the goods they needed at competitive prices. These policies were risky at a time when both French and English officials demanded exclusive trade agreements with their Indian allies. The European officials privileged exclusivity and military alliance at the expense of trade relationships, while trade remained the central motivation for Cherokees.

As tensions mounted, Cherokee leaders like Old Hop, Little Carpenter, and Oconostota engaged in a diplomatic balancing act by sending delegations to rival powers, utilizing rhetoric, and disclaiming alliances or diplomatic delegations as necessary. The power of trade, however, was primary for Cherokees. Different town leaders forged relationships with traders that could provide the most plentiful and high-quality goods. Towns with the best traders gained prominence in relation to surrounding towns, and the leaders of the most profitable towns also gained status for their ability to access and distribute prime goods. The efforts of both Virginia and South Carolina to maintain amiable relations with their Cherokee allies by meeting their trade needs were impeded by the governors' and assemblies' determination to keep taxes to a minimum and cut what they saw as useless spending, especially on Indian "gifts." Gifts had been part of the trading and military alliance between the British and their Cherokee allies from the beginning. It was standard practice among native people that gifts, which bound negotiating parties together in friendship, were part of the trading process. The practice of gift giving was so established that Indian nations counted on the gifts as a significant part of the goods they received in trade agreements, part of the price of doing business. British officials, however, saw gift giving as superfluous, bordering on bribery or extortion, and extraneous to the process of trade, a cost separate from the price of the goods for which they were to be paid market value. Indian allies, according to these officials, owed allegiance as a condition of the trading and military alliances. The alliances were reciprocal and therefore warranted no gifts or other payments. To them the military services of Indian allies should be forthcoming without exchange of gifts as simple fulfillment of an agreed-upon mutual arrangement. To the Indians, however, relationships, including trade and military alliances, required ritual reciprocity that displayed to the parties, as well as all observers, that the two were tied to one another and maintained obligations to one another. Gift giving was the outward manifestation of the relationship and the responsibilities each owed the other. Giving gifts therefore was a part of the relationship, performed with great ceremony and gravity, because it represented the renewal of a ritual kinship between the parties in which each owed the other obligations as ritual kin. These ritual relationships, however, were temporary and had to be renewed with each new trading or military expedition. Failure to perform the gift-giving ritual was to let the ritual kinship lapse and to fail to renew the relationship that bound them together. This contrast in views on gift giving, in which both sides felt strongly about how gifts should be treated, led quickly to tensions.[11]

Wars between the French and British had been ongoing throughout the early eighteenth century. The Nine Years' War blended into the War of Spanish Succession between 1689 and 1713. The French again fought the British as allies of the Spanish during the War of Jenkin's Ear in 1744, which ceased with the peace of 1748. However, both sides increased fortifications in their North American colonies with a jealous eye toward each other even in times of peace.[12] In 1754 Indian allies of the British, led by the Half-King, a Delaware headman, accompanied young George Washington and his troops on an expedition to try to convince the French to leave the Ohio Valley region. The Indian allies within the group attacked and killed French officers near Fort Duquesne. The incident spiraled quickly into a war that encompassed the French and British colonial claims in North America and spilled over into a war fought around the world.[13] In the colonial Southeast, conferences were called to induce native leaders to join one side or the other.

South Carolina's governor, James Glen, encouraged Cherokee leaders to heed the call for troops issued by Virginia's governor, Robert Dinwiddie.[14] Several hundred Cherokees joined Virginians in "protecting the frontier" from the French and French-allied Indians like the Shawnees.[15] In return for this military assistance, Virginia's governor promised to help build a fort near the powerful Cherokee town of Chota. This fort, garrisoned by Virginians, would augment Fort Prince George, built by Carolina in 1753 at Keowee town. Both of these forts, according to the Cherokees, were to be sites of trade and military protection, as well as symbols of the strength of the alliance between the governments. These forts were meant to bolster existing trade and remind the colonies of their commitment to provide the nation with plentiful goods.[16] Virginia finished building the fort in 1756 but left it ungarrisoned, and it was eventually burned by the Cherokees to show their disapproval of the neglect. Virginia had not followed through on their promises made and obligations incurred as part of the ritual kinship that formed the basis of the alliance. South Carolina built and garrisoned Fort Loudon near the Cherokee town of Chota in response to rumors of French plans to build a fort on the Tennessee River. This helped strengthen the relationship between Carolina and Cherokees, but it was done more as a strategic move by the governor in wartime than as a fulfillment of the obligations owed to their allies.

While fictive and marital kinship provided cross-cultural relationships that could yield benefits, the figurative relationships invoked in treaties revealed the importance of using kinship as a common language for diplomatic communication. Cultural differences in the definitions of those familial relationships created unintentional, or purposeful, misunderstandings. Treaty alliances were at their core understandings of kinship, since nonkin were usually assumed to be enemies. The political relationships between the governments described in these documents replicated the language of negotiators' interpersonal relationships.[17]

Treaties frequently invoked the familial ties upon which diplomatic relationships were built. Terms such as "brother," "father," "uncle," and "nephew" and even generational and rank designations such as "elder brother" and "younger brother" indicated power dynamics and obligations to adhere to specific, culturally defined kinship roles. These documents illustrated how Indian people expected international alliances to mirror kin-based power relationships and reciprocal obligations. These perceptions of the commonality of familial obligations provided a foundation for intercultural diplomacy, while culturally specific definitions of kin obligations enabled miscommunication.[18] The Seven Years' War generated many talks and treaties that used the language of kinship to describe the negotiating parties' expected affinity and obligations to one another. The cultural differences between matrilineal and patrilineal kinship systems, however, ensured that these kinship terms within treaties had different meanings for each side.

In 1756 the English colony of Virginia negotiated a military alliance with some Cherokees against the French, while some Cherokee towns continued to support a French alliance. The allied Cherokees agreed to provide troops in return for a substantial "gift" paid in trade goods. The Virginia alliance threatened South Carolina's trade monopoly with the Cherokees. Governor Dinwiddie commented on the depth of intercolonial rivalry to the treaty commissioners Peter Randolph and William Byrd, noting that "you will find the traders from South-Carolina, will do all they can to harass you in your treaty."[19] In his message "to the emperor Old Hop, and the other [Cherokee] Sachems, and Warriors," Dinwiddie spoke on behalf of "your Brothers the English," using the term "your Brothers" a total of seven times in his short speech. He also referred twice to "our Father" the king of England. The language Dinwiddie used reveals his desire to connect on a personal level with his Cherokee audience. It was also, however, derived from his own patriarchal culture. In Dinwiddie's society a father had authority over his sons, and brothers owed each other "love and friendship" that would bond them together against a mutual threat.

The speech, however, was received by a culture that assigned different obligations to those same terms. Cherokee fathers obtained the favor and ear of their sons by providing them with gifts, but they held no coercive authority. In matrilineal societies, fathers were not kin because they did not belong to the clan of their offspring. Brothers, then, born of the same father, owed each other the loyalty due to kin only if they shared the same mother. Even then, brothers often demonstrated competition in addition to loyalty. Brotherhood without the qualifiers "elder" or "younger" signified parity of position and power. The relationships Dinwiddie described in his speech held very different significance to his English and Cherokee audiences, which would shape the tenor of the alliance. Dinwiddie expected obedience and firm familial loyalty, but he had described a set of relationships that the Cherokees viewed as temporary, gift-dependent, and based on secondary, rather than primary, kinship ties. Had he eschewed his references to a common father, his calls to his "brothers" might have been received differently.[20]

The language of the other treaty talks and of the 1756 treaty itself utilized the same tropes to engender allegiance and amity. The treaty talks by the Virginia commissioners included the terms "brothers" or "brethren" an additional seventeen times, "our Father the King" an additional six times, and "dutiful children" an additional three times. Little Carpenter responded in kind using parallel language of "father," "brothers," and "children," but his comments illustrated how "duty" to a father was qualified: "I shall always remember my Father's [the king's] Commands, and shall *whenever I have an Opportunity*, give the strongest Demonstrations of *my Readiness* to obey them."[21] For the Cherokees to provide Virginia with troops, the Virginians had to follow through on promises the king and his governors had made to the Cherokees regarding consistent trade and the building of a fort in Cherokee territory. Little Carpenter argued again for the fort to be built and garrisoned so that the kin of the Cherokee warriors would be protected while the men were away at war:

> The King our Father told me, that we should mutually assist each other, and therefore, as we are unacquainted with the Manner of building Forts, and had not the necessary Materials, we thought ourselves justifiable in making our Application to Governor Glen [of South Carolina], who I must again repeat it, has forfeited his Word. I have a Hatchet ready, but we hope our Friends will not expect us to take it up, 'til we have a Place of Safety for our Wives and Children. When they are secure, we will immediately send a great Number of Warriors to be employed by your Governor, where he shall think proper.[22]

The king-father could suggest that the English and Cherokee brothers assist one another, but it was up to the brothers to follow through on their obligations. The metaphor of "brothers" reinforced the Cherokees' view of the parity of their chiefs and English governors in power. The treaty itself reiterated the relationship of the "brothers and faithful allies," promised Virginia's assistance in building the desired fort and prohibiting a corresponding French fort, and declared that in return the Cherokees would wage war against the French with four hundred able warriors.[23]

As is often the case, during wartime even friendly soldiers might commit atrocities. Virginia, to encourage warfare against French-allied Indians, put bounties on scalps taken from those Indians. Putting bounties on scalps taken from enemies was part of the colonial experience. Scalps were easier to transport than other body parts and retained, theoretically, the distinctive hairstyle of the enemy, providing evidence that the individual killed was indeed a member of an enemy, rather than allied, Indian group. Unfortunately, Cherokees and Virginians often failed to discriminate between those Indians who were allies or enemies of the British, taking scalps from both and further complicating the wartime political climate. To make matters worse, Virginia, like Carolina, remained tight-fisted and refused to give the promised goods to Indian warriors for their efforts. Some of those warriors took their pay out of the countryside by stealing cattle, horses, foodstuffs, and clothing from farmsteads on their trips home. The alliance during the early years of the Seven Years' War left both the Indian warriors and backcountry settlers with negative impressions of one another. By the 1760s, "Virginians" had become an epithet Indians used to refer to people who did not necessarily live in or hale from Virginia, but rather who acted like Virginians, that is, in a dishonorable manner.[24] Virginians, it seems, were people who had little regard for Cherokee rights, ways of life, or even the lives of Cherokee individuals. Instead they sought profit alone, through scalp bounties, inequitable trading practices, or encroachment on Cherokee lands.[25]

Cherokee frustration over continued poor trade with Carolina, Virginia's failure to pay Cherokee warriors, and backcountry attacks on Cherokees returning from war resulted in retaliation by raiding parties of Cherokee young men on the frontier towns of South Carolina, North Carolina, and Virginia. In October of 1759 several headmen from throughout the Cherokee nation traveled to Charles Town to apologize for the attacks and to seek a peaceful solution to both sides' grievances. South Carolina governor William Lyttleton had by that time decided to go to war against the Cherokees. Lyttleton ordered the delegation of seventy-eight prominent Cherokee leaders taken hostage, promising their release upon surrender of the prisoners the Cherokee were hold-ing as well as the men responsible for the raids on the backcountry. To avoid potential Cherokee attacks on Charles Town, the governor, prison-ers, and 1,200 troops traveled to Fort Prince George within the Cher-okee nation and waited for the Cherokee headmen who had not been imprisoned to comply with the demand to turn in the captives and the Cherokee raiders. Because the clans would have to voluntarily surren-der the culprits who felt justified in their actions and captives who had been adopted into their Cherokee families, Little Carpenter and other Cherokee leaders had to convince each clan to offer up their kin for the British to exact their retribution in the name of English justice. Little Carpenter had helped to negotiate the release of all but twenty-two of the headmen when the governor abandoned the fort due to a smallpox outbreak. Negotiations broke down, Cherokees attacked the fort, and the troops within the fort killed the remaining hostages in February 1760, beginning the open hostilities of the Anglo-Cherokee War.[26]

Cherokee forces surrounded Fort Loudon, the fort that had finally been built and garrisoned in Cherokee territory, but gave permission for the troops to march home to South Carolina on the condition that they left their arms in the fort. Unwilling to leave arms and ammunition in the hands of their enemies, the soldiers quickly buried as much as pos-sible before they were led out from the gates. When the Cherokees took the fort and discovered the subterfuge, they caught up with the fleeing soldiers and slaughtered them. Little Carpenter was able to find and con-ceal his close friend, and possibly adopted brother, Capt. John Stuart. That kinship connection saved Stuart's life as he escaped to the home of a kinsman of Little Carpenter and then made his way back to South Caro-lina.[27] Stuart would later repay that debt through diplomatic service to both the British and the Cherokees. Battles raged for the next two years against the forts and towns adjoining Cherokee territory.[28]

Although ordered to assist Carolina's war against the Cherokee towns, Col. William Byrd of Virginia undertook an expedition that concentrated on building roads and forts on its way to Cherokee ter-ritory. Reinforcements from Virginia never attacked the Cherokee Overhill towns near the Virginia border. Meanwhile, Carolina's troops under direction of Col. James Grant plunged deep into Cherokee terri-tory, destroying fifteen of the southern towns far from Charles Town and burning 1,500 acres of corn.[29] When the Cherokees sued for peace, the Virginia troops were close enough that Cherokee runners approached Byrd with the peace treaty before Little Carpenter and his delegation could get to South Carolina to conclude peace with Governor Lyttleton. The result was that the Cherokees made separate peace treaties with each of the colonies. Chief Standing Turkey, who negotiated peace with Byrd, requested that he "send an officer back with them to their country, as that would effectually convince the nation of the good intentions and sincerity of the English towards them."[30] Ensign Henry Timberlake volunteered to live three months in Cherokee towns, serving in essence as a hostage, in order to secure good relations between the colony and the Cherokees. His memoir left an account of his experiences and impressions of Cherokee culture.

Timberlake described the ritual process of restoring peace in the town of Settico in the spring of 1761. As he approached the town, he encountered a large group of as many of four hundred Cherokees, some of whom performed a ritual "welcome" that symbolized his status as a hostage and therefore a guest, but one at the mercy of his hosts. Six of them danced, "with eagles tails in their hands, which they shook and flourished as they advanced, danced in a very uncommon figure singing in concert with some drums of their own make, and those of the late unfortunate Capt. [Raymond] Damere." By flaunting the captured goods of Demere, the defeated and deceased commander of Fort Loudon, they provided an implicit threat that told Timberlake to tread cautiously or end up like the dead commander. The ritual then became even more explicit a warning to Timberlake himself: "This violent exercise [dance], accompanied by the band of musick, and a loud yell from the mob, lasted about a minute, when the headman waving his sword over my head, struck it into the ground, about two inches from my left foot; then directing himself to me, made a short discourse (which my interpreter told me was only to bid me a hearty welcome) and presented me with a string of beads.[31] Timberlake must have asked what was said, seeing the swing of the sword as directed toward himself in hostility. The interpreter's response must have been tempered to alleviate the anxiety of the "guest." The ritual more likely symbolized that he owed his life to the Cherokees, who by granting him life instead of death ritually adopted him as kin temporarily. Timberlake was then led into the council house, where he encountered five hundred more Cherokees. Cheulah, the town leader, "then made some professions of friendship, concluding with giving me another string of beads, as a token of it." This was followed by another dance during which "the peace pipe was prepared," which Timberlake was urged to smoke, followed by 170 or 180 additional pipes, which were offered to him by other Cherokees, probably to symbolize peace with their particular clans.[32]

Timberlake would later transition from temporary, ritual kin to a permanent kinship relationship by marrying a Cherokee woman and fathering a child that would become part of her clan.[33] In 1762 and again in 1764–65 he escorted a Cherokee delegation to England in an attempt to further cement Anglo-Cherokee peace.[34]

The conclusion of the Anglo-Cherokee War brought about many of the changes in trade policy for which the Cherokee leadership had hoped, but at a terrible price in death and destruction. Among the terms of peace negotiated by Little Carpenter was the guarantee that his friend and brother John Stuart be made the new superintendent for Indian affairs for the Southern District. Stuart owed his life to Little Carpenter, and his marriage to a Cherokee woman and fathering of several children who held clan membership further solidified his kinship connections that would ensure he supported Cherokees as an intermediary with the colonies. South Carolina's monopoly on trade was broken, and traders from Virginia set up stores in several Cherokee towns. The towns themselves had to be rebuilt in 1761 following the devastation wrought by Col. Grant. Many Cherokee lives had been lost in the hostage situation and in the resulting war. The treaty to end the war created newly defined boundaries that whetted the appetites of Virginians and Carolinians for land speculation.

Chickasaw and Cherokee efforts to secure steady access to trade were rooted in native traditions and were shaped by new realities brought about by contact with Europeans. Intermarriage proved one way to ensure that particular towns had regular access to European goods and that certain families maintained a degree of control over both the flow of goods and their relationships with the traders and governments that provided those goods. Matrilineal kinship also ensured that the clans could limit traders' influence in town councils, over their offspring, and over clan-controlled resources such as land. The marriage of Little Carpenter's niece Nancy to trader Bryan Ward illustrates how access to trade benefited their native families and how town councils restricted traders' political influence and access to native resources.[35]

Nan-ye-hi, also known as Nancy Ward, was powerful in her own right. A member of the Wolf clan along with chiefs Old Hop and Little Carpenter, Ward was among the women who accompanied Cherokee war parties and in the Battle of Taliwa had taken up the gun of her fallen husband Kingfisher to fight their longtime Creek rivals. Following his death, she married trader Bryan Ward to help reinforce the trading relationship between South Carolina and the town of Chota. Nancy's daughters, also members of the Wolf clan, married to facilitate diplomacy with English and American traders and officials.[36] By her actions in war and her role in facilitating trade, Nancy Ward gained power in traditionally male segments of society and became arguably the most powerful woman in the Cherokee nation. Her marriage and those of her daughters were not simply dictated by law or naïve admiration of the traders; rather, they were utilitarian unions designed to stabilize and regulate trade that was crucial to the survival of the town, their kin, and their tribe. Through their marriages, town leaders ensured the continued supply of goods. The traders' own power was restricted to observation in town councils, ensuring that the traders lived and ran their posts on land owned by their wives' clan and encouraging them to dress, speak, and act according to Cherokee traditions.[37]

Although cross-continental native trade routes had been consistently used for thousands of years, Europeans' access to those routes changed both the nature of trade and the demographics of native polities.[38] Pre-contact trade had been based largely on the exchange of prestige goods and rare resources through gift exchange. The slaving wars of the late seventeenth century increased migration and facilitated the "genesis" of native coalescent polities, including the Cherokees, Chickasaws, Creeks, and Choctaws. These new polities forged dozens of linguistically and culturally distinct polities into new political identities loosely bound together by kinship bonds, based on clan membership, adoption, and marriage.[39] Those wars had also proven that trade alliances, especially ones that provided arms and ammunition, could mean the difference between survival and extermination by neighbors. The slave trade had turned existing tensions between native competitors for natural and human resources into warfare that threatened dissolution of most native polities at the time. The deerskin trade continued to exacerbate tensions over natural resources by creating new demand for another limited resource, deer. Furthermore, trade alliances depended upon the forging of kinship ties, which had additional obligations to support one another in times of war.

Connections to trade were also important internally for Chickasaw and Cherokee societies. Native leaders vied with one another to gain influence within their towns and in councils with the leaders of other towns. These marriages provide a crucial kinship link between native families and sources of trade that gave them political advantage over their rivals and advanced the prestige of the family (clan). Rather than a cultural quirk or holdover from an antiquated past, matrilineal kinship served the needs of native communities in new societies that little resembled the hierarchical Mississippian chiefdoms of their ancestors.

The Chickasaws had long fought against the French ambition to fully control the Mississippi River from New Orleans north to the Great Lakes. Although the French had become allies of the Choctaws, the Chickasaws were a group that posed an obstacle to their plan. The French, along with their Choctaw allies, waged war against the Chickasaws, who were supplied with guns by English traders, throughout the early eighteenth century. The Chickasaws gained the reputation of the premier slavers for the English west of the Appalachian Mountains. They also participated heavily in the deerskin trade following the Yamasee War. By the 1730s, the Chickasaws had trading relationships with both South Carolina and Georgia, ensuring that trade and political competition remained intertwined.[40]

In January 1736, fifteen-year-old James Logan Colbert joined an expedition of Scottish traders to Chickasaw country led by John M. McIntosh. At age twenty he became the resident agent among the Chickasaws. By 1759, Colbert had married a Chickasaw woman from a prominent clan, and a year later his first son, William, was born. He would later marry two more Chickasaw women according to Chickasaw traditions of polygamy and have children with them as well.[41]

In 1754 Governor Glen of South Carolina commented, "The brave Chickasaws still stand their ground [against the French and Choctaws] and are determined to defend every inch of their country with the last drop of their blood."[42] Despite these ongoing battles along the Mississippi, the Colberts managed to bring a war party to the aid of the Lower Chickasaws, who joined with the English in the Anglo-Cherokee War. They would serve as scouts and warriors with Lt. Col. James Grant's force, which employed devastating total-war tactics against the Overhill towns of the Cherokees. Although they served as allies to the British throughout the French and Indian War, they dedicated small numbers of troops to help thwart the enemies of the British colonies to the east, including at this time the Overhill Cherokees. Their larger commitment continued to be opposing the French along the Mississippi River.[43] Chickasaw participation in the French and Indian War, therefore, was part of a longer struggle against the French in Louisiana rather than a discrete set of actions like those within the Anglo-Cherokee War. While the Colberts are particularly noted as allies of the British during the Anglo-Cherokee conflict, little has been written about them or other Chickasaws during the larger French and Indian War.

In 1702 Henri de Tonti had recorded an encounter with an English trader among the Chickasaws whose speech and dress mirrored those of the Chickasaws with whom he lived. Tonti described the trader as "holding a gun in his hand and a saber at his side. He had on a rather dirty blue shirt, no pants, stockings, or shoes, a scarlet wool blanket and some discs at his neck like a savage."[44] Although that seems to be an example of complete assimilation to Chickasaw culture, James Logan Colbert was selective in his adoption of Chickasaw ways. He learned the language and served as a translator, embraced plural marriage by marrying three Chickasaw women, and lived most of his life in Chickasaw territory. He also, however, enabled some of his children to get an education in the missionary schools and embraced a southern-planter lifestyle rather than life in a village. Indian agent Charles Stuart recounted Chickasaw complaints about Colbert and the other traders: "I am credibly informed that there are not less than 18 traders and packhorsemen now out a-hunting on the hunting grounds . . . which is contrary to all rule and of which the Indians complain much. . . . I am informed those hunters are divided into parties and that they are headed by Messrs. Colbert and Bubbie, and that said Colbert is contrary to His Majesty's instructions establishing plantations in that nation and that he has got cattle, negroes, etc. so as even to admit of his having an overseer."[45] This blending of Chickasaw and English plantation culture shaped the institution of slavery among the Chickasaws.[46]

The treaty that ended the Seven Years' War in 1763, negotiated in Paris, France, failed to include American Indians among its negotiating parties. Peace in the southern colonies was instead restored through a "Congress of the Four Southern Governors and the Superintendent of that District, with the Five Nations of Indians, at Augusta, [Georgia]," in November 1763. The commissioners in their treaty talks continued the tropes of "brotherhood" through "the great king, our common father."[47] The commissioners declared, "your lands will not be taken from you; and this is to be [said] before you all, and not in secret, that no nation of Indians may be ignorant of [the king's] gracious intentions, and of his fatherly care of the red as well as the white."[48] The Indians of the Southeast had significant experience by this time with the "fatherly care" of the English, including the punitive and disciplinary aspects of that relationship. They were well aware of what the negotiators meant, but that did not negate their own cultural definitions of the role of fathers.

The primary function of the treaty was to create peace between the colonies and their native neighbors as well as between the tribes that had gone to war against each other as allies or enemies of the English. James Logan Colbert, acting as a representative of the Crown, visited several towns to encourage the Chickasaws, Choctaws, and Upper Creeks to attend the congress and served as the interpreter for the Chickasaws and Choctaws. Colbert served an interpreter rather than a Chickasaw delegate. As opposed to his sons' later power as chiefs of the Chickasaw nation, James Logan Colbert himself was a trader, a soldier/warrior with the Chickasaws, and an interpreter, but he was not a chief representing the opinions of the Chickasaw nation.[49] The Chickasaws sent twenty-seven delegates; the Choctaws, two; the Creeks, nine headmen "and their followers"; the Cherokees, fifteen, including Little Carpenter; and the Catawbas sent "Col. Ayres and his followers." A total of seven hundred Indians attended the treaty.[50]

Englishmen and Indians used colorful kinship metaphors in the treaty talks. John Stuart, the superintendent of Indian affairs for the Southeast after the end of the Anglo-Cherokee War in 1761, noted that the purpose of the treaty was that "the great king's good disposition towards his red children is to be communicated to you, in the presence of one another."[51] James Colbert interpreted Payamatah's speech, saying, "He looks on the white people and them [the Chickasaws] as one; that they are good friends as if they had sucked one breast."[52] Payamatah's kinship metaphor would not have been lost on his audience since the Indians of the Southeast were matrilineal rather than patrilineal. The metaphor that the delegates had "sucked one breast" indicated a closer relationship than the "brotherhood" born of a shared father as described by the English in their treaties. Little Carpenter made talks not only to the English but also to the other Indian nations gathered at Augusta, saying: "He has now met all the red people of various nations, and will now give his talk to them. . . . He says, the governors, by the great king's orders, sent for them all together, and not to dwell together in enmity, but like friends and brothers."[53] After so many years of fighting against one another as allies of the French or British, some of which continued even through the congress itself, the native nations of the Southeast took this opportunity to make peace with one another publicly through speeches and giving strings of wampum. At this congress, another chief, The Prince of Chotih [Chota] "made overtures of peace and friendship to Pia-Mattah, the chief Chicasah; which being accepted, the prince of Chotih gave him a string of white beads."[54] Many Chickasaws, including Colbert and his sons, had fought against the Cherokees in the Anglo-Cherokee War. This congress enabled native leaders to discuss peace among themselves, continuing to use the rhetoric of "brotherhood," though the leaders that attended had to convince their towns and clans back home to accept those overtures.[55] The Treaty of 1763 and subsequent Proclamation Act were meant to placate Britain's uneasy Indian allies but failed to deter restless settlers and land speculators determined to turn the fertile hunting grounds of the Indians into financial opportunities for themselves.[56]

Kinship was important to the congress beyond rhetoric and language. Many of the traders and interpreters, like James Colbert, had been integrated into the tribes through marriage and adoption and owed the tribe the loyalty of kin. Likewise the superintendent himself, John Stuart, was Little Carpenter's close friend, possibly an adopted brother, who had married a Cherokee woman and fathered several children who held clan membership.[57] These personal relationships guided the proceedings and helped to mediate the tensions that grew out of opposing alliances during the Seven Years' War. These kinship ties would help to encourage factions within the Chickasaws and Cherokees to remain allies of Stuart and the British just over a decade later in the American Revolutionary War.

James Logan Colbert was listed as one of the seven traders and twenty-two packhorsemen operating in the Chickasaw nation in 1766.[58] Traders and their assistants were so prevalent in the nation that two years earlier Chickasaw chief Payamatah had requested in treaty negotiations that the number of traders be reduced to two favorites, noting that "Heyrider [John Highrider] and John Brown were enough, and that he desired no more."[59] Colbert served as interpreter at this meeting and was not among the traders Payamatah wished to keep in the Chickasaw nation. This indicates either that Colbert was not a valued trader or that his relation to the tribe made him one of them rather than a trader sent by South Carolina. His marriages, like those of Nancy Ward, existed within a state of competition in which traders, as well as native leaders, competed with their peers for influence over the trade. Colbert's connections to his Chickasaw families raised their prestige and his own. Those economic connections, however, existed within the broader context of clan prestige and individual performance in war and oratory as one factor among many that allowed individuals and families to gain influence among their peers. His actions as an aggressive military leader brought him renown but also criticism from other Chickasaw leaders as he operated independently and in competition with other factions and facilitated changes within the culture of the Chickasaws.

Just as with Indian and Anglo-American ideals toward marriage, expectations for treaty parties to fulfill kin-based obligations to one another were complicated by differing definitions of those obligations as well as contrasting definitions of kinship. Historians have described the contrast between the roles expected of fathers and sons in Anglo-American and those in matrilineal native societies. It is also true that "fictive" kinship relationships between "white people" and "Indians," like those forged in treaty purification rituals and reinforced in treaty language, held less sway over the actions of individuals than marriage ties that bound specific lineages together with mutual obligations to support one another in war or trade. Marriages of Indian women to traders like Colbert provided native families with seemingly more concrete assurances of reciprocity than the documents so prized by British officials.

Little Carpenter, Nancy Ward, and James Logan Colbert's marital family invested in personal relationships to reap the rewards of trading and negotiating in the highly competitive economic environment of the colonial Southeast. Their efforts were contested by other native leaders seeking to augment their own positions through trade with one or more European powers but also by leaders who sought to limit or eschew trade with Europeans altogether.

The kin-based divisions and factions in both the Chickasaw and the Cherokee nations served the larger purposes of their people by providing opportunities for active dissent against violent foes as well as providing a foundation for potentially valuable alliances. Repeatedly, factions expressed their extreme dissatisfaction with the trading practices of British traders through attacks on the traders themselves or on nearby Anglo-American settlements. In 1760, while Little Carpenter created a fictive kinship relationship with John Stuart and traveled to Charles Town to work toward a diplomatic solution to bring about better terms of trade for his people, other Cherokees sought to remedy the problem by taking the goods they had been promised from the countryside or allying with the French traders.[60] The marriages that brought Bryan Ward and James Logan Colbert into native families and towns helped to secure trade through marital alliance. Strategies of diplomacy and war among the Cherokees and Chickasaws were more than simple reactions to European provocations, such as unsatisfying terms of trade and requests for land cessions through treaties. Kinship strategies, born of deep and lasting cultural traditions, including reciprocal responsibilities, flexed with the needs of the people. Connections between kinship and politics served as a core part of the cultural identities guiding Cherokee and Chickasaw actions as their world continued to change through the colonial period.

Kinship connections provided the basis for key diplomatic and economic alliances for the colonial period and beyond. These relationships served as the basis for intercultural diplomacy that reorients the classic narrative of British colonial history in America. Kinship not only shaped but also determined Anglo-Indian relations in the American Southeast.

2 / Militant Families: Kinship in the American Revolution

In 1774 along the banks of the Watauga River near a small settlement of British settlers that had built on Cherokee lands, a group of hundreds of natives met with settlers who sought to make a land deal with them. As the elder chiefs considered the proposition to extend the use agreement they had with the Watauga settlers, Richard Henderson, a prominent land speculator, proposed that instead of lending the use of the land, the Cherokees should sell it to them. The Cherokee leaders heatedly discussed the possibility. As the discussions wound down, a younger man stood to be heard. Pockmarks from a childhood bout with smallpox gave the face of the determined warrior an especially serious look, but his words shook the crowd. Dragging Canoe had been known since childhood for his determination to go to war alongside his kinsmen. In this moment, however, he declared that war would be imminent if the treaty proceedings continued regardless of what the old men decided. Those who recorded the events of that day marked his words as saying, "You have bought a fair land, but you will find its settlement dark and bloody."[1] These words would become famous in the Cumberland River Valley as they would ring true for the next two decades. Richard Henderson was a land speculator without official title or sanction and thus was not authorized to call and negotiate a treaty at Sycamore Shoals. The agreement with which he later came forward would be rejected by the colonial authorities, but the coming of the American Revolution would give him another shot at legitimating the agreement. The Treaty of Sycamore Shoals was a golden opportunity for Henderson, if he could only hold onto control long enough to get to sell the land.

For the Cherokees meeting on the Watauga River, the treaty was a turning point in internal politics that illustrated the specific ways kinship shaped both internal and external political relationships. Elder Chiefs Oconostota and Little Carpenter were among those at odds over whether or not to accept Henderson's proposal. Dragging Canoe was the son of Little Carpenter, and, although his matrilineal kinship connections are unclear, he may have been the nephew or great-nephew of Oconostota. When his father voiced an opinion favorable to making the deal, Dragging Canoe rebuked his father in the midst of the negotiations and declared he would fight all those who sought to use the agreement to settle on Cherokee lands. Dragging Canoe, in this matrilineal society, owed his allegiance and overt respect to his mother's brothers rather than to his father. This moment highlights how matrilineality could be a determining force behind the beginning to war. For the Cherokees and other Southeastern peoples, clan lineages descending through the mother's line could create legacies of war or peace that would be passed down from generation to generation. In Dragging Canoe's case, his matrilineal kin responded to his call to war, and he, along with his supporters, moved into a new set of towns on the Tennessee River. They came to be known as the Chickamauga Cherokees, or Chickamaugas, and became infamous to settlers of the region for the frequency of their attacks on frontier outposts. Again and again throughout the period of the American Revolution, kinship served as a key means for families, regardless of culture, for mobilizing troop movements, securing alliances, and gaining political and economic ground during a time of great upheaval.

The American Revolution had a major impact on the trans-Appalachian West. As American Indians struggled internally over whether to pursue neutrality or an alliance with the British or Americans, they had to deal with Anglo-American settlers who both encroached on their territory and seemed to embrace the challenge against the British government. The two, pressure on Indian lands and political rebellion, became bound up together for those on both sides. As they confronted one another, both Indians and Euro-Americans fought alongside those they knew and trusted: their kin. For Euro-Americans who were determined to expand their territorial claims, kinship networks provided a means of securing land for future generations, creating land monopolies, and a way for migrating families to establish a level of security. These were benefits, or rights, they believed were denied to them by the king's government back in England. Likewise, American Indians drew upon kinship networks to defend their land militarily and diplomatically in the face of a flood of people strongly motivated to displace Indians from fertile lands. Understanding how kinship relationships shaped the Revolutionary era in trans-Appalachia is central to understanding what happened, and why.

The American Revolution on the Appalachian frontier reflected not only Britain's conflict with its colonies but also the Atlantic world context that had created that tension born of the Seven Years' War between Britain and France, as well as the strategic alliance of Spain with the Americans late in the war. The context of the Revolutionary War provided motivation and opportunity for native and Anglo-American families alike to use the contest to increase their families' collective power in the region.[2] Some historians have mistakenly interpreted most of these confrontations as minor skirmishes in the broader history of the Revolution, but these battles were actually central to the war west of the Appalachian Mountains.

Kinship networks provide a critical way of exploring this historical moment. From Lord Dunmore's War in 1774 through the 1783 treaties that ended the Revolution, kinship formed an essential foundation for military units, migration chains, and political action for both natives and non-natives. Kinship networks gave power, legitimacy, and autonomy to competing factions in Cherokee, Chickasaw, and Anglo-American societies. They facilitated Anglo-American land speculation and militia service and provided the foundation for Indian military resistance. The relationship between kinship, land, diplomacy, and war shaped the American Revolution as well as the battles for land and power that wracked trans-Appalachia for decades to come.[3]

Issues related to Lord Dunmore's War originated in the aftermath of the Seven Years' War. In 1763 the Court of St. James issued a proclamation that included an Appalachian boundary beyond which British colonial expansion was prohibited—both to limit military expenses and to maintain peace with Indians. Pontiac's War in the Great Lakes region reinforced Parliament's fear of the physical and financial consequences that would result from allowing unrestricted settlement on Indian lands. Even so, as Patrick Griffin has noted, a meaningful debate emerged in London over the permanence of the boundary restriction.[4] Fundamentally, it did little to deter Euro-American settlements beyond the Appalachians.[5] Land companies and even colonial governors sought to claim lands well beyond the crest of the mountains for themselves and their colonies.[6]

In November 1766, Sir William Johnson, the British superintendent of Indian affairs for the Northern District, called a treaty conference at Fort Stanwix, New York, because the Proclamation Line had failed as an effective boundary, stating:

> You all remember that three years ago I signified to you His Maty's [Majesty's] desire to establish a Boundary Line between his people and yours and that we then agreed together how part of that Line should run. . . . But [drawing the boundary] was a difficult Task, and generally unsuccessfull—for altho' the Provinces have bounds between each other, there are no certain Bounds between them & you, And thereby not only several of our people ignorant in Indian Affairs have advanced too far into your country, but also many of your own people through the want of such a Line have been deceived in the Sales they have made or in the limits they have set to our respective claims.[7]

Subsequently the Iroquois ceded "all their right south-east of the Ohio, and down to the Cherokee River"—including the entire Ohio Valley and extending as far south as the Tennessee River—to the British.[8]

The land cession certainly was not without controversy in Indian country. Several groups, including Shawnees, declared that, despite Iroquois hunting in the region, they had no right to sign away the lands of the Ohio Country. Iroquois hunting and war parties had occasionally traveled in the region, but Iroquois homelands were far to the north and east of the ceded lands.[9] Many other native groups hunted, lived, and fought upon these lands. During the negotiations for the treaty, amenable chiefs informed Johnson that they had received intelligence that "several of the Nations to the South and West [were] greatly alarmed at the Power and increase of the English and irritated at the ill treatment they had met with [and] had expressed a desire to meet the rest to deliberate on what was to be done." This meeting was all the more worrisome for Johnson and his Indian allies because "the Spaniards & French had for a long time urged them to take up arms and given them repeated assurances of a powerfull assistance [and] That they had now called [the disconcerted Indian leaders] to a meeting at the Mississippi near the mouth of the Ohio for that purpose . . . [and] that they were just ready to set out when Sir William [Johnson's] message came to them, and that they waited [for the results of] the event of the Treaty at Fort Stanwix."[10] The news that the group of chiefs received about the treaty would determine if they would ally themselves with the British or with the French or Spanish. Following the treaty, some tribes accepted the treaty, but many Shawnees in particular declared that the Ohio Country was the land upon which they lived and that they would not give it up. They resisted any attempts of Englishmen to settle in that region.

The Treaty of Fort Stanwix was only the beginning of treaties that would amend the Proclamation Line. To the south of the Ohio Country, John Stuart, the superintendent of Indian affairs in the Southern District, negotiated the Treaty of Hard Labor in 1768 and the Treaty of Lochaber in 1770. These treaties adjusted the boundary agreed upon in 1763 to accommodate settlements that had extended beyond that boundary in the ensuing years.[11]

In 1770 surveyor John Donelson was appointed by the colony of Virginia, on the authority of John Stuart, to gather the men he needed and to join with Cherokee chief Little Carpenter and his men to redraw the boundary between Cherokees and the colony of Virginia. Donelson and Little Carpenter spent weeks surveying the new boundary together. When they encountered geographic barriers, they worked around those barriers. To avoid the inconvenience of a treacherous overland route, the group agreed upon the water route of the Louisa River as the boundary line. This added thousands of acres to the land cession, and Little Carpenter, the Cherokee representative, agreed that five hundred dollars would be fair compensation. When the amendment to the treaty was brought before the Virginia House of Burgesses, they accepted the amended boundary but refused to pay the additional amount. The Cherokees never received their money for the additional land ceded through this change.[12] This encounter seems to have been the first between Little Carpenter and John Donelson. The families of these two men would soon be at war over other lands obtained in a similar fashion.

After the Lochaber line had been surveyed, Col. William Preston of the Virginia militia argued that "the Hunters or Settlers can now have no Excuse or Plead Ignorance in going over the Louisa or Infringing on the Indians Claim."[13] Despite the hopes of Preston and others like him, however, the amended boundary did not discourage settlement on Indian lands. Donelson would be among the land speculators who benefited from additional cessions. Over the next three decades his kin would use their familial ties to amass hundreds of thousands of acres in what would become Tennessee, Georgia, Mississippi, and Alabama.

The competition over boundaries that had plagued the British colonies inspired armed conflict between Virginia and Shawnees over claims to the Ohio Country that were based upon the Fort Stanwix land cessions. Lord Dunmore, the royal governor of Virginia, sent John Connolly into the Ohio Valley to claim Pittsburgh for his colony. As the colony of Pennsylvania also claimed the territory, the incident almost led to a major conflict between the colonies, including a clash of colonial militias each. Instead, the Virginia militia was diverted to respond to clashes between Indians and settlers on the frontier, and Lord Dunmore's War became a war against Shawnees instead of Pennsylvanians.[14] Dunmore proclaimed that "hopes of pacification can no longer be entertained . . . and that these People will by no means [be] diverted from their design of falling upon [or attacking] the back parts of this Country . . . it is necessary . . . that we Should have recourse to the only means which are left in our power to extricate ourselves out of so Calamitous a Situation."[15] The battles blended almost seamlessly into those of the Revolutionary War. Shortly after the expedition against Shawnees, Dunmore would call for loyalists, slaves, and Indian allies to support British regulars against Virginia's colonists in rebellion.[16]

Lord Dunmore's War began a decade-long struggle over land that coincided with the American Revolution. In trans-Appalachia, land acquisition inspired settlers to join American militias, while Indian resistance to encroachment blended with British objectives to retain control. Britain's failure to maintain control over the colonies led to a political vacuum that caused chaos, especially in the West. The American "Empire of Liberty" was born out of the audacity of land speculators pushing into native lands and the willingness of other Americans, including eventually the Continental Congress, to back those expansionist claims in the American Revolution.[17] Kinship served as a key avenue for mobilizing men to fight. But which side would best protect claims was not always clear. Dunmore remained allied with the British government, but many of his investors chose to cast their lot with the Continental Congress.[18]

The Watauga settlements that formed on Cherokee land between the boundaries of North Carolina and Virginia had been established in 1769 under the auspices of the Treaty of Hard Labor. When the boundary line was eventually drawn to mark the boundaries set by the treaty, the settlements were on the Cherokee side of the line. Rather than drive them off, local Cherokees allowed them to stay long enough to harvest their crops. Rather than breaking up at the end of the crop cycle, the settlements actually grew and pushed Cherokees to expand the terms of the agreement to allow them to stay longer. The settlements gained a reputation for fertile lands and drew more people through familial and community chain migration.[19] Several families from Halifax County, Virginia, for example, including those headed by John Donelson, Daniel Smith, and Hugh Henry, settled at Watauga before eventually moving west to help found Nashborough, which would become Nashville, in the Cumberland region.[20] The colonies of Virginia and North Carolina denied the legitimacy of the Watauga settlements because they claimed the settlement had violated Cherokee boundaries and had not been authorized by the proper colonial authorities.

After discovering the settlement, neighboring Cherokees refused to sell the land to the Wataugans, but they did allow the group to rent the land upon which they lived. Wataugans also were allowed to farm until the crops they had planted could be harvested—on the condition that thereafter they would move back across the boundary.[21] The Wataugans did not remove as promised at the end of harvest season, but the Cherokees did not drive them out by force. The settlement continued to grow in numbers, boosted by kinship-based chain migrations. In 1772, several years into this uneasy arrangement, the Wataugans, cut off from the political jurisdiction of both North Carolina and Virginia, formed a governmental body they called the "Watauga Association" that drafted a constitution of sorts called the "Watauga Compact" to facilitate community self-government and defense. They were part of the earliest wave of what Thomas Jefferson called an emerging "empire of liberty" in the West defined by its aggressive stance toward expansion and adherence to the ideals of democratic self-government.[22]

In 1774, North Carolinian Richard Henderson, who was not a member of the colonial government, sent word through Cherokee towns that he wanted to negotiate for the purchase of the Watauga settlements. Since the farmsteads had continued to creep outside of the leased area, Cherokees sought a way to halt the settlements and ensure peace. Several hundred Cherokees attended the treaty negotiation. Elders and chiefs stretched out the negotiations in the hope that they could reach an internal agreement. Chief Oconostota opposed the treaty and predicted that the pattern of encroachment and land cessions would repeat itself until native people disappeared entirely. He was recorded as saying, "Whole nations had melted away in their presence like balls of snow before the sun and had scarcely left their names behind, except as imperfectly recorded by their enemies and destroyers." According to John Haywood's account of Oconostota's speech, "He ended with a strong exhortation to run all risks and to incur all consequences, rather than submit to any further dilacerations of their territory."[23] Chief Little Carpenter, by contrast, seemed disposed to come to an agreement with Henderson. During the negotiations his son, a young warrior named Dragging Canoe, stood and declared that the chiefs had no right to give away the tribe's hunting territory. Dragging Canoe allegedly stood during the negotiations and declared to the Wataugans, "You have bought a fair land, but you will find its settlement dark and bloody."[24] Wataugans found the outburst startling because Dragging Canoe rebuked his own father, a man of great prestige in the tribe, in open forum. They perceived Dragging Canoe to be an enraged young man breaking from his father's guidance. In reality, they had witnessed a split between the peace and war factions over the treaty. Each town had chiefs whose voice held particular influence in matters of war or peace. Often those positions were generational. In this case the war faction would not bow to the wisdom of their elders but rather vowed to resist this encroachment violently.[25]

The break between father and son was not as unusual as it was portrayed. Cherokees, like most of the Southeastern Indians, were matrilineal. A father did not control or discipline his children because that role belonged to the children's maternal uncle. Their mother's brother provided their education and served as their closest male relative. Fathers were not even related to their children by clan, which provided people with their central familial identity. Dragging Canoe owed allegiance and respect to his uncles rather than to his father—who was just another elder, albeit one with great influence. This matrilineal kinship system based in clan identity would provide a foundation for Dragging Canoe's influence, enabling him to create kin-based military units and even towns dedicated to resistance of settlement of the "Henderson Purchase."[26]

Dragging Canoe followed Oconostota's lead, claiming authority to resist the settlements for the good of his clan, his town, and his nation. Oconostota might have been Dragging Canoe's great-uncle, but little evidence is available to confirm this. The connection between their speeches opposing the treaty is interesting and hints that such a kinship connection was possible, but they may just have shared disgust for Henderson's treaty and at the negotiations that threatened the Cherokee land base. A decade later Cherokees disputed the land cession in the Treaty of Sycamore Shoals on the grounds that "Richard Henderson says he purchased the lands at Kentucky, and as far as Cumberland, but he is a rogue and a liar, and if he was here I would tell him so. . . . If Little Carpenter signed this deed, we were not informed of it; but we know that Oconostota did not, yet we hear his name is to it. Henderson put it there, and he is a rogue."[27] The Cherokee negotiators in 1788 had oral traditions about who had signed or not signed the document and thus believed the signatures on the document to have been forged. Southeastern Indians created a balance between war and peace, between those who could provide the best outcome for their people through war or treaty negotiation. In this moment, Dragging Canoe declared that he, not his father, best served the needs of the people. Dragging Canoe became the leader of new towns on the Tennessee River, known as the Chickamauga towns. The war and peace factions of the Cherokees would operate separately from one another through the next two decades, each pursuing what they asserted was best for the tribe, each rooted in tradition and legitimate authority, but often acting in contradiction to one another. The spiritual and ideological legacies of resistance that native leaders drew upon during the American Revolution often created alliances that bridged tribal differences, all the while creating divisions with others of their own cultural background. Understanding kinship connections between key resistance leaders, and the cultural context of those connections, helps to explain how this process took place and why it happened the way it did. The Chickamauga Cherokees became a separate set of towns removed both physically and philosophically from the Overhill Cherokees. The Chickamauga towns would be the home base for Cherokee warriors to launch campaigns against the Cumberland settlements.[28]

In the end, through the 1775 Treaty of Sycamore Shoals, Richard Henderson and his land company claimed all Cherokee hunting grounds north of the Cumberland River, including what would become upper Middle Tennessee and Kentucky. The colonial governors of Virginia and North Carolina repudiated the treaty immediately because Henderson was not an "Officer appointed to superintend Indian Affairs." Josiah Martin, governor of North Carolina, issued a stern warning to colonists in 1775:

> I DO hereby forewarn all, and all Manner of Persons, against taking any Part, or having any Concern or Dealings with the said Richard Henderson, touching the Lands for which he is said to have entered into Treaty with the Indians as aforesaid, or with any other Person or Persons, who have engaged, or may engage, in Projects of the like Nature, contrary to the Tenor of his Majesty's Royal Proclamation aforesaid, as every Treaty, Bargain, and Agreement with the

Indians, repugnant thereto, is illegal, null, and void, to all Intents and Purposes, and that all Partakers therein will expose themselves to the severest Penalties.[29]

Virginia's governor, Lord Dunmore, like Martin, also opposed Henderson's treaty because, according to British law, treaties had to be made by colonies through the superintendent for Indian affairs. Moreover, the Treaty of Sycamore Shoals threatened to overlap, and therefore impinge on, Virginia's claims gained through the Treaty of Fort Stanwix.

After the Declaration of Independence, Dunmore continued to represent the Crown in Virginia. Henderson embraced the cause of Independence and applied for, and received, formal recognition of the treaty by the new *state* governments of Virginia and North Carolina. The Revolution signaled a shift in power that included reinforcing land rights of those in rebellion against the British government and repudiating those of loyalists. Henderson took advantage of the political divisions created by the American Revolution to seek approval for his treaty by the pro-expansion continental government, which would go on to create "an empire of liberty" based on the premise of maximizing Indian land cessions by whatever means necessary.[30]

In June 1776, Col. William Christian of the Virginia militia suggested to William Preston Smithfield that they could prevent an alliance between Indians and the British by convincing settlers swiftly to move off Cherokee lands: "The Cherokees are drawing on their destruction; should they make War, an army will be sent directly against them; and I fear it is now too late to send messengers into their towns to undeceive them, especially as the Agents seem to have such an ascendancy there. . . . Is it not some pity that the poor Savages should be ruined by the intrigues of our own Nation[?]"[31] Heedless encroachment would drive the Cherokees to join the ranks of American Indian allies supporting the British. Christian himself would soon lead American troops in battle against Cherokees.[32] Wataugans and the proponents of the Treaty of Sycamore Shoals were both solidly in the American military camp, which meant that the Cherokees who opposed the controversial land cession were certain to meet with fervent armed opposition by those settlements closest to them. The resulting clash became known as the Cherokee War of 1776.

In 1776, Dragging Canoe and his kin-based military attacked the Watauga settlements, killing several settlers and taking others hostage. Little Carpenter, leader of the peace faction, had worked to bring peace back to his town but had failed as the Wataugans declared war on the towns closest to them. Little Carpenter's niece Nan-ye-hi, later known as Nancy Ward and Ghigau (Beloved Woman), worked to assure the Americans that their people were indeed neutral. Nancy Ward, like her uncle Little Carpenter, was a matrilineal descendant of the prestigious Wolf clan. "Beloved woman" was a rare honor in Cherokee society that gave Nancy Ward the right to speak and make speeches in councils and other diplomatic situations as well as to declare captives free.[33] Ward had extended the family's kinship connections beyond the Cherokees when she married trader Bryan Ward in the mid-1750s.[34] Those ties influenced her to protect her husband's people in western North Carolina when war broke out. In July 1776, Nancy Ward warned the Watauga settlements of an impending attack by her first cousin Dragging Canoe and six hundred of his followers.[35] She then rescued one of the women captured in her cousin's attack, a Mrs. Bean, who was apparently slated to be burned.[36] Her actions mirrored those of her uncle Little Carpenter, who also worked toward a peaceful resolution.

Cherokees acted on behalf of, or against, the British government according to their own interests. These interests, however, deeply reflected social ties, especially personal relationships such as kinship and friendship, in both Anglo-American and American Indian contexts. Dragging Canoe, his brothers, his nephews, and others like them, claimed to have joined the British cause, but in reality they accepted British arms to fulfill their own purposes in fighting the Americans. John Stuart, the British superintendent of Indian affairs, repeatedly implored Dragging Canoe and his troops to hold off on their attacks so they could be coordinated with British troop movements. Dragging Canoe continued to fight on his own terms, but British officials continued to supply them with ammunition.[37]

Kinship networks served as the basis for forming and legitimizing the actions of competing Cherokee factions, but it also provided the basis for forming militia units for the Americans. Capt. John Donelson Jr. and Lt. Hugh Henry Jr., along with Ensign Moses Hutchings (Thomas Hutchings's brother and Donelson's future brother-in-law), commanded a company in 1777 to combat "Indian outrages."[38] For Euro-American families, their relationships with one another provided shared identity, support, and security in a time of war, as well as the opportunity to distinguish themselves in battle.[39] The kinship networks settlers brought with them from the East were reinforced and supplemented by fictive kinship relationships forged in the heat of battle with their "brothers-in-arms."

Battle distinctions served the men of the Donelson family well, as they translated militia service into military commissions and social capital that added to their prominence in the region. The Donelson family network became known for their bravery in war, their founding of Nashville, and their influence within the community as military leaders, lawyers, surveyors, and plantation owners. This same family speculated heavily in the postwar years in lands gained during the Revolution and through Henderson's purchase. The Donelsons turned their kinship network into an effective economic network through land speculation and participation in local legal and political systems.

By 1777 the war between Cherokees and the American forces had turned brutal. Older chiefs like Little Carpenter, who had long professed peaceful intentions toward the Anglo-Americans, resolved to end the violence plaguing their towns. They signed treaties with North Carolina, South Carolina, Georgia, and Virginia in 1777, promising to "bury the hatchet and to reestablish peace." The treaty with South Carolina and Georgia even specified that "The Cherokee nation acknowledges that the troops that . . . repeatedly defeated their forces . . . did effect and maintain the conquest of all the Cherokee lands eastward of the Unacaye mountain."[40] Furthermore, each treaty delineated new boundaries and demanded cessions of Cherokee lands that added up to more than 5 million acres. Signing this treaty would be one of Little Carpenter's last acts. His death was recorded in 1777.

As part of this new peace, Nancy Ward's daughter Betsy married Joseph Martin, the newly appointed U.S. representative, or Indian agent, to the Cherokees. Martin took up a second residence in Indian country while retaining a residence, wife, and children in Virginia. He would presumably pursue the interest of both sets of kin over the next decade.[41]

While some Cherokees declared peace with their Anglo-American neighbors, the treaties formally created a rift between them and those who vowed to continue fighting. The war faction, led by Dragging Canoe, withdrew to the river towns near the southern bend of the Tennessee River. Cherokees in the Overhill and Middle Towns claimed to remain peaceful; the war faction in the Lower Towns became known as "Chickamaugas." Although it is likely many Cherokee young men from the Overhill and Middle Towns joined the Chickamaugas in raids and battles and then returned to the peace towns to the east, Cherokee chiefs claimed no knowledge or support of Chickamauga activities. In the 1780s and 1790s those chiefs would even provide intelligence on impending Chickamauga attacks in order to save their own towns from reprisals.

The Cherokee nation, by declaring peace, was forced to disavow the actions of the Chickamauga movement, even though many Cherokees agreed with Chickamauga aims and even their methods of resistance.

After these treaties, Dragging Canoe and the Chickamauga towns were no longer sanctioned by the Cherokee nation but became an entity unto themselves.[42] Essentially, this dedication temporarily trumped the connections of these Indians to their sacred towns. Dragging Canoe and the rest of the Chickamaugas claimed to serve the Cherokee people by pursuing the return of native lands and expulsion of intruders upon those lands. Similarly, the Cherokee peace towns claimed to support Cherokees' best interests, adopting the opposite philosophy that peace would ensure stability and economic success in the Cherokee nation by moving beyond previous land cessions and conflicts.[43]

Chickamaugas used the imperial tensions inherent in the Revolutionary War to their advantage by making alliances and receiving supplies from British, Spanish, and French supporters. The Chickamauga resistance movement joined with the enemies of the Anglo-American settlers, including the British during the American Revolution and several pan-Indian efforts, to check the ongoing settler encroachment.[44] The main goal of the Chickamaugas was to discourage Anglo-American settlement of the Henderson Purchase.[45] They did this through raiding settlements to drive settlers away, pillaging horses and captives, and encouraging slaves to run away from their masters to join Chickamauga towns. John Wimbish wrote to Capt. Joseph Martin in August 1777 with a description of a runaway slave and a request for Martin's assistance in "apprehending the fugitive" who was hiding or captive among the Chickamaugas.[46] These strategies of economic sabotage hurt the Americans economically as well as physically. Although they had officially declared peace with the Cherokees earlier that year, the raids resulted in a renewed campaign by the Americans against a new target—the Lower Towns where the Chickamaugas resided. At times, however, militias again retaliated for Chickamauga raids by attacking peaceful eastern Cherokee towns, declaring that Cherokees had aided and abetted the war faction. Many militia men were tired of "half-way peace" and were determined to end the attacks one way or another.[47]

Kinship networks continued to shape both diplomacy and warfare for Cherokees, dissident and otherwise. While Nancy Ward and her daughters cemented their alliances to Anglo-Americans through intercultural marriage, networks of brothers, uncles, and nephews continued to provide the foundation for Dragging Canoe's support. Dragging Canoe himself had drawn from the legacy of Oconostota in declaring war upon settlements that encroached upon Cherokee territories. His brothers Turtle at Home and Little Owl (or White Owl's Son) and his nephew (or son) Young Dragging Canoe fought alongside him.[48] They were joined by The Tassell and his nephew Watts (or John Watts). Many others fought according to their conscience, politics, or simple self-interest. By 1780, the population living in the river towns included not only warriors but women and children as well.

To some degree, Cherokees split along generational lines, following traditions of kinship and dissent that had served their society well in the past.[49] Dragging Canoe and the other young warriors followed in the footsteps of Oconostota, who had been the tribe's great war-chief during the Anglo-Cherokee War. Little Carpenter had served as a great peace chief in that conflict, just as he continued to push for peace in the 1770s. The old men argued that they could not control the young men's actions and that they wished to be at peace with the Americans. They told the truth but may have given unspoken support to those who fought for political autonomy and the traditional geographic boundaries that had ensured their economic stability in the stiff competition for resources that dominated the region in the eighteenth century. The generational split was not complete, as many young men remained in the peace towns. Nancy Ward, of the same generation as Dragging Canoe, actively campaigned for peace. She attempted to limit the damage inflicted by American militias by reporting impending attacks on Anglo-American towns, supplying the settlers with food, and encouraging her daughter to marry Joseph Martin.

Nancy Ward's daughter Elizabeth "Betsy" Ward helped to improve the relationship between the Upper Towns and their American neighbors by agreeing to the marriage. Martin's son William recounted how his father had married Betsy Ward shortly after being appointed Virginia's Indian agent to the Cherokees. The two lived together at Long Island on the Holston.[50] If this marriage took place in 1777, as this source reported, Martin's marriage would have forged familial ties between the two governments just after the peace treaty was signed between Virginia and the Cherokee nation, and during the height of Dragging Canoe's Revolutionary War–era resistance. Martin himself led military expeditions against the Chickamauga towns while attempting to insulate the Upper Towns from settler retaliation.

Cherokee allegiances were divided between supporters of the Americans and the British. The actions of Dragging Canoe, Nancy Ward, and

Betsy Martin represented two contrasting but complementary strategies. Dragging Canoe orchestrated devastating raids on the unwanted
settlements while Ward and Martin attempted to limit counterattacks
through diplomacy and denial of Dragging Canoe's legitimacy. Together
these strategies might have accomplished the goals of reinforcing Cherokee territorial boundaries and power in the region. Although the two
sides often disavowed one another, they shared the goal of protecting
the political sovereignty of the nation, one through war and the other
through peace. While Ward's faction found neutrality the most palat-
able option, Dragging Canoe, like other resistance leaders, sought active
roles in opposing the settlers moving into traditionally Cherokee territory.[51] American militias, however, treated the Cherokees as a one-
enemy nation and waged war on the peace towns and war towns alike.
Over time, many American forces came to see all Indians as enemies
and attacked accordingly.[52] Although the actions of these cousins appear
directly opposed, examination of their actions within the Cherokee cultural context reveals that their efforts followed accepted traditional strategies of creating peace and war factions to deal with outsiders.

As previously noted, Chickamaugas drew support and arms from
the British throughout the Revolutionary War. John Stuart, the British superintendent for southeastern Indian affairs, supported Dragging Canoe in waging war against the Americans. A large contingent of
Creeks led by Alexander McGillivray, a Creek leader whose father was a
Scottish trader, likewise received support from Stuart and waged war on
behalf of Creeks against the encroaching Americans.[53]

By contrast, Chickasaws attempted to remain largely neutral, despite
their long-standing trade alliance with the British. British trading companies dominated trade with the Chickasaws and sought to maintain
a permanent presence among their allies. James Logan Colbert, for
example, had married into the tribe and became thoroughly integrated
through marriage and possibly adoption. During the Seven Years' War,
Colbert fought alongside his Chickasaw kin and other Englishmen in the
region against the French, as well as traveled east to help fight alongside
South Carolinians against the Cherokees in the Anglo-Cherokee War.

In 1777, Colbert, his sons, nephews, and other English loyalists
engaged in patrols of the Mississippi River, in the process asserting
Chickasaw (and possibly English) control over the waterway. Like Cherokees, Chickasaws had a matrilineal culture. Colbert's influence reflected
his marriage to Chickasaw women and connections to a Chickasaw clan,
his proven military ability, and his access to trade goods. He used his

personal influence to forge a coalition of loyalists and Chickasaw kin in order to keep the Mississippi River clear of Americans and, later, their allies the Spanish. These patrols, although largely inconsequential in scope, convinced Americans like Thomas Jefferson that Chickasaws were a significant threat to American ambitions in the Mississippi Valley. These patrols would ultimately result in efforts by Americans to take control of the Chickasaw Bluffs, near present-day Memphis, which destroyed Chickasaw neutrality and provoked their wrath against the Americans in the midst of the Revolutionary War.[54]

After the American Declaration of Independence, the state legislatures of North Carolina and Virginia initiated efforts to survey boundaries beyond the Appalachian Mountains. Each state named surveyors that would run the boundary line together. In 1779 Richard Henderson, William B. Smith, Daniel Smith, and Thomas Walker were appointed. They proceeded to create two separate lines, reflecting the interests of the two different states. While the colonies of North Carolina and Virginia had denied the validity of Henderson's Treaty of Sycamore Shoals, the states of North Carolina and Virginia had no problem incorporating the lands into their states. Henderson was respected enough by the legislature to represent North Carolina in surveying the boundary. By the time the surveyors began to run the line, Henderson had already attracted several investors to his Transylvania Land Company and was taking possession of tracts of land on the Cumberland River.[55] The other surveyors were also active land speculators who benefited personally from the land cession.

After the state government of North Carolina approved the Henderson land cession, the settlers from Watauga chose to purchase and move onto lands gained through the Henderson Treaty in the autumn of 1779. The settlement of these lands would place Americans on strategic waterways, including the Cumberland River, thereby claiming a foothold along the fertile but hard-to-defend riverbanks. Male settlers would double as militia troops who defended their claims and the families they brought with them.

James Robertson and John Donelson would lead the founding party into the fertile lands along the Cumberland River. Robertson would guide the smaller party of well-armed men along the shorter overland path through the Cumberland Gap and then over the "dark and bloody ground" defended by Chickamaugas. Robertson's group planned to reach the Cumberland region first and prepare dwellings and fortifications at the place they named Nashborough before the second group arrived. John Donelson led the second group, in which a smaller number of men escorted a large number of women, children, and a few slaves along the water route to the Cumberland settlement. Other family would arrive later, over the next several years, in a pattern of chain migration. Altogether, twenty-six of the eighty-two travelers were immediate family or related by marriage to Donelson revealing the centrality of kinship networks to this migratory journey.

Although traveling along the Tennessee River to the Ohio River and then to the Cumberland—as people had done throughout the eighteenth century—was infinitely easier than overland travel during the time, the plan was complicated by the Chickamaugas' intense, unexpected attacks on the flotilla. Embarking on December 22, 1779, the boats and rafts contained more than eighty-two people, their livestock, and food, goods, and tools.[56] It encountered obstacles almost from its embarkation. They encountered low water, high water, outbreaks of disease, and resistance from Chickamaugas, whose major towns were along the Tennessee River. The transition from traveling through the territory of Cherokee neutrals to the territory of Chickamauga Lower Towns was marked by the exit of a very nervous Cherokee translator named Archie Coody from the boats just before the group came upon Chickamauga towns. Dragging Canoe's forces repeatedly and devastatingly attacked the flotilla as it passed by their towns, but they did not pursue them. Altogether, the group lost at least thirty-four people to disease, warfare, and accidents, amounting to possibly 40 percent of the original group. Of those that arrived exhausted and terrorized on April 24, 1780, most would stay to help establish an Anglo-American foothold on the trans-Appalachian frontier.[57]

In April 1780, just as the Donelson flotilla arrived at the Cumberland settlements, George Rogers Clark established Fort Jefferson on the Mississippi River at the Chickasaw Bluffs. Thomas Jefferson, then governor of Virginia, had ordered the fort built in an effort to stop the patrols of the British-allied Colbert faction and gain control over the river.[58] Although the patrols had been a nuisance more than a barrier to American travel on the Mississippi, Jefferson viewed the Chickasaws as a potentially powerful military opponent. His preemptive efforts created rather than averted a crisis. Chickasaws laid siege to the fort and the accompanying settlements for over a year.

The Colbert kinship network once again rallied into a military unit, this time with the open support of the broader Chickasaw leadership, to pursue both British and Chickasaw goals of eliminating the American fort from the banks of the Mississippi in Chickasaw territory. James Logan Colbert was himself wounded while attacking the fort. On August 10, 1781, John Floyd, resident commander of the fort, wrote to Clark: "The Savages are constantly pecking at us & in a few weeks this handful of wretched People will be invaded on all sides by them & their Infernal Leaders. Nothing has hitherto prevented it but the expectation of a Campaign against them. The reason that the Country is not now left waste is the inability of the Settlers to remove having already lost most of their Horses, and the Ohio only runs one way. The Militia are entirely without Ammunition and I find it impossible to procure any."[59] The situation for Fort Jefferson was desperate, and by October 1781, the fort and settlements were evacuated.[60] The Chickasaws had defeated the Americans, reclaimed the fort and the land, and, for the moment, triumphed over the encroachment.

Spain remained neutral until near the end of the Revolution, when they sided with the Americans. This alliance prompted the Colbert faction to capture Spanish ships on the Mississippi, even taking prisoner the wife of Governor Esteban Miro of New Orleans. Indeed, in April 1782, James Logan Colbert "and his band of Loyalists and Indians," including his son William (whose mother was Chickasaw), began attacking Spanish ships on the Mississippi River. In capturing one of these ships, he took prisoner Madam Nicanora Ramos Cruzat, Miro's wife, and her four children. Colbert subsequently released Madam Cruzat, along with a message to the governor requesting the prohibition of scalp buying at Mobile and an exchange of prisoners. Governor Miro refused, sent an expedition to capture Colbert, and demanded the leaders of the Chickasaws turn Colbert's band over to him. The leaders argued that the raids were by loyalist Englishmen and refused to hand over Colbert's party but agreed instead to give up some Natchez refugees who had escaped into Chickasaw towns. Colbert's kinship connections protected him, all the while allowing the Chickasaw chiefs to claim that his identity as an English loyalist muted their own culpability. The ambiguous identities of Colbert and his children served both his agenda and those of the Chickasaw chiefs.[61]

Colbert's military faction also attacked the Spanish "Arkansas Fort" near St. Louis. His forces consisted of "eleven Indians, sons and nephews of Colbert, five Negroes, one Frenchman, and enough English and Americans to make the number eighty-two."[62] This human accounting reveals that Colbert's military raiders were not simply "English loyalists." Rather, they were a blend of people whose aims matched Colbert's.

The core of this group were Colbert's "sons and nephews," illustrating the importance of kinship in the forming of military units for the Chickasaws. Colbert drew upon both marital and blood kinship relationships as he entered into battle against the Americans. The faction may or may not have been acting as representatives of the Chickasaw tribe, but they pursued agendas that reflected larger Chickasaw interests of maintaining control over the Mississippi River.[63]

At Nashville and at Chickasaw Bluffs settlers sought to settle lands obtained in the Henderson Treaty. In effect, Americans sought to take advantage of Revolutionary chaos to undermine British limits on expansion and to justify their attacks on tribes that claimed neutrality.

The 1783 Treaty of Paris made no mention of the fates of Indian allies of either side. The American government subsequently sought to reestablish peace in the Southeast through treaties with each tribe. Joseph Martin and John Donelson represented Virginia in treaty negotiations across the Southeast. These treaties demanded land cessions, as well as the return of prisoners and property taken during the war. In theory, they also promised a stable and mutually beneficial trading relationship between the parties. These treaties, however, were never ratified because in 1783 the jurisdiction to make treaties with Indian tribes transferred from the domain of the states to the control of the federal government. Donelson was actually investigated with regard to these treaties under the charges that he pursued personal interests and sought private land cessions as part of the treaties.[64] Donelson and Martin both denied these charges and they were dropped. The U.S. government in 1783 had no desire to replicate the complicated and controversial negotiations of the Treaty of Sycamore Shoals. The Federalists in particular sought instead to end the war with Indians in ways that were concrete and legally defensible while shoring up the power of the federal government over the rights of individual states.

Not until the Hopewell Treaties of 1785 was peace formally reestablished between the United States, the Chickasaws, and the Cherokees. By then land speculators and settlers had streamed into the region. Indians increasingly sought federal and state assistance in stemming the tide and regaining profitable trade relationships. They hoped that the new republic would be able to create and enforce boundaries that would protect Indian lands and provide quality trade goods at competitive prices. In return, they promised to give up land, to return property and captives taken during the Revolution, to trade exclusively with the United States, and to uphold the peace.[65]

Neither side fully honored the stipulations of the treaty. War factions like Dragging Canoe's Chickamaugas and Alexander McGillivray's Creeks continued to attack Anglo-American settlements through 1794, when many of their key towns, and those of their allies in the Northwest Territory, were destroyed. Additionally, after the Revolution the United States had to compete with Spain for the loyalty and trade of Chickasaws, Chickamaugas, and even the Anglo-Americans in the region. Throughout the eighteenth and into the nineteenth century, kinship remained central to military and diplomatic strategies for American Indians and Anglo-Americans as they wrangled over who would control the land west of the Appalachian mountains. As Americans attempted to expand their control and jurisdiction over Indian lands, native peoples would continue the war they began in the Revolution for several more decades through alliances founded in shared anger at American encroachment. Kinship networks helped native people forge these alliances. Meanwhile Americans would use their own kinship networks to acquire land through war, trade, and treaties.[66]

Kinship connections shaped the contours of battle in the backcountry as military units were forged upon the foundation of kinship associations, as it motivated Americans to claim Indian lands and encouraged Indians to fight for the land of their ancestors for their children. As kinsmen fought side by side for Revolutionary ideals of land and liberty, other groups of kinsmen violently opposed their forts and settlements. The battles in the backcountry during the American Revolution were only the beginning of these contests. Kinship continued to play a key role in how the competition for the frontier played out. The British and Spanish connections with American Indians who resisted American encroachment would reemerge in the years immediately following the Treaty of Paris in the "Indian Wars" of the 1780s and 1790s.

3 / Ongoing Warfare: Indian Resistance and Accommodation

During the 1780s and 1790s, the American Revolution in Indian country raged on long after Britain and America had signed the peace treaty ending the war. Elizabeth "Betsy" Ward Martin followed in the path of peace forged by her mother, Nancy Ward, and her great-uncle Little Carpenter. She had married Joseph Martin in 1777 as part of the peace that ended the Overhill Cherokees' war against the Americans. Their marriage represented a political alliance between the Overhill Cherokee towns and the states of North Carolina and Virginia, both of which were represented at different times by Joseph Martin.

Following their marriage and the peace treaty, Betsy waited for word on the outcome of battles between her new husband and her cousins who had joined Dragging Canoe in waging war against American settlements just to the west of her home. He also served as a treaty commissioner from the United States to the Cherokees and routinely pressured Betsy's people to cede land to the states. Joseph Martin himself benefited directly from these cessions so that by 1788 he had plantations in Virginia, South Carolina, and Georgia.[1] The irony that he was both treaty commissioner and Betsy Ward Martin's husband, obligated to fulfill the responsibilities of a kinsman, must have created tense situations for Betsy in dealing with her family.

By the time he married Betsy, Joseph Martin had already married and divorced Savannah Emory, the daughter of a prominent Cherokee woman and an Anglo-American trader. Marriages in Cherokee country were fluid and could be constituted and dissolved easily according to the desires of the couple. While married to Betsy Ward Martin, he also maintained a marriage back east in Virginia and fathered a total of twenty-three children with four wives, two of those children with Betsy.

In 1788 Betsy Martin found herself caught in the middle when tensions between North Carolina and the newly seceded "State of Franklin" boiled over. John Sevier, the governor of the self-proclaimed state, decided to attack the Overhill Cherokees in retribution for Chickamauga Cherokee raids that had taken place. Betsy's home at Long Island on the Tennessee River was among the places attacked by the Franklinites. Betsy herself was wounded in the attack. She and her children moved to the safety of one of her husband Joseph's many plantations to wait out the turmoil at his home. He dug into his personal stores to send corn and other supplies to her kin and then set out to exact his own revenge on Sevier.[2] Receiving orders from North Carolina's governor to capture and retrieve the troublesome Sevier, Joseph Martin set out after the man whose raids had injured Betsy and her kin as well as devastated her home.[3] This was the same year that Joseph Martin married Susanna Graves following the death of his first Virginian wife, Sarah Lucas. The following year in 1789 Joseph Martin would leave Cherokee country to return to his home in Virginia.[4]

Betsy and her children would see him again on the occasions that he made special trips back into Cherokee territory. Martin made arrangements for at least one of his Cherokee sons to be educated in Virginia.[5] On his last such trip in 1808, Martin "visited many scenes of his early years and also his former friends among the Cherokee."[6] Those former friends would have included his Cherokee wives, children, and, by that time, fifty-seven grandchildren who lived in Cherokee territory. Sources related to Martin's life barely hint at the lives of those like Betsy who lived and died as Cherokees, but their actions and experiences fundamentally shaped the motivations of Martin and others who were memorialized for their role in the intercultural diplomacy and warfare of the time. Although few sources exist that directly reference Betsy Ward Martin, those that do indicate the complicated nature of intercultural relationships, the disastrous effects of the political turmoil of the time, how kinship shaped the motivations and methods of warfare, and the role kinship played in alleviating the hardships caused by war. How Betsy or Joseph Martin felt about those events and the familial relationships that were built, and then left, remain subjects for historical speculation.

Following the official end to the Revolutionary War with the Treaty of Paris, kinship remained the foundation upon which the members of each society built their relationships to political, economic, and social institutions. Key crises such as Chickamaugas' sieges of the Cumberland settlements, the conflict between North Carolina and the State of Franklin, and the Northwestern Territory wars of the 1790s illustrate that fragmentation continued to serve factional interests in each of these societies. The family case studies in this chapter represent the disparate perspectives in these dramas and show how kin-based factions turned the upheaval of the post-Revolution era to economic advantage.

As the Donelson family and others clamored to buy and survey former Indian lands, "mixed blood" American Indian families like the Wards, Ridges, and Colberts made names for themselves as intercultural negotiators working to reinforce their nations' political boundaries and economic stability, some by engaging directly in the Anglo-American market economy. Others, like Dragging Canoe and his supporters, resisted encroachment militarily and took the spoils of war. These economic strategies reflect the political atmosphere of the trans-Appalachian frontier but also reveal how these government leaders and their families carved out places for themselves in the highly competitive economy that resulted from the new power dynamics of the post-Revolution Southeast.

Some native families worked to halt westward expansion through diplomacy. The new Federalist government encouraged Indians to become "civilized," or like the Americans in culture, through adopting Anglo-style dress, learning and speaking English, practicing Protestant Christianity, and embracing similar rules of government. These new "civilized" Indian governments intended to maximize the benefits Indians received in trade from the United States as a result of engaging in the practices of "civilization" such as through growing, spinning, and weaving cotton or flax. To represent themselves to Americans as "civilized," Indian officials adopted cultural markers that their diplomatic counterparts in the United States felt were signifiers of civilization while maintaining the key cultural components that made up their Chickasaw and Cherokee identities. Whether their actions benefited their people or themselves, however, quickly became a topic of debate, accompanied by accusations of bribery and fraud. Others used military opposition to reverse the encroachment by making the losses in Anglo-American lives and property unacceptable to those living on the contested borderland of the trans-Appalachian frontier. Whether native families embraced strategies of alliance or resistance, their political and economic strategies worked toward the goal of reinforcing Chickasaw and Cherokee political sovereignty and land retention in the face of immense pressure from their Anglo-American neighbors, like the Donelsons.

The negotiations of 1783 failed to produce viable treaties between the United States and the Southeastern Indian nations. John Donelson had been brought before the Virginia governor charged with betraying the state's interest in order to pursue his own agenda.[7] Although Donelson was not found guilty of such indiscretion, when new treaties with the Chickasaw and Cherokee nations were negotiated, he was not among the new U.S. treaty commissioners.

The Treaty of Hopewell, convened at the town of Hopewell on the Keowee River on November 28, 1785, highlighted the roles of Little Carpenter and his descendants, Nancy Ward and Dragging Canoe, in pursuing familial economic strategies. Cherokee chief The Tassell, or Old Tassell, rejected the validity of the 1775 Henderson Treaty during the Hopewell treaty negotiation. He denied outright that several Cherokee chiefs, including Oconostota and Little Carpenter, had signed the document and accused Henderson of forging the signatures.[8] Beyond a testimony of the roles of Attakullakulla and Oconostota's fervency against the treaty, Old Tassell's outrage indicates not only that the oral tradition of the Cherokee contested the written historical record of the Henderson Treaty proceedings but also that the Cumberland region was as thoroughly contested in the 1780s as in 1776. Nancy Ward then spoke before the assembly declaring: "The talk that I give you is from the young warriors, as well as from myself. They rejoice that we have peace, and hope that the chain of friendship will never be broken."[9] The Treaty of Hopewell was intended to end the hostilities between the Cherokee and the Cumberland settlements, thereby returning the parties to their former trading relationship. However, it failed to address the central issue of those hostilities—the appropriation of the Cherokees' valuable hunting grounds in the Cumberland region through the highly suspect and contested Henderson Treaty.

The commissioners—Benjamin Hawkins, Andrew Pickens, Joseph Martin, and Lachlan McIntosh—insisted that the cession was valid and that this treaty would reinforce the boundaries established by the Henderson Treaty. The treaty also demanded the return of slaves, property, and prisoners taken in attacks on the Cumberland settlements. Dragging Canoe, representing his own group of young warriors who had claimed those people and property as the spoils of war, did not sign this treaty but rather began anew the siege of the settlements.[10]

Although Little Carpenter had died prior to this treaty, his authority within the tribe remained part of the oral history, and his niece replicated his efforts to create a lasting peace between the Anglo-Americans and the Cherokees. Dragging Canoe replicated and intensified Oconostota's resistance to the imposed boundaries. Kinship helps explain how Cherokees reacted to the both the Henderson Treaty and the reinforcement of the boundaries drawn there through the Treaty of Hopewell a decade later. Each side represented differing kin-based economic agendas.

The Chickasaw nation also signed a treaty at Hopewell just over a month later on January 10, 1786. This treaty likewise delineated the tribe's boundaries, required that prisoners be returned, and promised that the United States rather than the states would be authorized to regulate trade. The Chickasaws, however, lacked the motivation to continue warfare against the United States once Fort Jefferson was abandoned. Instead, the agreement provided the potential for a valuable trade relationship.[11] They had signed a treaty with the Spanish on June 23, 1784, establishing a similar trade relationship.[12] The Chickasaws, consciously or unwittingly, utilized various kin-based factions to take advantage of several governments vying for their trade.

Joseph Martin, Virginia and North Carolina's appointed agent to the Cherokees, married Elizabeth "Betsy" Ward in 1777 to improve diplomatic and economic relations between the two formerly warring governments by becoming a relative of one of the most prominent Cherokee families. To fulfill his political obligations, Martin embraced Cherokee cultural norms that drastically differed from, and even contradicted, Anglo-American beliefs about marriage and gender roles. Despite Christian doctrine against polygamy and sexual relations outside of church-sanctioned marriages, Martin maintained one family in Virginia and others in the Cherokee towns of Long Island and Citico.[13] Establishing diplomatic ties through his familial connections and honoring his obligations among the Cherokees required rejecting Anglo-American definitions of marriage and gender norms at least while he remained within the Cherokee Territory. His actions contrasted sharply with those of Creek agent Benjamin Hawkins, who worked to make his agency a model of Anglo-American cultural norms so that Creeks might emulate "proper" marriages and gender roles. However, Martin's behavior, rather than Hawkins's, more readily reflected the pragmatic responses of Anglo-American traders and diplomats to the demands of transacting political or economic business with American Indians in the Southeast in the late eighteenth and early nineteenth centuries. Because Indian politics revolved around kinship categorizing people into "kin" and "enemies,"

Martin and others found that they needed native kin to do their jobs as agents, diplomats, or traders.[14] Gaining native kin trumped the dictates of their own culture that made marrying native women taboo at best and threatened to jeopardize one's very soul at worst.

Martin's position as an intermediary between the Cherokees and the Anglo-Americans made him vulnerable to both sides. He found himself leading military expeditions against both the Chickamauga towns and against the Franklinite militia that burned Cherokee towns. This ambivalence made him the target of many North Carolinians' disdain.[15]

After North Carolina extended its laws over the Watauga and Cumberland settlements in 1783, Martin was appointed the Indian agent to the Cherokee for North Carolina.[16] The following year, representatives of the Watauga settlements declared their independence from North Carolina, forming what they called the sovereign state of Franklin. Sevier and several other prominent men in the Watauga settlements in 1783 began pushing for statehood separate from North Carolina's government because, they argued, North Carolina was not defending communities west of the Appalachian Mountains from their Indian enemies. After declaring themselves a separate state and electing their own government officials, the Franklinites met federal opposition in addition to North Carolina's. North Carolina called upon loyal military men like Joseph Martin in an attempt to enforce its laws, including taxation, on the Franklinites. The Franklinites refused to yield to North Carolina's jurisdiction and continued to pursue their own political and military agendas.

As previously noted, John Sevier led a Franklinite militia on an Indian campaign against the Upper Towns of the Cherokee, destroying several towns and wounding Betsy Ward, Martin's Cherokee wife, in the process. Martin, who had recently been appointed brigadier general by North Carolina's Governor Caswell, recommended military action against Sevier and the Franklinites for their rebellion against North Carolina and their attacks against the Cherokee allies of that state. Those recommendations were approved, and Martin himself led the expedition to detain Sevier for questioning. Sevier ultimately escaped. The Franklinites finally conceded defeat in 1788, dissolving the fledgling state government, but they were in part vindicated a year later when the federal government created a new territorial government called the "Territory South of the River Ohio" for the lands North Carolina had claimed beyond the crest of the Appalachian Mountains.[17] Martin remained the agent to the Cherokees and one of the commissioners for treaties between that tribe and the U.S. government through 1789.

The marriage of Joseph Martin and Betsy Ward illustrates the ongoing commitment of the Wolf clan to maintaining peace between the Upper Towns and the neighboring governments of Virginia and North Carolina. Interestingly, however, Martin himself frequently launched military expeditions against his wife's cousin Dragging Canoe in the Chickamauga towns during his time as Indian agent. Martin served as the agent to the Cherokee, remained married to his wife in Virginia, and pursued some land speculation in the Cherokee lands at Muscle Shoals. Similarly, some accounts hint that Wolf clan men, including Nancy Ward's brother and son, occasionally slipped away from their Overhill towns to fight alongside the Chickamauga warriors. Officially, they were pledged to be at peace with their American neighbors. Unofficially, some joined the raids by the Chickamauga towns as an outlet to express their frustration and to try to drive those neighbors from the area.[18]

The failure of the 1783 and 1785 treaties between the Cherokees and the United States to address the reason for Chickamauga military resistance, the contested Henderson Treaty, resulted in perpetuating that resistance. Whereas negotiation between diplomats promised the potential for peaceful coexistence of modern democratic republics, the U.S. government's commitment to territorial expansion, settlers' disrespect for treaty boundaries, and the frontier violence that resulted gave the lie to these promises for peace.

Violence continued to wrack the region. Col. John Donelson was killed in the spring of 1786, possibly by Indians, while traveling from Kentucky to the Cumberland region.[19] His travelling companions claimed the group was attacked by Indians from whom they had fled. Donelson's body and horse were found, but the saddlebags were not. Even after British support had disappeared with the close of the American Revolution, Dragging Canoe and his relations pursued a concerted effort over decades to resist that encroachment by making settlement of native lands economically infeasible. Kinship networks became military units that made Chickamauga warfare against the Cumberland settlements possible. The Chickamaugas used warfare as a means to achieve the economic ends of reclaiming valuable hunting grounds. Their raiding served as a profitable economic strategy, simultaneously depriving Anglo-Americans of their property and supplying the Chickamauga towns with horses, slaves, and trade goods.

Cherokee attitudes toward slavery and race shaped Chickamauga Cherokee strategies for resistance. Slaves in Cherokee society prior to 1800 held less value as laborers than they did as barter for trade, which yielded concrete and immediate gains to the captor. Slaves became more valuable as market demand increased, first for Indian slaves and later for black slaves. Slaves were kidnapped from one part of the frontier to be sold to plantations in another part. As the opportunity for profit from selling captives grew, warfare increased among native groups, often instigated by white resident traders.[20] Blacks rarely became allies of American Indian groups because of the stigma of inferiority attached to blacks by whites as well as frightening stories about Indians told to slaves on plantations. The Cherokees perceived such an alliance as disadvantageous in their dealings with the whites. Such reluctance toward an alliance with blacks did not exist among the Chickamaugas, who had little need of white approbation.[21] Chickamauga Cherokees inherited views of blacks as alien and exploitable from their Cherokee roots, but their purpose of expelling the white population trumped older ideas, including racial prejudices and ancient rivalries against other indigenous and European political powers. The Chickamaugas created several multiethnic communities in their hideaway towns on the lower Tennessee River that included enslaved and freed blacks. Slaves became a focal point of the Chickamauga plans of destruction along with the lives and other property of the enemy.

Chickamaugas took every opportunity to pillage and inflict losses on their enemies. Dozens of letters from the Indian agents to the Cherokees demanded the return of slaves taken from white estates. William Blount, governor of the Territory South of the Ohio River, wrote to the Cherokee chiefs, "I would advise you to deliver up at the Tellico block house, to John McKee, without delay, all the deserters, prisoners, negroes, and horses; then the people of Kentucky can have no more cause to invade your country."[22] John Sevier wrote to the "Chiefs and Warriors of the Cherokee Nation" that he required the return of "some black people that was taken from the same place [Kentucky] (a woman and three children that belonged to general Logan of that country)."[23] He wrote again less than three weeks later, requesting the return of some slaves taken from George Colbert of the Chickasaw nation: "You know it is wrong to stop people for horses, for negroes is not horses though they are black. . . . I wish you and the Chickasaws to live as brothers and good neighbors, but you can't expect this to be the case, if you keep their people from them."[24] Sevier reminded the Indians that they already knew that stopping people for, or robbing travelers of, horses was wrong and then essentially said that taking slaves was basically the same thing. The Chickamaugas refused to give up the slaves. Nearly a year later, in May 1797, Louis Phillippe, the future king of France, related in his journal of his travels through Chickasaw territory George Colbert's argument that the Chickasaws' relationship with the Cherokees was strained because "the Cherokees resent the Chickasaws for their neutrality in the last war with the Americans, and they hate the major [George Colbert] for several reasons: 1st because with his brothers he served in the American army, 2d because he married a Cherokee woman who owns livestock and is well off, and 3d because they stole two Negroes from him that they do not want to give back."[25] The allies of the United States, including the Colberts, were not immune to the Chickamaugas' economic strategies that aimed at the destruction and demoralization of their white enemies through relieving them of their financial assets. Louis Phillippe had also noted that the tension was in part caused by the marriage of Colbert to a Cherokee woman, which resulted in the tribe losing control over her land and resources, which belonged to her through matrilineal inheritance. This comment revealed several economic and political motivations for the animosity between these Chickamauga Cherokees (Louis Phillippe did not distinguish between them and their Overhill relatives) and George Colbert.[26]

After the defeat of the Chickamaugas at Nickajack, Governor Blount replied to Chickamauga chief John Watts: "I understand that [the Chickamaugas] wish an exchange of prisoners; to this I agree. . . . All negroes in your hands, whether captured, or absconded from their masters, are to be considered as prisoners in your hands, and are to be delivered up."[27] The Chickamaugas saw slaves as a weakness in their enemy. They therefore proceeded to exploit that weakness through abduction and encouraging desertion of the slaves. Theft of slaves served as an economic blow to Anglo-American settlers but also provided labor or even allies for the Chickamaugas.

The economic strategies of Dragging Canoe and the Chickamauga Cherokees derived from their knowledge of the regional economic system. Their raids for horses and slaves were a continuation of previous Cherokee economic tactics that modified Anglo-American economic practices to fit the Cherokee culture, wherein, for example, the opportunity for military bravery and exchange value trumped slaves' labor potential. The Chickamaugas also destroyed property and lives to make the cost of remaining in the Cumberland region unacceptable to the settlers. Although Chickamauga resistance has been noted by historians as among the military pan-Indian traditionalist movements, which rejected anything to do with Anglo-American culture including trade goods, the tactics of Dragging Canoe and his followers reflect their familiarity with the economic system.[28] They understood Anglo-American economic strategies and how to best inflict damage that would make settlement economically infeasible.

In 1788, U.S. commissioners again had the opportunity to meet the Chickamaugas' demands and thereby end the constant warfare. Federal officials wanted to clarify boundaries between the Territory and native groups to decrease the friction between them. These talks gave the Cherokee and Chickasaw leaders a chance to bargain for rights or trade negotiations they had not secured in the earlier Treaty of Hopewell. Cherokee headmen at Ustinale wrote to Richard Winn, superintendent for the Southern Department of the War Office, that "Congress is determined to have our hunting grounds open so that our young men may hunt" and that plans had been made "that a friendly talk will soon take place . . . [to] put a stop to all Hostilities and for the time to come to Live like Brothers and friends."[29] Dragging Canoe and John Watts, both prominent Chickamauga leaders, signed this talk, indicating that they approved of the message and the peace that would result from a return of hunting rights to the Cherokee hunters. This was a compromise that asked not for the previous boundaries to be restored, but just for their people to have a right to hunt in the territory. This clause, however, never made it into a ratified treaty, and the Chickamauga Cherokees continued their warfare against settlements in Kentucky and on the Cumberland River. Meanwhile other Cherokee towns and clans, including Chota, home to Nancy Ward, Dragging Canoe's first cousin, would declare themselves at peace with the settlers, disavowing the actions of the Chickamaugas. Talks, treaties, and warfare worked together as Cherokees and Chickamaugas sought to protect their sovereignty in the ongoing intercultural contest. If one method did not work, another might. Although the two strategies at times worked in tandem, Cherokee peace chiefs frequently expressed frustration at the Chickamauga tactics, especially when they resulted in retaliations inflicted upon the peace towns.

The Chickasaws also found themselves in treaty talks in 1788 and 1789 in response to the formation of the new Territory South of the River Ohio. Following the close of the American Revolution, the Colbert family, familiar with the formerly British settlers in the region, seemingly ended their alliance with the British government and supported friendly relations with the United States. The Colbert faction, however, was not alone in negotiating for the Chickasaws. "A talk delivered [to] General Joseph Martin by Piamingo chief warrior of the Chickasaw Nation for His Excellency Samuel Johnson [Governor of North Carolina]" in 1789 reaffirmed the alliance between the Chickasaw and the United States and requested ammunition from his North Carolina allies to provide Chickasaw warriors with the means to fight against the Creeks. The "Elder Brothers of North Carolina" were asked to provide his warriors with ammunition in exchange for furs or horses. Piamingo ended the talk by saying, "my Talk is short [so] I hope [you] will Remember me and my People we are not able to help ourselves without you as we do not know how to make powder and are verry [sic] unwilling to apply to the Spaniards for it, they are people we never loved they have Sent to us often to come to them but we will not if we can help it."[30] The Chickasaws fought the Creeks as enemies of the United States but also as enemies of their own people. They would fight the Creeks whether or not North Carolina gave them arms and ammunition. Whoever provided the arms would prove themselves the better trade and military ally to the Chickasaws in a time of intense competition between the Spanish and Americans for control over the Southwest Territory. The Spanish were supplying the Creeks and Chickamaugas as enemies of the Americans and would not hesitate to arm the Chickasaws in the hope that they, too, would turn against the Americans in the backcountry.

Piamingo's Spanish trade alternative was no mere threat. The Chickasaws negotiated official treaties with the Spanish in 1784, 1790, 1793 and 1795 that included assertions on the part of Spain that trade goods would be provided to the Chickasaws "under the most equitable prices."[31] Signatures on the U.S. treaties did not match those on the Spanish treaties, indicating less political centrality than that implied in the treaties. The Colberts did not sign any of the Spanish treaties. Different kin-based factions negotiated with different imperial powers, ensuring that the Chickasaws reaped trade benefits from multiple sources. The 1786 Treaty of Hopewell likewise delineated Chickasaw boundaries and an exclusive trade relationship between the Chickasaws and the United States. Each set of leaders could uphold their trade agreement with their imperial ally because those factions functioned separately. Together the U.S. and Spanish treaties reveal divergent groups pursuing separate interests with competing imperial powers. Colbert's band was only one of several groups claiming political authority; Piamingo's was another.[32] Even as

Piamingo negotiated, the Colberts fought alongside other Chickasaw raiding parties against the Creeks. They, too, would request aid form the United States to fight this war against the Creeks. As will be described later, this would become a factor in their negotiations with the United Sates over compensation for their service in the battles in the Northwest Territory.

The years 1788 to 1794 marked an intense period of warfare from the Great Lakes to New Orleans. In the newly formed regions of the Northwest Territory and the Southwest Territory, Americans pushed onto lands gained through the Treaties of Hopewell and Greenville signed after the American Revolution. In both places, the settlers, militias, and U.S. Army met resistance from American Indian groups that claimed that the treaties and requisite land cessions were invalid. Throughout the period, kinship helped bind resistance factions together and facilitated cross-regional warfare. Southern Cherokee Indians traveled north to fight with the Shawnees, and the latter returned the favor by coming south as allied warriors against settlements on the Cumberland River. Kinship served as the foundation for Indians, like the Chickasaw Colberts, who fought alongside the U.S. Army against the resistance coalition. Kinship connections in the 1790s wars in the Northwest and Southwest Territories shaped the internal dynamics of how these groups coalesced and crossed regional boundaries.

Joseph Brown's capture by the Chickamaugas in 1788, described in this book's introduction, was not an isolated or random incident but was rather part of a war that spanned the region from the Great Lakes to the Gulf of Mexico. Joseph Brown's captivity narrative presents his perspective on his adoption in the midst of warfare. At the age of fifteen when he was taken, Brown would have been very cognizant of the ongoing brutal conflicts in the region and would have been deeply affected by the murder of his family members.

Adoption was one way kinship was used during what became known as the "Indian Wars," but this was only one way that native peoples sought to utilize kinship during this period of warfare. American Indians often incorporated individuals from other tribes into their own through warfare, especially when their numbers had thinned significantly. Sometimes captives became slaves; sometimes they were adopted. If slaves, they were set apart as a symbol of the Other, of their dominance over enemies. They were not kin, but women especially could become kin through intermarriage if they convinced someone to marry them and thereby extend the protection of his clan over her. More often, Cherokees and other tribes incorporated women and children into the tribe through adoption. They changed the appearance of the adopted and put them through rituals of disassociation to separate them from their past and of incorporation that captives often did not understand. Scratching with snakes' teeth, changing their clothes, and painting them to make them look like Cherokees were some of the rituals of incorporation. For many captives, this was traumatizing rather than incorporating. Many times these adoptions took place to replace warriors killed in battle. The captive adoptees then took on the name, the identity, and familial connections of the deceased. In this way, Indian tribes attempted to restore balance to the tribe—balance that had been stripped away by too many deaths from wars and reoccurring epidemics.

While Joseph Brown and his sister were still living among the Chickamaugas as captives, the men of those villages were launching a series of attacks on the Cumberland region from which Brown was taken. Even as the Chickasaws were fighting the Creeks, the Chickamaugas allied with the Creeks to attack the Cumberland settlements, especially in 1791 and 1792.[33] The attack on Buchanan's Station, five miles outside of Nashville, was one of many made on stations and homes throughout the region in an effort to drive settlers back east. This battle is symbolic of how such resistance movements united former enemies and how Indians in the Northwest Territory joined with those in the Southwest Territory who wanted to push back the Americans. This pan-Indian alliance served as a sort of predecessor to Tecumseh and Tenskwatawa's efforts to forge a pan-Indian movement just prior to the War of 1812. It also, however, foreshadowed the fragmentation and internal strife that would plague later movements as John Watts struggled with his Creek and Shawnee allies over battle strategy and ultimately saw his objective of attacking Nashville dissolve as his troops scattered during and after the battle of Buchanan's Station.

Buchanan's Station, like stations throughout the region at the time, was a small fort composed of a collection of four blockhouses connected by a palisade fence of sharpened logs to deter those who would attempt to enter uninvited. Outside lay fields and forests, livestock, and the flowing creek. Inside, in times of peace, the Buchanan family lived and worked, but in times of war their neighbors gathered there to protect themselves and their families. On the night of September 30, 1792, roughly twenty neighbors had gathered at Buchanan's Station. They had been warned that an attack was imminent.

Settlers and American Indians in the region had complicated relationships with each other. Many of the earliest settlers had formed friendships with the native people they met. Some had intermarried, and those couples had raised their children in the Indian towns along the rivers. These marriages would directly impact the events on September 30. Local leaders of native towns and the Cumberland settlements often visited in peace as they traveled through each other's territory. However, this relationship was complicated by the tension that grew out of competition for the lands of the region. As more settlers entered the region, some native leaders felt they were approaching a point of no return when Cherokee, Creek, and Chickasaw people would be pushed from their homelands altogether. Given the right circumstances, chiefs who normally advocated for peace could change their minds.

For over a decade, since Dragging Canoe had declared the Cumberland region would become "dark and bloody," militant Cherokees had violently opposed settlement of that region. They attacked the Cumberland settlements throughout the summer of 1792 and for two weeks after the attack on Buchanan's Station.[34] The Battle of Buchanan's Station was part of a much larger story of Indian resistance to settlement on disputed lands, but not all the Indians in the region were unified in this resistance.

William Blount, governor and Indian agent for the Southwestern Territory, received letters about Buchanan's Station between September 15 and November 5, 1792. Cherokee chiefs, The Breath and Charles, opposed the plan to unite the Cherokees with the Creeks and Shawnees to escalate the war against the Cumberland settlements. They sent warnings to Blount on September 15 and 17, noting, first: "We are sorry to inform you . . . that, there was a great number of Creeks passed by here for several days; it was out of our power to stop them; they said there was several hundreds crossed the river low down, and had with them 500 lbs of powder and lead accordingly; they said they were going to Cumberland; it is not the principal head-men of the Creek nation, but young fellows, and indeed a great number of them boys."[35] Later they also informed Blount that a group of Cherokee Indians had joined with the Creeks and a group of Shawnees who sought to attack the settlements. Richard Finnelson, a "mixed-blood" Cherokee, and a French Canadian named Joseph Deraque had been traveling with this group and learned of the specific plans for the attack. Having decided not to participate in the assault on the Cumberland settlements, probably because they had family and friends in those settlements, they reported what they knew of the plans to Blount just two days before the attack on Buchanan's Station occurred.[36] Meanwhile, most Cherokees remained at peace with the settlements.

As a result, Blount compiled a list of short biographies of Indians mentioned in Finnelson's report, noting his personal relationship with each and often recording kinship connections when he found them relevant. He noted "Tolottiskee . . . is the nephew of the old Tassell [and] has ever breathed resentment for his death. . . . Watts is also the nephew of the Tassell; but after the treaty, he declared he would no more think of revenge; that he had already sought and obtained it."[37] Blount would soon find that both would seek additional revenge.

After Dragging Canoe died in 1792, informant James Carey told William Blount that "the brother of the late Dragging Canoe, the same that the Council at Estinaula declared should succeed to his brother's honors and command, came to Estinaula after the War pipe which he had brought down from Detroit."[38] John Watts was a nephew of Old Tassell, a chief and elder for the Chickamauga towns. Watts, rather than a closer member of Dragging Canoe's kin, took Dragging Canoe's place in the eyes of their enemies as the person most associated with leadership of the Chickamauga war parties. While matrilineal kinship patterns ensured that leaders passed down their knowledge, skills, and even their names to their nephews, the transition of power from Dragging Canoe to Watts illustrated that tribal perception of merit ultimately decided who would continue the fight against the Cumberland settlements. Nonetheless, kinship remained a factor as Watts fought to avenge his uncle's death. Although the Chickamauga towns were destroyed by 1795, Watts continued to negotiate as chief of what was left of the Chickamauga "river towns" into the nineteenth century after they were reabsorbed by the Cherokees.[39]

Because of the reports of the Cherokee peace chiefs and informants Finnelson and Deraque, the militia had been patrolling the area around the station in the weeks before the attack. The settlers inside Buchanan's Station were prepared for, and therefore largely unharmed by, the attack.[40]

Gen. James Robertson, one of Nashville's founders and leader of the militia informed Blount of what occurred there:

> On the 30th September, about midnight, John Buchanan's Station, four miles south of Nashville, (at which sundry families had collected, and fifteen gun-men) was attacked by a party of Creeks and Lower Cherokees, supposedly to consist of three or four hundred. Their approach was suspected by the running of cattle, that had taken fright at them, and, upon examination,

they were found rapidly advancing within ten yards of the gate; from this place and distance they received the first-fire from the man who discovered them, (John McRory). They immediately returned the fire, and continued a very heavy and constant firing upon the station, (blockhouses, surrounded with a stockade) for an hour; and were repulsed with considerable loss, without injuring man, woman or child in the station.

During the whole time of attack, the Indians were not more distant than ten yards from the blockhouse and often in large numbers round the lower walls, attempting to put fire to it. One ascended the roof with a torch, where he was shot, and, falling to the ground, renewed his attempts to fire the bottom logs, and was killed. The Indians fired 30 balls through a port-hole of the overjutting, which lodged in the roof in the circumference of a hat, and those sticking in the walls, on the outside, were very numerous.

Upon viewing the ground the next morning, it appeared that the fellow who was shot from the roof, was a Cherokee half-breed of the [town of] Running Water, known by the whites by the name of Tom Tunbridge's step-son, the son of a French woman, by an Indian, and there was much blood, and signs that many dead had been dragged off, and litters having been made to carry their wounded to their horses, which they had left a mile from the station. Near the blockhouse were found several swords, hatchets, pipes, kettles, and budgets of different Indian articles; one of the swords was a fine Spanish blade, and richly mounted in the Spanish fashion. In the morning previous to the attack, Jonathan Gee, and [Mr.] Clayton were sent out as spies, on the ground, among other articles left by the Indians were found a handkerchief and a moccasin, known one belong to Gee, and the other to Clayton, hence it is supposed they are killed.[41]

The fort's attackers who were killed or wounded included several Indian leaders, most notably John Watts. According to native custom, even a few deaths were often deemed unacceptable to Indian raiding parties, and they retreated hoping to cut their losses and perhaps attack again when they had regained the element of surprise. They never fully regrouped. After the attack, the small groups of Indians attacked other outlying homes but caused minimal damage, shooting at individuals but not usually killing them. Robertson's militia of three hundred men waited to engage the Indians as they traveled through the country, but it did not encounter the group of hundreds of Indians that had supposedly entered the Cumberland region and attacked Buchanan's Station. Blount wrote that Robertson's express "further informs me that the Cumberland people are in good spirits; and employ every hour, when they are not embodied for the common defense, in erecting block-houses and stockades, the better to ensure safety to their families."[42] The Cumberland settlements continued to be vigilant after this battle and would proclaim the heroism of those within the fort for a century. No concerted Indian attack emerged after this battle, and the Indians lost momentum in their efforts to protect their lands from invasion and encroachment.

Blount's description of Indians killed and wounded in the attack once again described the kinship connections that he found important. He mentioned that an Indian shot while trying to set fire to the roof, Chiachatalla, was "known by whites by the name of Tom Tunbridge's step-son, the son of a French woman, by an Indian." Shawanese [Shawnee] Warrior, who had formed a Shawnee town alongside the Chickamauga towns on the Tennessee River, was also killed. Another killed warrior was listed as "a Creek Chief." John Watts, who had been the main leader for the attack, was wounded, as was "the Dragging Canoe's Brother the White Owl's Son." Also present, said Blount, were "John Walker and John Fields, two young half breeds, who have been raised among and by the white people [who] acted as the advance, or spies to Watt's party."[43] Blount carefully noted kinship in this report just as he had only days before the attack. Kinship proved a motivator for nephews seeking revenge for their uncle's death and garnered loyalty from others like Dragging Canoe's Brother.

After the battle, Blount argued that the battle had not been over disputed land claims: "The Creeks having never had the color of claim to land on the north side of the Tennessee . . . [a]nd if the Cherokees ever had a claim, it has been extinguished by two public treaties. . . . But, by the best information I can collect, the claim of the Cherokees to the lands lying on Cumberland is a recent thing; . . . Richard Henderson and Company purchased from their claim to the lands lying on Cumberland, as well as nearly all those included within what is now the limits of Kentucky."[44] Instead, he argued, they had been stirred up by the Spanish governor to fight against the Cumberland settlements in hopes of gaining power and the spoils of war. In truth, this resistance began in 1775 and had not diminished. The Spanish helped to fuel the flames of resentment and provided arms and ammunition to the group.

Blount also argued, correctly, that the "lack of government" or decentralization of the tribes was part of the issue. Leaders from the Cherokees, Creeks, Shawnees, and many other native groups forged alliances out of the shared desire to reclaim their lands from settlers. However, those alliances also often divided the tribes themselves between those who chose to fight to keep their former boundaries and those who signed treaties with the Americans seeking peace. Even the Indian alliance's fighting force in 1792 appears to have split into many small bands of warriors more interested in creating fear among the settlers to drive them out than in killing them. Family connections between these groups, evident in the roles of "half-breeds" in the attack on Buchanan's Station, complicated relationships between the settlers and natives as George Finnelson warned of the impending attack while Tom Tunbridge's son, or Chiachatalla, apparently used his dying breath to fan the flames at the outer wall.

Prior to 1794, Chickamauga Cherokees put forth formidable resistance to the encroachment of the white settlers onto their lands. From 1788 to 1794, some backcountry settlers in the territory that would become Kentucky and Tennessee flirted with the idea of seceding from the United States and joining Spain. Spain had recently closed the Mississippi River to non-Spanish trade, which severely impacted the economic potential of lands west of the Appalachian Mountains. Gaining the favor of the Spanish government at New Orleans would help to reopen the Mississippi as a trade route. To court the favor of the Spanish Governor Miro of New Orleans in the hope of securing access to the Mississippi River, they named the region north of the Cumberland River the "Mero District," misspelling the governor's name. Joining Spain would at the very least provide them with access to the Mississippi River for trade and squelch the Indian threat by removing the reason for Spain's supplying native raiding parties with arms. Many were convinced that the federal government was either uninterested in or unable to provide protection for the western settlers against Indian attacks. However, they hinted at secession rather than outright defecting, and the Cumberland residents chose to fight back against the Indians, a decision that would eventually pay off.[45] The federal government took their concerns seriously and negotiated to reopen the Mississippi to trade.

Ultimately, the connections between the Cherokees and the Cumberland settlements would overcome the resistance movement, just as the birth connections of Joseph Brown trumped his adoption into Chickamauga kinship networks. In 1794, a group of Cumberland region residents, led by Maj. James Ore and guided by Brown, attacked and destroyed the Chickamauga towns of Nickajack and Running Water near Muscle Shoals, the heart of the Chickamauga Lower Towns. The towns, founded by Dragging Canoe, had served as the military base for the highly effective attacks against Nashville. Brown's vow to avenge the deaths of his father and brothers was fulfilled, and the Chickamauga attacks largely ceased. In the same year, Gen. Anthony Wayne's troops decisively defeated the pan-Indian army at the Battle of Fallen Timbers in the Northwest Territory, breaking apart the alliance and draining most of the warriors of their will to continue the fight.

Following the defeat of the Indian resistance coalitions at the Battles of Fallen Timbers, Nickajack, and Running Water, on August 19, 1795, General Wayne wrote to Arthur St. Clair, then governor of the Northwest Territory. Wayne indicated that the coalition was breaking up and Indians returning to their own regions. He excitedly proclaimed that it had been "two days since a Cherokee Chief with some young warriors arrived here from the head waters of the Scioto, bearing a talk from Coona Miskey . . . in which he solemnly promises . . . that he will withdraw all the remaining Cherokees from this side of the Ohio, in the Course of this fall and return to his own nation! That the greater part had left the [Scioto] very early in the Spring, in order to settle in their own Country!"[46] Wayne declared that he knew the previous party had arrived back in the Southwest Territory because he had seen a letter from the territory's governor, William Blount, stating, "a Considerable number of Cherokee warriors with their families, arrived on the 27th of May at the Tellico Block House that they had forever abandoned the Hostile tribes Northwest of the Ohio, determined to remain peaceable in future."[47] Families emigrated together out of the Northwest Territory just as they had once moved into the region together to form the coalition fighting against American encroachment. Kinship networks facilitated the transition back to their peacetime roles.

After the armies of the Northwest and Southwest Territories defeated the resistance movements at Fallen Timbers, Nickajack, and Running Water, the United States signed treaties with the affected tribes. The Chickasaw Colberts, however, were not quite ready to end their war against the Creeks. In the early 1790s, the Colbert family heeded the U.S. commissioners' request that the Chickasaws aid in the campaigns of Arthur St. Clair and Anthony Wayne against the American Indian coalition in the Northwest Territory. As in the Revolutionary War, the Colberts went to war as a kin-based faction. However, when Creek allies of the northern Indians attacked the Chickasaws and the Colberts retaliated, Secretary of War Timothy Pickering argued that the assistance of "a few Chickasaw warriors" was not enough to convince him to back the Chickasaws in a war with the Creek Indians. Rather than lending military support to their Chickasaw allies, Pickering advised that the United States stay out of the conflict because "the four Southern nations of Indians have, in precisely the same terms [in treaties], put themselves under the protection of the United States. Two of them are now at war with each other. And from the terms of their treaties each has an equal right to demand protection."[48] Pickering later had to accept the consequences of that decision when he "found Major Colbert singularly difficult to please: perhaps because the President could not gratify his wishes in making open war against the Creeks." He agreed to provide Colbert and his fellow Chickasaw delegates with clothing and "to furnish their families with clothing," adding: "To grant his request and to soothe him under his great disappointment I have given Major Colbert four hundred dollars to buy an elegant stallion: but he seemed to consider this sum as hardly sufficient. As I said before it was not easy to please him."[49] Both Colbert's actions as a military commander and as a negotiator revolved around his kin relations. Pickering recognized that mollifying Major Colbert required also providing for Colbert's family.

Some contemporary American officials, and later historians, have argued that the Colberts operated as corrupt officials demanding bribes and hijacking the treaty process to the detriment of their people. Others see this family as one important faction among others in a decentralized society. To gain the support of these multiple factions, the United States was often forced to accept Chickasaw terms of trade, paying more for native lands and services than the U.S. commissioners would have liked.

In 1795 the federal government signed the Treaty of San Lorenzo, settling the border with Spain, lifting the ban on American transportation on the Mississippi River, and allowing American goods to be "deposited" in New Orleans. As Spanish support of the Chickamauga and Creek resistance to the Cumberland settlement and trade with Chickasaw factions diminished, Anglo-American economic and territorial expansion increased and families like the Donelsons profited.[50] By 1797 those listed in Cherokee territory as "not natives of the land" included people who were of American, Spanish, Scottish, French, English, Dutch, African American, Shawnee, and Creek ethnicities.[51]

For both allies and enemies of the United States, kinship provided the foundation for military action. Kinship relationships in many cases also provided the motivation for alliances. Those relationships existed within specific cultural contexts that guided individuals to claim alliances with one side or the other during this time of war. Through evaluation of kinship networks, the "Indian Wars" of the 1780s and 1790s are revealed to be much more complicated than simply a series of conflicts between the army and militias of the United States on the one side against different Indian resistance coalitions on the other. Instead, the extent to which Indians in the Northwest and Southwest Territories traversed the regions to fight as allies becomes evident. Meanwhile other kin-based military units, such as the Colberts of the Chickasaws, fought alongside American troops. By adding these nuances to historical understandings of the battles that took place during the post-Revolutionary period, the importance of interpersonal relationships, especially kinship, in the period and the impact of local events on regional, tribal, national, and international events during the time becomes more evident.

Following the American Revolution, the political and economic climate of the trans-Appalachian frontier changed significantly. The Chickasaws and Cherokees sought to play Spanish and American diplomats against one another to secure profitable trade alliances. The Chickamaugas fought to regain lost Cherokee territory, accumulating significant spoils of war in the process. In the meantime, the Donelsons built familial wealth through land speculation. As U.S. political clout and commitment to territorial expansion increased during the nineteenth century, the Indian families turned their attention even more toward securing their territorial boundaries and political sovereignty against the U.S. expansion strategies.

4 / The Donelsons: Social, Political, and Economic Expansion on the Frontier

The 1791 marriage of Andrew Jackson to Rachel Donelson united a man who had been orphaned at an early age with the family of one of the most prominent men in the region. Rachel Donelson's father had led one of the two expeditions to found the town that would become Nashville, Tennessee. The marriage bound Andrew Jackson to a network of in-laws who would smooth the way for him to gain contacts among the regional elites. In addition to being well-connected, the Donelson family had ambitions to capitalize on the burgeoning land markets in the region. The huge amount of land speculation, litigation, and wide-open commercial markets drew them to invest heavily in the opportunities available in the frontier economy. Their investments were not simply monetary but involved significant diversification of personal and familial job skills to take advantage of the opportunities. The family would boast members who could operate at every level of the land speculation process. They had soldiers who fought and pushed Indians to cede lands, treaty commissioners who negotiated the terms of the treaties to encourage large land cessions, surveyors to record the boundaries, lawyers and judges to try the cases, and politicians to encourage ongoing expansion. Eventually the family would even include the secretary of state for North Carolina and the president of the United States.

Rachel Donelson Jackson and her sisters and sisters-in-law supported these ventures by helping to run the plantations while their husbands were out surveying, soldiering, or establishing additional plantations. They churned out almost daily correspondence at times to keep their loved ones abreast of the financial situation at home. They raised the children, managed the household staff, cared for the ill, and maintained an active presence in the local community. Although the official sources largely ignored the role of these women, personal correspondence gives insights into the active role women played in the maintenance of family assets and the planning for future familial endeavors. Letters between Andrew Jackson and Rachel Donelson Jackson reveal an affectionate marriage in which Rachel was the dutiful and caring wife at home at the Hermitage, their home. She inquired after his health and sought news on his activities, but she also had her hands full at home with her responsibilities.

Their marriage epitomized what was possible in familial networking. Jackson gained an army of brothers, literally, and together these members of the kinship network created an efficient system that provided profits for all. Few other frontier families would employ family networking quite so effectively, but while their strategies were exceptionally efficient, they were also representative of the types of networking that was going on, usually on a smaller scale.

After the American Revolution, many families attempted to profit from the Indian land cessions and increased Anglo-American presence in the region by investing in commercial enterprises, plantation agriculture, and booming transportation market. The ongoing work of the U.S. Army as the primary builder of roads and an active military presence on the frontier enabled some families to become suppliers for the U.S. Army. Anglo-American demand for property in the Cumberland region also led to American Indian families adopting complementary as well as divergent economic strategies.

After completing the trip to the Cumberland region during which they braved the rapids, arrows, cold, disease, and hunger together, the Donelson family united to pursue common economic and political goals. The family pooled their talents as land speculators, lawyers, planters, soldiers, and businessmen to advance members of the network in their social and economic investments. By 1797 Nashville had a population of between 250 and 300 inhabitants, of whom at least 39 were relatives of John Donelson.[1] The Donelson family was one of many families that invested heavily in the land speculation market during the land boom of the 1780s and 1790s. The economic strategies of Anglo-Americans on the trans-Appalachian frontier were not simply an extension of the commercial economy of the eastern seaboard but were predicated on continued U.S. territorial expansion and Anglo-American emigration. Kinship-based networks enabled the Donelsons, and others like them, to capitalize on the land-speculation and business opportunities that both thrived on and drove the territorial expansion of the new United States.

After the death of Col. John Donelson in 1786, his widow, Rachel Stockley Donelson, rented rooms to the local lawyers John Overton and Andrew Jackson. By doing so, she gained economic stability for herself and her three children still living at home. One of John Donelson's daughters, also named Rachel, gained permission to leave Kentucky and return to the Donelson homeplace on the Cumberland River after having a falling out with her husband, Lewis Robards. That short-term separation became a permanent divorce, and Rachel fell for the man boarding with her family. At a time when divorce required an act of the state legislature, the widow Donelson must have supported her daughter Rachel's decision to get a divorce and marry Andrew Jackson. The widow Donelson's economic activities and her possible role in initiating or encouraging profitable marriage alliances for her children are equally obscured, leaving a deceptively strong impression of the importance of patriarchs, such as Col. John Donelson and Andrew Jackson, in creating and sustaining the Donelson family network.[2]

The marriage of Andrew Jackson and Rachel Donelson Robards in 1791 created significant controversy. Apparently both Jackson and Robards believed her first husband had granted her a divorce when they eloped at Natchez. When it came to light that Rachel Robards had not received the divorce, the couple reapplied for the divorce and then remarried in Nashville. This incident resulted in repeated accusations of bigamy and fornication that drove Andrew Jackson to engage in several duels, one with Tennessee governor John Sevier.[3] Jackson would later claim that these accusations led to the death of his pious wife, who he claimed could not endure the frequent assaults on her character.[4] His marriage into the family had the happy consequence of allying the aggressively ambitious Jackson with the equally ambitious Donelson family in a fast-growing land market. This association ensured that the sons and sons-in-law of John Donelson created one of the region's most economically and politically dynamic kinship network.

After the Revolution, the *state* of North Carolina chose to appropriate Richard Henderson's Treaty of Sycamore Shoals in order to pay its debt to Revolutionary War soldiers by assigning them land grants as their payment for war service. By doing so, North Carolina simultaneously undermined Henderson's claim and affirmed the treaty. North Carolina officials claimed that Indians, particularly the Cherokees, had forfeited their lands by allying with the British. Soldiers who completed their full period of enlistment would "receive a prime slave and two hundred acres of land . . . located in that part of the western country which lay to the north of the Tennessee River and west of Cumberland Gap."[5] The warrants benefited land speculators more than veterans because most veterans could not afford to claim their warrants and move their families west and so sold their claims for well below market value.[6] The Donelsons readily took advantage of veterans' willingness to sell their land warrants. Between July 21 and July 26, 1794, Robert Hays, husband of Jane Donelson and brother-in-law to Jackson, bought seven of these warrants, each containing 640 acres. Similarly John Donelson bought five military certificates on August 20, 1794, worth a total of 1,865 acres. Samuel Donelson was named as co-assignee with John on one of these warrants. On April 18, 1796, William Donelson purchased the warrant from James Scurlock for 550 acres awarded for military service.[7] Stockley Donelson bought and sold these warrants frequently. Through such warrants, members of the Donelson family bought up and later resold much of the region, building personal empires from land sales.[8]

Donelson land speculation in the Cumberland region was an extension and drastic expansion of the types of investments John Donelson had made in Virginia. The economic environment of the Cumberland region, and the aspirations of the Donelson clan, revolved around land: land speculation, land surveys, and land-ownership disputes. Land speculation was central to the establishment of Nashville. Because trans-Appalachian leaders and their allies in the North Carolina government were deeply involved in large-scale land speculation, the issue dominated local politics and strongly influenced those of the North Carolina, Southwest Territory, Tennessee, and U.S. legislatures. Stockley Donelson and John Donelson were among the most prominent land speculators in the region, along with James Robertson, with whom John Donelson Sr. had coordinated the initial settlement expeditions to Nashville.[9]

In the 1790s, when Washington's administration found that aggressive land speculation and the corresponding escalation of warfare had cost the country too much in revenue and lives, the Federalists backed off of their enthusiastic support of unbridled expansion. Ultimately, this break helped lead to the ascendancy of the Jeffersonians, who continued to support territorial expansion. The party would gain long-term political dominance in the state. Essentially, the interests of land speculators determined the direction of the state vote at a critical juncture.[10] As conflict between officials declined and the effectiveness of Indian resistance to the encroachment diminished, resolution of conflicting legal claims through the judicial system became an important part of the land speculation industry dependent upon the actions and decisions of lawyers, judges, and surveyors.

Land markets for the Donelsons were alive with possibilities for speculation and incredible financial gain.[11] Their ideals of market possibilities revolved not around credit and wage or slave labor, though both were part of their ventures, but around exploiting the cheap land and lack of mercantile competition to its fullest. Personal relationships in the Donelson family network produced real gains in wealth and stature for its members that defied strict definitions of markets. The right investments in the marital market could be the best way for a family to capitalize on the booming economic opportunities available. Connecting two prominent land-speculating families could create profitable economies of scale and scope that could make the kinship network vastly richer.[12] The Donelson family integrated land speculation, legal careers, and other economic ventures to take advantage of the interconnected opportunities for vast profits based upon the booming land market.

Early tax lists for Tennessee indicate that between 1796 and 1815, members of the Donelson family network owned land in Davidson, Wilson, Williamson, Maury, Knox, Grainger, Sevier, Robertson, White, Sumner, Montgomery, Campbell, Blount, and Greene Counties in Tennessee.[13] Members of this family network also speculated heavily in lands that would become parts of Georgia, Alabama, Florida, and Mississippi.[14] Wide-ranging land speculation became the foundation of the Donelson family wealth, resulting in several large plantations that were passed down through the generations. This speculation was largely successful and was facilitated by the family network and predicated on the ability to obtain land cessions from Indians.

A surveyor on the trans-Appalachian frontier faced dangers as well as opportunities. Many surveyors lost their lives to Indian attacks, and that danger caused most surveyors to make out plats for military warrants and other lands without ever seeing the property itself. The secretary's office at the land office issued grants in such numbers that they did not question the accuracy or methodology of the surveyors.[15]

The Donelsons likely faced somewhat less danger as many of the tracts they surveyed existed on the boundaries of properties that they or their brothers already owned. Surveyors' positions yielded great rewards in an economy based upon land speculation. Col. John Donelson utilized these skills both in Virginia and in the new Cumberland settlements. At least three of his sons, John, Stockley, and William, and at least two of his sons-in-law, Thomas Hutchings and Robert Hays, were also official surveyors.[16] These skills helped to build the Donelson family holdings. The Donelsons had political connections that facilitated their connections to the land office, including at least five surveyors in the family network. Stockley Donelson, secretary of the state of North Carolina, frequently traveled to and from the state capital to visit family or check on his holdings in the Cumberland region. His trips provided the rest of the Donelsons with a convenient means of getting documents to the land office there. Similarly, individuals who could survey the land for themselves, as many of the Donelson men did, were not required to pay survey fees at all and knew where to find the best lands. John Donelson Sr., John Donelson Jr., and Stockley Donelson achieved high surveyor positions within county and state governments, receiving appointments as principal surveyor, assistant surveyor, and surveyor general respectively. These positions generated not only higher economic status but also prominent social and political positions that resulted from growing social networks built upon land speculation markets.[17]

The Donelsons also collaborated by buying and selling land to members of their family and to outsiders, as well as granting power-of-attorney to one another to make such sales. One example of this interconnection in land sales involved a purchase made by Stockley Donelson and William Terrell Lewis from the state of North Carolina and then sold to Thomas Hutchings:

Stockley Donelson & William T. Lewis—Feb 26, 1798

North Carolina Grant No. 356. For 10 lbs per 100 acres paid by **Stockley Donelson** and William T. Lewis was granted a tract of land containing 640 acres in Davidson County on the south side of Cumberland River in Jones Bent about one quarter of a mile above **Donelsons Ford** and Jones Bluff. **Surveyed** for said Donelson and Lewis by **John Donelson** 3/1/1792, W.No. 321. Located 3/1/1784. Dated (no date given).[18]

Thomas Hutchens [Hutchings]—May 14, 1798

> This indenture made 4 Dec 1797 between Stockley Donelson of
> Chatham county, State of North Carolina of the one part and
> Thomas Hutchens of Davidson County of the other part. Stockley
> Donelson conveyed unto Thomas Hutchens 320 acres of land on the
> south side of Cumberland River in Jones Bent, being and undivided
> part of 640 acres in joint with William T. Lewis and joining Jones
> Bluff and John Donelson's corner. Wit: John Hutchens [Hutchings]
> and Daniel Small. Signed by John Donelson, attorney for Stockley
> Donelson. Apr Term 1798.[19]

John Donelson, brother of Stockley Donelson and brother-in-law to
Thomas Hutchings, surveyed this piece of land and then later certified
the transaction between the in-laws as Stockley's attorney. By utilizing
the positions of surveyor and lawyer as collective assets, the Donelsons
built their separate fortunes and furthered those of their family members. Each person benefited individually, but their familial ties enabled
the whole to prosper through such advantages as proximity, lower fees,
trusted legal witnesses, and reliable neighbors.

In 1797 Stockley Donelson was implicated in a land fraud scandal
along with his father-in-law, James Glasgow. When Glasgow, North
Carolina's secretary of state, was accused of issuing grants of land
based upon forged military warrants, Donelson, his longtime partner,
was implicated as well. Andrew Jackson tried to direct the charges at
his political rival John Sevier but in the process snagged his brother-
in-law in the turmoil of scandal and investigations. An undated letter
from Stockley pleaded with Jackson: "I woud thank you to write Me, by
the first oppertunity your friendly advise, I now and Continually want
some New occurrences, Seem to be awaiting me of a Singular Nature. I
forbear to Mention. I have no doubt but Some other Judgements will be
this Court Obtain againt me."[20] Andrew Jackson was not successful at
diverting the scandal away from his brother-in-law and toward his rival.
It became a controversy that damaged Jackson's reputation at the time.[21]

In 1801 Andrew Jackson wrote to Stockley's wife, Elizabeth, requesting her to convince her husband to move to the Cumberland region,
where "here his friends are disposed to serve him as far as is in their
power, at least I speak for myself." He also notes that "Col. Donelson
has shown me your letter and the information communicated to you.
with respect to the sentiments of his friends relative to you, rest assured
is not well founded. The respect they have for you and his happiness

would always make you a welcome guest with them" despite the unfortunate events that had befallen Stockley. Jackson seems to have perceived Elizabeth Glasgow Donelson as both the barrier to the couple's move to the region and the remedy to the possible resistance of her husband to the idea.[22] Although family members could prove valuable partners, the land speculation business itself often proved quite risky. Jackson was convinced that if the couple moved closer to the rest of the family, the situation could be resolved more easily. Elizabeth Donelson would serve as a crucial kinship link, either to her natal family or her marital family. The couple did eventually move to Davidson County, Tennessee.

Not all economic interchange even within the Donelson family network ended positively. In an 1803 case before the Superior Court of Tennessee, Thomas Hutchings sued his brother-in-law Stockley Donelson, claiming that the latter had in effect stolen a plat belonging to Hutchings and sold it as his own to pay his debts to the firm of Mayberry, Jackson, and Miller. The case abated due to the deaths of both Hutchings and Donelson before a verdict was reached.[23]

The economic environment of the new Cumberland settlements, especially the booming land speculation market, enabled men of modest means to acquire, through utilizing social and political networks, the capital and personal connections necessary to invest in land. Lawyers had the opportunity to collect capital that could be invested in wildly profitable land deals. In early Nashville, men of modest beginnings could rise socially by studying law, collecting capital, and making the right connections. Only with the right connections could a lawyer become landowner and then a politician with local, regional, state, and national possibilities. Wealth and power grew out of large landownership, and landownership grew out of the right investments and connections with individuals who would assist in the advancement of interests common to himself and his associates. While familial networks were not the only social networks that knit together frontier elites, they were among the most effective and durable of those networks. The addition of several lawyers to the Donelson family network of land speculators and surveyors only served to strengthen their position in the litigious competition for land and influence in the Cumberland region.

The land speculation–based economy generated an abundance of litigation over overlapping boundary lines and contested deed ownership. Surveyed land did not always guarantee clear title or undisputed boundaries, especially when land was surveyed from the inside of a fort. In Kentucky, land claims were frequently embroiled in ongoing controversy and lawsuits over conflicting and overlapping borders and uncertain titles.[24] Tennessee faced similar problems, but for the Donelson family such litigation brought prosperity more often than ruin. Surveyors were employed to verify boundaries in such claims, and the Donelson family had more than its fair share of surveyors.

Similarly, having lawyers within the family could be of use to those involved in land purchasing. As well as being knowledgeable about land law, the lawyers in the family, Andrew Jackson, Samuel Donelson, and Robert Hays, provided a form of insurance for those involved in speculation. They could be witnesses to contracts (such as in Thomas Hutchings's 1798 contract with Stockley Donelson), trusted with the power-of-attorney to execute deals or collect debts, and counted upon to take the cases of family members involved in land disputes.

The Donelson lawyers also leaned upon one another for professional support. Stockley Donelson, in particular, frequently prevailed upon his brother-in-law Andrew Jackson to take cases regarding Donelson's land claims or those of men for whom Donelson scouted or surveyed pieces of land. For example on August 3, 1792, Stockley sent a request to Jackson:

> Their is a writ of Ejectment Sevd. on Capt. John Kearnes and Capt. John Sawyears for the Wright of the Land & possession whereon they now live which Land I sold them and am bound to make the Title to them therefore have to defend the Suit the one Servd on Kearnes I leave with this letter for your Perusal and wish you to take Such measures as is Most adviseable Also woud be glad youd call on Kearns and Sawyears; The Suit is Brought by one Jeremiah Chamberlain claiming by the advantage of Obtaining the first Grant by fraudulently obtaining the Same by Suprenumery warrants. My wrighs were by early Special Entries in Armstrongs office Pray Sir Enter yourself as attorney for the Defendants Sawyears & Kearns and Not Suffer a Judgement Immediately to be obtaind, I Shall be at the Court but Perhaps late.[25]

In sending such a letter, Stockley Donelson gave Jackson little room to refuse or defer to another named individual. He further gave Jackson power-of-attorney to handle land deals for him on September 10, 1792, calling him "my Trusty friend."[26] Donelson made similar requests of Jackson throughout their relationship, which lasted until Stockley Donelson died in 1805.[27]

Jackson also intervened on behalf of another brother-in-law, Alexander "Sandy" Donelson, in a dispute with the heirs of Anthony Bledsoe over title to a piece of land in August 1797. Jackson gave his brother-in-law Robert Hays power-of-attorney "to Receive from the Treasurer of the United States, all Sums of Money due & Oweing to me, for my Services done and performed as Attorney General."[28] Samuel Donelson, while on a buying trip for the mercantile firm he co-owned with Jackson, asked his partner to take over a court case for him, and "If you should not go down to Tenessee Court you will get Mr. Searcy [a friend of Jackson's] to do my business in that Court."[29]

Future generations of the Donelson family continued to join the legal profession, including Stockley Donelson Hays in 1812, Andrew Jackson Donelson in 1823, and a future namesake of Samuel Donelson who served as the clerk of the Criminal Court of Donelson County in 1878.[30] As members of the Donelson family network, these lawyers were obliged to assist family members with their legal concerns, as well as their docket loads.

The Donelson family network filled a variety of governmental positions, mostly within the judicial branch, that gave them access to knowledge and power that supported their familial economic agendas. Many Donelsons and Donelson in-laws became justices for the county and state courts. Brothers-in-law Capt. John Donelson and Robert Hays both served as justices for the Davidson County Court in 1789. The next year, Andrew Jackson was appointed attorney general for the Mero District of North Carolina, also known as the Cumberland region, shortly before he married Rachel Donelson. Hays also served as chairman for the "Inferior Court of Pleas and Quarter Sessions at Nashborough" in 1791. In 1792, Jackson was appointed judge advocate for Davidson County.[31] In 1796, Samuel Donelson became a justice for the Davidson County Court, followed in that position the next year by his brother William Donelson and brother-in-law Thomas Hutchings. Jackson served as a state Superior Court judge from June 1798 through June 1804, when he resigned from that position after being appointed the major-general of the militia. William Donelson also served as justice for the Davidson County Court in 1805 and 1828. With these positions, the Donelson family network created ties within all businesses and government offices related to land speculation, which brought them immense profit.

The legislative and executive positions occupied by the Donelsons helped to ensure that the local, state, and federal governments supported U.S. territorial expansion. Col. John Donelson had been elected to the Virginia House of Burgesses just prior to the American Revolution.

In 1790, John Donelson Jr. and Robert Hays were appointed justices of the peace for Davidson County.[32] Stockley Donelson was appointed by President George Washington to be a council member in the Upper House of the Territorial Legislature for the Territory South of the Ohio River.[33] Upon Tennessee achieving statehood in 1796, Andrew Jackson was named a representative for the state in Congress. He immediately followed this yearlong appointment with another year as one of Tennessee's U.S. senators but he resigned in June 1798 to serve as a judge for the Superior Court of Law and Equity for Tennessee.[34]

Samuel Donelson's father-in-law, Daniel Smith, also served as a U.S. senator for Tennessee from December 3, 1798, to March 3, 1799, and from December 2, 1805, to March 3, 1806. Daniel Smith was a reluctant part of the Donelson family network. The marriage of Mary Smith and Samuel Donelson in 1796 inspired scandal in the region. When Daniel Smith forbade his sixteen-year-old daughter to marry thirty-seven-year-old Donelson, the two eloped with the help of Samuel's brother-in-law Andrew Jackson. Smith disowned his daughter and refused to speak to either of them. He relented a year later, when his first grandchild, John Samuel, was born. The couple would name their second and third sons Andrew Jackson Donelson and Daniel Smith Donelson respectively.[35] Kin connections between these early political offices reinforced the Donelson network's influence.

Jackson's six years as a Superior Court justice were followed by a commission as major-general of the state militia, the highest military office in the state. John Donelson had held a similar military commission in Virginia. The militia offered the Donelson family network prestige and connections to other prominent men in the area, which often translated into business connections. Military victories on the frontier were also often accompanied by Indian land cessions, adding to the value of military service for the Donelsons. Militias on the trans-Appalachian frontier took on especially important roles for the community, providing a semblance of protection and acting as the proving ground for a man's reliability, bravery, and leadership skills. These qualities, or their absence, in a leader meant life or death for the men in the company. The militia became a symbol of masculinity and a stepping-stone into local politics. If a man could prove his manhood and leadership skills in the militia, he gained credibility with the populace. Deference on the trans-Appalachian frontier was accorded to men of property, but men could gain a political following by proving their worth on the battlefield and convincing their regiment of their leadership skills.[36] The Donelson family had the advantage of both avenues for political advancement. Marksmanship and courage in battle were among the traits most valued in the Cumberland region. Due to the fierce resistance of Chickamaugas to Anglo-American settlements, the Donelson men had plenty of opportunities to prove their worth on the battlefield.

Of the eleven sons and sons-in-law of Col. John Donelson, at least eight of them held military titles, including (Gen.) Andrew Jackson, (Col.) Robert Hays, (Col.) Stockely Donelson, (Maj.) Alexander Donelson, (Capt.) John Donelson Jr., (Ensign) Samuel Donelson, (Col.) John Caffrey, and (Col.) Thomas Hutchings.[37] William Donelson, Stockley Donelson, and Robert Hays received commissions as lieutenant colonels within the Davidson County militia.[38] Such family dedication to military involvement was a testament to both the importance of the military to the community and to the importance of militia activity in attaining local prominence.[39]

Indian relations constituted another important political sphere for members of the Donelson family who secured positions as U.S. treaty commissioners and agents to the Southeastern Indians. Col. John Donelson, Gen. Andrew Jackson, and Gen. John Coffee all served as commissioners, representatives of the U.S. government, at treaty negotiations with the Chickasaws, Cherokees, and other tribes. Prior to his death in 1786, Colonel Donelson was a U.S. commissioner traveling to the Southeastern nations, including the towns of the Chickamauga Cherokees, endeavoring to negotiate a peace that would deliver the Cumberland settlements from the ongoing siege. Andrew Jackson was a treaty commissioner for several treaties with the Cherokees and the Chickasaws from 1816 to 1818. John Coffee was a commissioner for the 1816 treaty with the Choctaws and for the 1832 treaty with the Chickasaws. Daniel Smith was a commissioner for the 1804 and 1805 treaties between the United States and the Cherokees and witnessed several other treaties. John Coffee was also the U.S. agent to the Chickasaws during and after the War of 1812 and Creek War. These positions completed the vertical integration of Donelson family careers in the land speculation business. They fought the native peoples, negotiated the treaties to end the fighting and demanded native lands as the price of war, surveyed the newly available lands, bought those lands, litigated over disputed boundaries, adjudicated the cases, and made and kept laws within the region that had been carved out of Indian lands. In these positions, the Donelsons most often came into contact with members of Cherokee and Chickasaw elite families, including the Colberts, Little Carpenter, and Dragging Canoe. This does not mean that the members of the Donelson family network supported one another uniformly, that all battles against Indians were actually about securing more land for the family to speculate in, or that judges were automatically predisposed to ensure the success of cases brought by family members. It did, however, mean that members of the family had knowledge of many business, legal, and government positions associated with land speculation. It also meant that the family was poised for economic success even where individual members failed or fell to the physical or economic dangers of the contested region.[40]

General-stores, or "mercantile ventures," in the outlying areas around Nashville also offered potential profits to the Donelsons. Samuel Donelson and brother-in-law Andrew Jackson formed a partnership to this end, opening a mercantile store in 1795 near Jackson's home at Hunters Hill. The store served dual purposes: it provided Jackson, Donelson, and their associates with easy access to the goods they wanted or needed, and, with little local competition, the store promised decent profits. Jackson was forced to sell the store in 1796 to pay debts incurred when an associate for whom he had cosigned proved insolvent.[41] Jackson attempted to get another brother-in-law, Robert Hays, to join him in a similar venture in late 1797 and early 1798, though Hays does not appear to have been receptive.[42] Later Jackson found another more amenable family member in John Hutchings, son of brother-in-law Thomas Hutchings, with whom he would partner. The two opened a store in 1803 at Hunters Hill as well as branches in Gallatin and Lebanon in 1804–5.[43] John Coffee ran a store in Haysborough, and in 1804 he joined Jackson as a partner in his Clover Bottom business, "comprising a store, tavern, boatyard, and racetrack."[44] Five years later, Coffee married Jackson's niece Mary Donelson, the granddaughter of Col. John Donelson. Coffee would become one of Jackson's best friends as well as an integral part of the Donelson family network. He engaged in the family businesses of land and mercantile speculation, military leadership, and the Indian trade.

Jackson seems to have been the most enthusiastic of the members of the Donelson network in opening mercantile stores, but he at least shared the opportunity to engage in this type of speculation with his family members. By 1805 three of the ten Donelson brothers and brothers-in-law had died, and Jackson began to look to his nephews rather than to his brothers-in-law as business partners. Following the War of 1812, Jackson's political career transformed his business relationships as his business ventures, legal career, and land speculation became secondary to his political aims. At this point, the younger generation sought to use their familial ties to capitalize upon his fame and power.[45]

The legal, military, and governmental offices filled by members of the Donelson family helped to establish the family's esteemed place in the region. Their positions as lawyers, military officers, and government officials proved their dedication to the community while also strengthening the Anglo-American hold on the Cumberland region. Together law, economic opportunity, and family reveal much about the economic strategies of the Anglo-American local elite on the trans-Appalachian frontier. In this newly opened region, land and mercantile speculation could be augmented by the possibilities afforded to men who embraced a career in law. The Donelsons used their familial network to take advantage of the many possibilities opened by a booming land speculation industry and the new markets that industry created in the frontier community of Nashville. U.S. territorial expansion, and land speculation particularly, directly opposed the motives behind the economic strategies of the Chickasaw and Cherokee families: land retention and reinforcing native political sovereignty.

While not all of the Donelson family networking and economic strategies worked out perfectly, those strategies had enabled the family to become one of the wealthiest in the region. The family continued to pursue strategies in the nineteenth century similar to those they had in the eighteenth century. The Donelsons had found economic strength in numbers. But this story of familial economic partnerships and vertical integration belies the fraught political and military environment within which it took place. While the Donelsons and others like them worked to acquire new lands, native kinship networks and alliances sought to disrupt those acquisitions and to protect their own economic status and lands. They continued the fight they had begun against the expansionist Americans during the Revolutionary War and worked to protect their economic well-being through engagement in or disruption of the new market economy in the region.

5 / Family Strategies and "Civilization"

George Colbert was among the richest men in the Tennessee River Valley. His home was set atop a bluff overlooking the expanse of the Tennessee River, where he could watch the horses loading and unloading freight onto the ferry. Colbert's ferry was among the most lucrative enterprises west of the Appalachian Mountains. People from all walks of life paid to have their goods cross the treacherous river safely aboard the ferry. Because of the location and the need for the ferry, treaty negotiations were often held at his house. Hundreds gathered together to hear the words of the "great white father" and to provide input on matters that would affect their towns. Colbert and his brothers, the children of marriages between Scottish trader James Logan Colbert and women of a prominent Chickasaw house group, occupied the cultural borderland between the Anglo and Chickasaw worlds. Although George Colbert himself ranked among the wealthiest Chickasaws, he did not speak English. He hosted the most powerful men in the region, including Andrew Jackson and Joseph Martin, as his houseguests, feasting them and giving them rest within his home. The diplomatic world of intercultural negotiation quite literally came to rest at his doorstep. His relationships, and those of his kin, helped to define the diplomacy of the colonial and early modern eras. Their political and economic networks came to dominate the political landscape for the Chickasaws. More and more, the Colbert family came to resemble the plantation owners and politicians with whom they negotiated. By the 1830s, the Colberts maintained slave-based cotton plantations that were among the most valuable and most profitable in the

Southeast. Their efforts at becoming "civilized"—that is, mirror images of white elites—had the irony of incorporating Chickasaw leaders into the brutishness of chattel slavery while embracing the "Christian ideals" of the southern planters.

Tumultuous international politics at the beginning of the nineteenth century meant that families on the trans-Appalachian frontier had to be flexible and adaptive to make the most of the opportunities and address the challenges inherent in a region in political flux. Jay's Treaty and the Treaty of San Lorenzo, or Pinckney's Treaty, in 1794 and 1795 created a peace that diminished the ability of Native southerners to tap into British and Spanish resources and their desires to keep a buffer between the Americans and their own colonial claims in North America. These aims had made the British and Spanish governments valuable allies to those native groups who also wanted to prevent American expansion prior to 1795. In the new political environment that emerged after these treaties, playing one power against the other failed as a strategy, and many native leaders chose instead to strengthen their relationships with the Americans. Prominent native families, such as the Colbert and Ridge families, utilized long-standing kinship networks and traditions to navigate new social and political environments as the United States' power grew in relation to its European rivals. These Chickasaw and Cherokee families reinforced their alliances with the United States by using diplomatic and economic tactics that paralleled some of the Donelson family's economic strategies, such as building plantations, practicing Christianity, and incorporating written documents more fully into their culture. The Colberts and Ridges emphasized their "civilization" in an effort to capitalize on the United States' rising power and willingness to trade goods for "civility."

At the turn of the nineteenth century, France, Spain, and England adjusted their territorial claims according to shifts in their global imperial strategies. Louisiana, claimed by Spain since 1763, was transferred back to France in 1800 and was bought by the United States in the Louisiana Purchase of 1803. At the same time, Jefferson sought to implement new policies toward Indians that encouraged them to take up plantation agriculture, spinning and weaving, and animal husbandry so that they would become self-sufficient yeoman farmers who would abandon hunting as an economic activity. With their fragmented diplomacy strategies curtailed by diminishing European power in North America, many Chickasaw and Cherokee families chose to reinforce their relative political position by strengthening their alliance with the United States. The War of 1812 gave these families, native and non-native alike, the opportunity to prove their worth as allies to the United States.

Although the power dynamics in the Southeast went through significant changes, Chickasaw, Cherokee, and Anglo-American families held onto many of the strategies that had been successful over the previous decades. As in the past, the United States and the British relied upon Indians as allied forces to supplement their troops in order to fulfill their military agendas in the region. Kinship remained the bonding mechanism for war parties and political factions within Chickasaw, Cherokee, and, even to some degree, American governments. The competition between kinship networks in all three societies continued to ensure that some families were more prominent than others in the historical record and, therefore, presumed by historians to have had more power. The family of The Ridge, also known as Major Ridge, received more attention in the historical records of the early nineteenth century than did the descendants of Little Carpenter and Dragging Canoe, thus shifting this chapter's focus toward The Ridge's family network. The descendants of The Ridge (or Major Ridge) took Ridge as their surname and represent cultural changes during the nineteenth century. The Ridge family also ran a trading post and a ferry. Major Ridge's son and nephew attended mission schools nearby and in Connecticut. They went on to be active voices for "civilization" in Cherokee politics and through the first Cherokee newspaper, the *Cherokee Phoenix*. The Ridge had a major influence on both his nephews and his son as his kinship network operated as signers of the Treaty of New Echota, the document that was the basis for Cherokee removal from the Southeast. His influence and that of his children and nephews significantly shaped Cherokee history. However, historians have yet to uncover the historical records describing The Ridge's matrilineal ancestry. While The Ridge was a key actor in the period from 1800 to 1815, his ancestral kinship network remains behind the scenes. Kinship networks served as the enduring structure supporting these families as they adjusted their strategies to cope with the changing political and economic environment of the early nineteenth century. By hanging onto kin-based strategies, these families built upon what they knew in order to deal with the new circumstances in which the old balance of power politics no longer applied.

Through the seventeenth and eighteenth centuries, Cherokees and Chickasaws utilized familial networking to create and maintain simultaneous alliances between their peoples and multiple European and native allies in order to hedge their bets, ensuring that some of their people would come out to the good in conflicts or trade agreements. These alliances were predicated on the desire of European allies to translate trade agreements, first, into physical security for their colonies as Indian allies provided military support and buffer zones against enemies, and, second, into a profitable market that provided raw materials such as deerskins. Through 1763 Cherokees and Chickasaws balanced their alliances with the English against those with the French in Louisiana and the Spanish in Florida. With the end of the Seven Years' War, the Spanish took over control of the Mississippi River and transferred its claims to Florida to the British. In treaty negotiations in 1800 Spain returned possession of Louisiana to France. Just three years later Napoleon sold France's claims to Louisiana to the United States.[1] Florida went through similar imperial transitions. It was claimed by Spain until 1763, by Britain from 1763 to 1783, and once again by Spain from 1783 until it ceded that land to the United States with the Adams-Onís Treaty of 1819.[2] These imperial shifts at the turn of the century meant that native leaders had to stay abreast of the global political movements and changing European territorial claims that affected their trading relationships and their own claims to regional power.

Colbert family actions between 1800 and 1803 illustrate the ways Chickasaws continued to try to play powers off one another even in the midst of the shifting imperial claims. The Colberts' role as liaisons to the British and the U.S. governments likely increased their standing within the Chickasaw nation, especially as such negotiations became critical to the survival of the polity. Malcolm McGee, an interpreter in the nation at that time, told Lyman Draper: "George Colbert was never Head Chief, but was asked by the King to act as principal chief in all matters with the U.S. government—as his knowledge of English better fitted him for such services. Levi Colbert was appointed precisely as was George and for the same purposes."[3] In contrast, U.S. politician William Anderson in 1809 referred to George Colbert as "the Bonaparte of that Nation."[4] As long as multiple imperial competitors remained in the region, the family independently forged an economic strategy that was most advantageous to them despite the efforts of U.S. Indian agents to ensure their sole allegiance to U.S. political agendas.

Samuel Mitchell, the U.S. agent to the Chickasaws, expressed frustration that he could not convince William Colbert to cease war with the Osages west of the Mississippi River:

I have done every thing in my power to cause this Nation to make peace with the Osages. When any mischief is done the Osages by this or the Chactaws Nation, they retaliate on the white hunters from the different Spanish post. I have not a doubt but the whole of this Nation[,] William Colbert excepted[,] would willingly make peace, he is opposed to the Nation, having fell in the estimation of his people, and will do all in his power to thwart their design, and has declared his intention of going to war against the Osages, but do not believe he will raise many . . . warriors.[5]

Colbert apparently refused to let U.S. desires stand in the way of his quarrel against the Osages and raised warriors from his clan rather than a large united Chickasaw force.

Mitchell also described the Chickasaws' concern at the reoccupation of New Orleans by the French on January 23, 1803: "Some appeared alarmed by the report from Orleans that the port was shut against the United States, and expecting that the French would take possession (who have never been friends with the Chickasaws) would set either the Creeks or Cherokees or both nations against the Chickasaws and thereby destroy their Nation."[6] In this instance, Mitchell represented U.S. military support against a potential enemy. George Colbert assured Mitchell that to counteract the French threat the Chickasaw nation would be willing to allow the United States to establish a post on the Tennessee River.[7] When the Louisiana Purchase eliminated the French threat, it also ended talk of building that fort.

Getting the best prices for trade goods remained a high priority, and the Spanish presence enabled Chickasaws to use competition to their advantage. Mitchell noted in May 1803 that he had trouble getting the Chickasaws to agree to a federal trading post, or "factory," at the Chickasaw Bluffs because "goods bring much lower [prices] in Mobile, and which they [who] can get goods at reduced prices will trade in Mobile."[8] The Chickasaws were aware of the fluctuating imperial power dynamics and continued to make adjustments to take advantage of Euro-American competition as long as that competition existed.

Following the transfer of Louisiana claims to the United States in 1803, the Cherokee and Chickasaw political systems retained their traditional format in which leaders shared and competed for power. Leaders still had to prove their worth to have influence and credibility with the nation itself. When leaders stepped over the line, they did not represent the nation long.

In 1807 Cherokee chief Doublehead abused his treaty-making power by getting tracts of land dedicated in his name in treaties and then reselling the land to the United States. Several "young chiefs," including The Ridge, assassinated Doublehead for this transgression. Just two years later, efforts to get the Lower Towns to negotiate an exchange of their lands for others in Arkansas resulted in the nation's repudiation of those chiefs' power to sell land. The Ridge played important roles in both of these events, consolidating treaty-making power as the purview of a National Council.[9] These events constituted a move toward becoming a modern nation-state.[10] However, the new Cherokee national council added new requirements of residency within specific boundaries and loyalty to the representative government as prerequisites for Cherokee citizenship. The enforcement of a common Cherokee purpose contrasts against the pluralistic political practices that had held up through the end of Spanish claims to Louisiana in 1803. After the withdrawal of the Spanish from the region, younger leaders like The Ridge felt that the practice of separate parties negotiating without consent of the governing body would no longer work to their advantage because U.S. officials represented one interest rather than competing colonies.

These changes in perspective did not, however, invalidate the importance of kinship and clan membership to Cherokee identity and political decision making. To remain political leaders, proponents of "civilization" still had to represent the ideas of the town, clan, or nation by convincing their audiences that adopting some components of Anglo-American culture could benefit their people through added political clout and protection of their lands and sovereignty. The unbalanced way Cherokee and Chickasaw political leaders adopted the trappings of plantation agriculture and its attendant wealth was not so very different from the economic disparities between American political leaders and the majority of their constituents. While The Ridge and his supporters gained enough support to remain political leaders and to avoid retaliation through kin-based vengeance, other chiefs continued to express dissenting views that led some to relocate into Arkansas even before the 1817 treaty that enticed a large portion of the Cherokees to move west of the Mississippi River.[11]

In the 1780s the federal government had little power to enforce its edicts, as was evident in the Regulator movement, the State of Franklin secession, and armed conflict between Franklin and North Carolina. By the early nineteenth century it had embraced the expansionist mission that had fueled many of those rebellions as a sanctioned national project.

Nonetheless, figures like Andrew Jackson continued to defy the U.S. president and Congress in favor of their own interests and desires. By the end of the War of 1812, the United States was beginning to look less fragmented and more united in its vision for the nation and its approach to achieving that vision through acquiring native lands.

Thomas Jefferson's presidential election in 1800 marked the beginning of a new era in U.S. Indian policy that contrasted sharply against the Federalist efforts to minimize conflict between native and non-native frontier inhabitants. The Jeffersonian election and consequent changes deemed the "Revolution of 1800" created a significant shift in the approach and intensity of "civilization" rhetoric with negative repercussions for native land retention.[12] While historians recognize the power that Jefferson's ideals had on U.S. internal and diplomatic policies from the election onward, it is important to recognize that his vision for America was highly contested during the election and beyond. Robert Troup, one of Alexander Hamilton's aides, noted: "The election was extremely warm and contested. . . . Never before have I witnessed such exertions on either side before."[13] Federalist support of an industrial American nation continued to contest Jefferson's vision of a nation of small-scale commercial farms. However, upon Jefferson's election that vision directly shaped the diplomatic relationships between the United States and American Indian groups.[14]

Fascinated by the cultures and languages of native peoples in North America, Jefferson collected information on native vocabularies and grammar and shared it with the American Philosophical Society, an organization of early American intellectuals in Philadelphia. According to Jefferson, better knowledge of American Indians would permit better diplomatic negotiations between the new United States and those native polities: "I have long believed we can never get any information of the antient [sic] history of the Indians, of their decent & filiation, but from a knowledge & comparative view of their languages. I have therefore never failed to avail myself of any opportunity which offered of getting their vocabularies."[15] It would also facilitate the religious and cultural conversion of those people from their "savage" state to one of "civilization" that would permit their incorporation into American society.[16] This plan for "civilizing" American Indians was meant to be both altruistic and self-interested. The transition, he believed, would benefit Indians tremendously by elevating them to join "civilization." "Civilization" as defined by Jefferson and his contemporaries essentially meant Anglo-American culture, including among other things their manner of dress, religion, language, and culinary choices, which they saw as the pinnacle of cultural evolution. Jefferson argued that "experience and reflection will develop to them the wisdom of exchanging what they can spare and we want, for what we can spare and they want. In leading them to agriculture, to manufactures, and civilization; in bringing together their and our settlements, and in preparing them ultimately to participate in the benefits of our governments, I trust and believe we are acting for their greatest good."[17] If native people needed less land, particularly their hunting grounds, they would happily sell that land in massive quantities to the U.S. government for a pittance. The U.S. Treasury would fill with revenues gained from selling these lands to Anglo-American yeoman farmers, bringing to fruition Jefferson's dream for the American economy.

Jefferson advocated encouraging American Indians to become "civilized" by adopting plow agriculture, spinning and weaving, and embracing animal husbandry in place of the Indians' existing diversified economic strategies that combined hunting, fishing, and trading with small-scale agriculture and animal husbandry. By 1800, many families had already added animal husbandry and wage-earning activities, such as assisting traders or surveyors for a fee, to their varied economic activities. They already practiced agriculture and eagerly requested the opportunity to learn new weaving and blacksmithing skills. Although they were glad to add new skills, native families were less willing to relinquish hunting activities and their traditional gender roles that were central to their social structure and cosmological understanding of the world. Ultimately, Jefferson's administration was committed to separating American Indians from their land through the policy of "civilization," while native people utilized the concept of "civilization" to augment their existing economic strategies and to reinforce their claims to their land. The tensions between Jefferson's definition of "civilization" and those definitions embraced by Chickasaw and Cherokee leaders provided a space for negotiation, agency, mutual misunderstandings, and conflict.

Treaty talks and treaties in this period illustrate the ways U.S. commissioners and native leaders negotiated "civilization" to serve their own purposes, continued to use the rhetoric of familial relationships, and gained financial advantage through treaty-related enterprises. Some of the leadership of Cherokees, Chickasaws, and other Southeastern Indians, including the Colbert and Ridge families, embraced "civilization policy" (according to their definition rather than Jefferson's) and made some structural changes to their societies to accommodate their U.S. allies. These changes, however, were interwoven with existing native understandings of politics, kinship, gender roles, and economy. The experiences of the Colbert and Ridge families illustrate how their definitions of identity based around conceptions of "kin" and "other" shifted according to the degree of their greater involvement in the U.S. economy. Rather than buying into "civilization," these families used Jefferson's political ideals to further their own economic and political agendas while pursuing their particular visions for their own governments. Such families were usually of elite economic status rather than typifying native economic adaptation.

In treaties between the Cherokee and Chickasaw nations and the new United States, "civilization" was often one of the reasons for distributing certain trade goods at little or no cost to the tribe. Cherokees and Chickasaws had been trading with Europeans for over a century to obtain goods such as blankets, clothing, knives, salt, sewing items, guns, ammunition, cooking paraphernalia, and ornamental items such as beads and silver jewelry. In fact, by 1775, native peoples could no longer live without trade goods.[18] Some American Indians were quite ready to become "civilized" if it meant an abundance of these goods at little or no cost. The U.S. government's offer to supply cotton cards, spinning wheels, and even skilled weavers and blacksmiths seemed like a great opportunity for American Indian communities to get more of what they had already incorporated into their societies for a much lower cost. However, the Jeffersonian focus on land acquisition meant that trade transactions became more focused on gaining Indian land, rather than peltry, for trade goods or money. Treaties and treaty talks serve as some of the clearest statements of U.S. intent to "civilize" the Indians and reveal a kind of dialogue on the subject between the two sides. Article 14 of the treaty between the Cherokees and the U.S. government concluded on July 2, 1791, promised to send up interpreters and goods to "furnish, gratuitously, the said nation with useful implements of husbandry; and further to assist the said nation in so desirable a pursuit [of civilization], and at the same time to establish a certain mode of communication [to better encourage positive relations with the tribe]."[19] Likewise, on October 21, 1801, Gen. James Wilkinson invited the representatives of the Chickasaw nation to "state to us freely [the] situation of your nation and what you wish on the part of your father the president to better your condition in trade, in agriculture and manufactures."[20] In response, "A Talk from the King

Chiefs and Warriors of the Chickasaw Nation to the Secretary of War, delivered by Tisshamastubbe, Speaker for the Chickasaws" requested spinning wheels, cotton cards, and weavers:

> Father, our first Father the then President [George Washington] advised us to settle out, raise Stock, and become farmers and that he would give us assistance, nearly all our people have left the old towns & Settled over our Country raising stock and working like white people many of our women have learned to Spin to make our own Cloathing [sic], we have been furnished with some wheels & cards, but not enough we raise Cotton this year with a hope that we shall be furnished, and we want weavers.

Tisshamastubbe further complained that U.S. citizens "brought, into our land, between forty & fifty head of Kattle and dry goods and trading with the Indians, to the Injury of George & Levi Colbert."[21] This talk reaffirmed that the Chickasaw leadership sanctioned certain aspects of "civilization," such as spinning and weaving, and requested that the promised related goods be forthcoming. Samuel Mitchell, agent to the Chickasaws, wrote in 1802 that "more than half the nation have settled and made small farms with good fences and receive the benefit of their Stocks ~ they are much in the spirit of farming and raising of stock, and will settle the road tolerable."[22] Other aspects of "civilization" promoted by the U.S. officials, such as Anglo-American gender norms, would meet with less enthusiasm. This talk also protected the financial interests of the Colbert family, who, as important traders and leaders in the nation, helped to shape the definition of "civilized" Chickasaws while insisting upon limiting competition from rival traders.

Plantation agriculture provided Indian and Anglo-American leaders with similar lifestyles. By adopting plantation agriculture and securing wealth in land and slaves comparable or superior to that of their Anglo-American rivals, the Ward, Ridge, and Colbert families attempted to achieve status and respect from U.S. officials that placed their governments on similar terms with the U.S. government. According to one missionary, the Ridge built "the usual log cabin of the frontier settler. . . . And here . . . the Indian warrior and his bride, forsaking the habits of their race, [set] themselves to ploughing and chopping, knitting and weaving and other Christian employments" including the purchase of slaves.[23] William, George, James, and Levi Colbert amassed wealth in the form of plantations and slaves mirroring those of the most affluent Anglo-American planters of the time. By 1835 Levi Colbert had acquired

150 slaves, roughly equivalent to the number owned by Andrew Jackson. At the turn of the nineteenth century, several native-owned plantations operated in Indian country that mirrored those of elite southerners like the Donelsons.[24]

While they professed determination to become "civilized" following Jefferson's election in 1800, people like the Ridges and Colberts actually modified the adopted goods and practices to meet their societal needs and norms, as they had in generations past. For example, some leaders combined Anglo-American-style jackets and pants with breechcloths, turbans, and feathers. While Jefferson envisioned thousands of new American Indian yeoman farmers, some who adopted the Anglo-American agricultural model took up plantation agriculture rather than small-scale farming. Although some southern Indians ran small farms without slaves, elite leaders patterned their economic adoption after Jefferson's example rather than that of their Anglo-American neighbors who often struggled to feed their families. Perhaps the U.S. congressmen, governors, and presidents were pleased that the lifestyle of the American Indian leadership began to mirror their own, or perhaps they were threatened by these men who utilized the plantation model to become competitors in the American economic system.

To some extent, Indian adoption and modification of the plantation model even fit with existing gender roles that were rooted in a cosmology of balance. Southeastern native people believed that the world depended upon a careful balance between opposites: male and female power, the over-world and the under-world, spiritual and physical beings, life and death, etc. Throwing that balance off, for example by mixing or confusing male and female power, according to native beliefs created distinct imbalances that unleashed chaos in the world that would have negative repercussions in their lives.[25]

Adopting European-style agriculture and its U.S. southern corollary, chattel slavery, enabled southern Indians to claim to be "civilized." Native groups in the Southeast had long had slaves and even interacted with the U.S. American variant through strategic kidnapping or harboring of runaway slaves. After the turn of the nineteenth century, the Cherokee and Chickasaw economies, along with those of other southern tribes, grew ever more intertwined with the institution of chattel slavery. The adoption of chattel slavery sustained the traditional gender roles among Southeastern Indians. European-style agriculture threatened native gender roles that gave women ownership over, and responsibility for, the fields while men were the hunters and warriors. Rather than pursuing subsistence agriculture, which would make men the farmers in a household, as envisioned by Jefferson's civilization policy, American Indian elites embraced plantation agriculture. Plantation agriculture ensured that slaves did the physical work of planting that had traditionally been a female responsibility, emasculating male slaves but not their native owners. Plantation, rather than subsistence, agriculture provided an amenable intersection of the Anglo-American economic system and the matrilineal gender-role traditions for Cherokee and Chickasaw elites. Many Indians, however, heeded the call to adopt Anglo-style agriculture but did not have the means to procure the slaves necessary to keep their traditional gender roles intact.[26]

These understandings of slavery changed as plantation agriculture took root in Cherokee and Chickasaw societies. These societies with slaves became more and more intertwined with the institution. Native slaveholding plantations came to mirror those owned by Jefferson and Jackson. The institution grew much more race-based, labor intensive, and hierarchical than in previous American Indian variants that prevailed into the early nineteenth century. Slavery divided black and Indian peoples in response to the economic and social pressures exerted by U.S. proponents of "civilization policy."

Generations of historians have highlighted the economic gap between native political leaders who adopted "civilization" strategies and nonelites who at times suffered from poverty and starvation.[27] They argue that "civilization policy" and its supporters created a breach between "hunters" and "elites." Mixed-blood elites, supposedly, turned their backs on their societies' core values in favor of self-interest and a newfound greed for Anglo-defined wealth. Such dichotomies, however, rarely existed in practice. "Civilization" had proponents and opponents but also many whose opinions balanced somewhere in between. Nonetheless, some individuals refused to adopt small-scale agriculture. Anglo-style agriculture without slaves disrupted matrilineal gender roles and dispossessed women of their traditional authority over farms. Whether elites' embrace of private material goods was a diplomatic strategy derived from the selfless virtue of the native politicians that put the good of the polity (or kin) above themselves or whether it was from selfish personal interest was debatable. According to the rhetoric of the time, however, it did help to alleviate the cultural distance between leaders of the United States and leaders of the Chickasaw and Cherokee governments.

While some tribal leaders adapted "civilization" policy to their needs, others eschewed the system altogether. The nature of the historical record highlights those who embraced the system, but the challengers to the system appear between the lines. Treaties between the United States and the Chickasaws after 1805 included clauses rewarding certain chiefs for their "long services and faithful adherence to the United States Government," indicating that such loyalty was valued by the United States and contested by other native political leaders.[28]

The Colberts again received special consideration in the 1805 and 1816 Chickasaw treaties. The 1805 document noted that the Chickasaws were parting with tracts of land because "the Chickasaw nation of Indians have been for some time embarrassed by heavy debts due to their merchants and traders, and being destitute of funds to effect important improvements in their country."[29] George Colbert received a special payment of one thousand dollars, "granted to [him] at the request of the national council, for services rendered the nation."[30]

As in the colonial period, treaty talks composed by Anglo-Americans invoked the father/child relationship, but that language took on a hard edge as treaty commissioners sought to dictate to the Indians their definitions, terms, and even the location where the treaties would be held. The new context of negotiating the definitions and benefits of "civilization" encouraged native leaders to assert their authority in the face of Anglo-American pressure to change. U.S. officials, in turn, worked to get Indian leaders to accede to their wishes and their definitions. On August 15, 1801, U.S. commissioners James Wilkinson and Benjamin Hawkins sent a letter to the Cherokee chiefs convening at Eustinale declaring that the newly elected President Thomas Jefferson "will neither violate your lands or suffer them to be violated while you behave yourselves as you have done like dutiful and affectionate children who look up to him for protection. . . . Your father has a right to name the place where he will speak to you and you have no right to object to his invitation, since he has for object your own good as well as that of his white children."[31] While for the Anglo-Americans the paternal relationship represented authority, benevolent rule, and disciplinary action for disobedience, the same relationship to Cherokees and Chickasaws represented at most goodwill gained through generous gifts of a father to his children rather than his authority over them.[32] The rhetoric of fatherhood in Anglo-American treaties had always contained implicit connotations of enforcement. As American pressure on the cultural and territorial boundaries of American Indians increased, that rhetoric transformed its implicit threats into explicit ones. This became especially true when warfare threatened the Southeast as it would once again in the 1810s.[33]

Treaties provided the terms of peaceful negotiations between governments, but they were also windows into the economic activities of the region. Treaties set the terms of trade, secured permission for the building of roads, granted exclusive rights to operate ferries and inns, determined who would accompany the surveyors of the new boundary lines, and determined how and to whom payment for land cessions would be paid. The process of treaty negotiations was itself quite expensive as treaty commissioners, interpreters, and surveyors all received fees for their services. At times the negotiations began with gift giving and supplies had to be provided for all who attended the proceedings. The Colbert and Ridge families took advantage of these economic engines by running ferries and inns, providing supplies for survey crews, treaty negotiators, treaty attendees, and the U.S. Army, as well as served as interpreters and boundary surveyors. While these activities brought significantly less capital than plantations and trading posts, they illustrated the extent of intercultural contact in the region, the economic impact of treaties, and the families' broader connections to one another.

The Colbert family embraced "civilization" through their early economic and military alliances with the English, their running of trading posts, taverns, and ferries, and their later support of economic and military connections with the United States, all the while serving as leading Chickasaw chiefs. In 1801 the Colberts helped to secure permission for a "Great Road"[34] to be built through the Chickasaw nation with the condition that only Chickasaws could own or run taverns on the road to service the travelers, a clause that benefited the Colberts tremendously. Agent Samuel Mitchell wrote about the negotiations that he did not believe he "should have been able to do any thing had not George Colbert came in from the river who gave his opinion in favour of the Stages. . . . The Indians they have appointed to Settle on the road are well disposed men, and have property and if they will hire honest white men as they have promised me, they will be able to keep good houses."[35] The Colbert family lobbied to ensure that treaties guaranteed the continued preeminence of their trading posts, inns, and other economic activities. The Colberts maintained ferries over the Duck and Tennessee Rivers that derived great profits from the building of the "Great Road."[36] They often hosted treaty negotiations and entertained U.S. officials as houseguests. The ferry was such an integral part of their economic strategies that after Indian removal the family built a new "Colberts' Ferry" over the Red River between Indian Territory and what would soon become the Republic of Texas. Major Ridge of the Cherokees ran a ferry in Cherokee territory on the Eustinale River. In 1836 George Lavender signed a "certificate in relation to the value of Major Ridge's Ferry" in which he noted that "some six or seven years ago the Ferry was very valuable, and considered to be a ferry as valuable as any within the Cherokee Nation . . . [when it] made from three to four dollars pr. day."[37] The Colbert and Ridge families successfully integrated these profitable transportation-related industries into their diversified economic strategies.

Councils at which treaties were negotiated also required a variety of economic activities just to make sure the negotiations ran smoothly, from providing food and supplies for attendees to hiring assistants and interpreters for the survey crews laying new boundaries and provisioning the U.S. Army and others as they built new roads or trading posts on native land. When the U.S. commissioners planned to make a treaty within the Chickasaw nation, "Major [George] Colbert . . . informed [U.S. officials] that abundant supplies of provisions could be furnished by the nation."[38] His brother James Colbert, who frequently made the U.S. Army payroll as an interpreter, requested a pay increase because he said the out-of-pocket expense, incurred by the requisite entertaining of parties for which he interpreted, interfered with his ability to provide for his family.[39] Family members earned wages through these activities that contributed to the economic strategies of their families.

The Ridge and Colbert families' embrace of elements of Anglo-American economy and culture through "civilization" highlight both what they gained from these changes and how those elements blended with native social and economic traditions.[40] These families gained prestige within their tribes through their roles as liaisons to the U.S. government. Both the Colberts' political standing and the intergovernmental relationship were strengthened by the family's "advancements in civilization." In some cases, they enjoyed special recognition and monetary compensation for their political and military loyalty to the United States. Both families show evidence of emerging patrilineal influence as fathers, Major Ridge and Levi Colbert, influenced their sons' educations, but they also show evidence of the continued importance of clan prestige and matrilineal relationships between uncles and nephews. How the Ridge and Colbert families responded to U.S. "civilization" efforts reflects the personal and tribal benefits that could be gained through adoption of U.S. economic practices, as well as how they modified "civilization" to fit into their existing economic and cultural frameworks. While what constituted "Cherokee" or "Chickasaw" identities changed as the tribes became "civilized," crucial elements including gender roles and political sovereignty remained important to the economic and political strategies of these families.

The Colbert and Ridge families by the early nineteenth century shared many economic and social characteristics with the Donelson family, including their embeddedness in the regional market economy. While the diplomatic climate favored emphasizing the similarities between societies built upon the rhetoric of "civilization," the points at which these family strategies diverged illustrate clearly how the effectiveness of native "civilization" strategies (modified from the Jeffersonian definition) was limited by the persistence of Anglo-American expansion. The booming land speculation market depended upon continued land cessions by the native polities. Land speculation, and the U.S. support thereof, were in direct opposition to American Indian efforts to use modified "civilization" strategies to retain their lands and political sovereignty. Ironically, although native people tried to use "civilization" to help them secure their place as allies and peers of the United States, in reality the rhetoric and imagery of "civilization" policy served to facilitate the trope of the vanishing Indian in such a way as to promote U.S. nationalism at the expense of the public image and political effectiveness of Indians. Their ability to participate in the markets of the Southeast and create a democratic political system based on America's own constitution also positioned native people as perceived economic competitors in the eyes of some Anglo-Americans.[41]

The familial economic strategies described in this chapter, whether the similar strategies of plantation agriculture and treaty negotiation, or the contrasting strategies of land speculation and military opposition to expansion, illustrate the families' resourceful uses of kinship to support their families' economic goals during the Jeffersonian era. These strategies intertwined with national politics as well. As representatives of their governments, these families pursued the good of both their kin and their polity. These disparate, sometimes conflicting, economic strategies reflected the contested nature of politics in each of these societies. "Civilizationists" became a term that referred to those who pursued strategies embracing American culture in the hope that they would gain respect and favor of American politicians with whom they worked. They sought to create a sense of parity and mutual respect between their native governments and the United States. They drove hard bargains at the treaty table, pushing for the right to send a native representative to Congress and discussing the possibility of creating a native state that would join the United States. Others within native communities argued that such negotiations were futile and that only military opposition would stop encroachment on Indian lands and ensure native political sovereignty.

6 / Creek War Family Networks

Shawnee headman Tecumseh ventured down the Mississippi River into the Deep South in search of allies who would heed the message of his brother Tenskwatawa, the Shawnee Prophet, and turn toward war against the encroachment of whites. This call to arms would become part of the larger War of 1812, which formally began when the United States declared war on Britain, partially to try to push remaining British troops out of U.S. territory and to bring an end to British impressment of Americans at sea into the British navy. By the time of this declaration of war, Tecumseh and his brother Tenskwatawa were already engaged in leading an allied force of northern Indians in a war to resist the persistent U.S. encroachment on their lands. Tecumseh and Tenskwatawa had used their powers of persuasion to unite disparate Indian groups in the rejection of white ways based upon spiritual visions from the Great Spirit. Their words created a shared vision among native peoples anxious about the future safety of and sovereignty over their lands. The successes of these Shawnee leaders in creating a pan-Indian alliance in the Ohio Valley led Tecumseh to embark upon a southern tour to seek to engage native peoples of the South into the cause of pushing back the Americans and rejecting the trappings of whites. Kinship ties played an important role here. Members of the Muscogee Creeks, related to Tecumseh through his mother's lineage, were the most receptive among Southeastern Indians to hearing his message. These distant kinsmen chose to join the fight against white encroachment and threats to their sovereignty.

Beginning a cleansing purge of their lands, whites and Creeks dedicated to embracing "civilization" found themselves at the wrong end of the war club. These warriors became known as the Red Sticks or Red Stick Creeks, deriving their nickname from the war club itself. Cherokees, Chickasaws, and even other Creeks refused the call to arms. As war broke out in Creek territory, Americans joined the fray to protect their settlers on the frontier. Chickasaws and Cherokees took the opportunity to demonstrate the value of their alliance with the Americans by sending hundreds of troops to fight alongside Andrew Jackson's militia. This conflict in the South, known as the Creek War, was both part of the War of 1812 and a conflict unto itself.[1]

The Chickasaw Colbert and Cherokee Ridge families were among those who fervently rejected Tecumseh's call to arms, proclaiming dedication to the "civilization" project within their nations. Return J. Meigs, the Cherokee Indian agent, noted: "Three Cherokee chiefs [including The Ridge], men of property and considerable information, came into the council and observed, that there would be war between the United States and the English, and that they thought it would be for the advantage of their nation to offer their aid to our government; and that they wished each to raise a number of young warriors, and offer their services."[2] Rather than joining the Red Stick Creeks, they fought as allies of the U.S. Army against them. Their strategic military alliances, like the Colberts' alliances in the 1790s against the "northward Indians," were intended to solidify the families' relationships with the United States and boost the prestige of the individuals, their families, and their governments. The Donelson family network, including Generals Andrew Jackson and John Coffee, also used the war as an opportunity to gain prominence. The close of the Creek War and the Battle of New Orleans left the United States with the dilemma of how to reward their Indian allies and at the same time translate the destruction of the Red Stick Creeks into large, profitable land cessions. They were successful in the latter at the expense of the former.

After 1803 the United States drew upon the weakening position of its English, Spanish, and French rivals to encourage Indians to make a series of treaties and land cessions, but the British, especially, remained an economic and political player in American intercultural politics. The impressment of American sailors into service on British ships and the continued British encouragement of American Indian resistance to American encroachment on their lands provided the motivation for the young republic to once again declare war on Britain in the War of 1812.[3] War hawks hoped that decisive victories by American troops would lead to fewer Indian wars, safety for American vessels on the seas, and possibly even the opportunity to expand U.S. territorial claims into Canada and Florida. Instead, the U.S. Army met with defeat after defeat and suffered the demoralization of its soldiers, who were unsure of exactly why or even sometimes against whom they were fighting. Troops often could not tell friendly Indians from enemy ones and ended up being fired upon by people they thought were "friendly Indians." Such setbacks significantly demoralized the American troops.[4]

With the outbreak of the War of 1812, many Indians took the opportunity, as they had during the Revolutionary War, to express their displeasure with the encroachment on their lands by siding with the British. Tecumseh and his brother the Shawnee Prophet inspired a coalition of tribes in the Ohio Country to fight with British aid to drive the Americans from their lands and then sought Southeastern Indian converts to his message of native religious renewal and military resistance. Most of those who heeded Tecumseh's call to arms were his distant kin among the Upper Creeks, but his message resonated with many who felt the U.S. pressure to relinquish lands had simply become too much. Both George Colbert and The Ridge claimed to have heard Tecumseh's appeal, rejected it, and actively raised troops to fight alongside the Americans against the Red Stick Creeks.[5]

The Colberts proved their alliance to the United States once again by forming military parties to march against the Red Sticks on the Alabama River. According to historian James Atkinson, "William, George, Levi, and James Colbert later raised a military force of about 230 Chickasaw warriors, which left in March 1814 to join Colonel Russell at Fort Claiborne in present-day Alabama."[6] In return for their assistance, James Robertson ordered additional fortification of the Chickasaw nation, including troops sent to protect Colbert's Ferry, against Red Stick retaliation.

The Ridge was among the strongest Cherokee supporters of the U.S. campaign against the Red Sticks. He received a commission as lieutenant at the beginning of the conflict and was promoted to major by its end.[7] The Ridge noted that his troops had been at Hillibee and Fort Armstrong with Jackson's troops. Charles Hicks requested remuneration for losses of two large barrows and six large hogs sustained by The Ridge during his wartime absence when the U.S. Army foraged for provisions as it trekked through Cherokee country.[8]

Like their Chickasaw and Cherokee allies, Andrew Jackson and John Coffee drew upon their kinship network to fill the ranks with trusted family members. Jackson and Coffee had been friends for decades and had recently become related by marriage when Coffee married Jackson's niece. Jackson's brother-in-law Robert Hays was the muster master and deputy inspector general for the West Tennessee militia during the Creek War.[9] Jackson's nephews served in strategic support positions: Maj. Alexander Donelson (Jackson's aide who was killed in the Battle of Emuckfaw during the Creek War);[10] Stockley Donelson Hutchings (quartermaster sergeant in Coffee's cavalry regiment);[11] Stockley Donelson Hays (quartermaster general for Jackson's army);[12] Lt. John Donelson Jr. (company captain for Coffee's mounted infantry at the Battle of New Orleans);[13] Lt. Thomas Hutchings (often a messenger for the family);[14] and Maj. Robert Butler (nephew by marriage, brevet colonel and Jackson's adjutant general through 1821).[15] Although Jackson and Coffee commanded thousands of nonkin, their family ties encouraged them to place family in positions of power, creating interesting parallels between their commands and the kin-based war parties of the Colberts and The Ridge.

The Creek War campaigns ended shortly after the Battle of Horseshoe Bend. Tennessean Ephraim Foster crowed, "How pleasing is the thought, that while in the North, everything means the face of discomfiture, & disgrace, the American coulours wave triumphant in the south: while Wilkinson, Hampton, & Harrison are either lying inactive, or moving to no purpose but to their shame, the great & immortal Jackson, leads the valliant & daring sons of Tennessee to victory & to glory."[16] Cherokees and Chickasaws had fought in several crucial battles and suffered losses alongside the U.S. Army. Eighteen Cherokees were killed and thirty-six wounded in the Battle of Horseshoe Bend. Chickasaw losses and Cherokee losses in other battles were not recorded.[17] Although the Cherokees returned home after the battle, some of Jackson's Chickasaw allies joined him in fighting the British at New Orleans.[18] The Ridge and the Colberts would claim their part in the Creek War as proof of their valor and loyalty to the United States for decades to come. Jackson would translate his role into a dynamic political career and a profitable resurgence in his land speculation activities.

To punish the Red Stick Creeks, Jackson forced the tribe to cede most of the Creek lands covering much of the Southeast. That cession, to the dismay of Jackson's Indian allies, included significant amounts of territory claimed by the Lower Creeks, the Chickasaws, the Cherokees, and the Choctaws. Native leaders protested to Congress against Jackson's unfair redistribution of lands, and Congress rewarded their outrage by revoking Jackson's unilateral decision. The nations would once again bargain at the treaty table to retain their territorial sovereignty. In choosing the "winning side," Indian allies expected to be rewarded for their assistance monetarily and through U.S. reinforcement of their political boundaries. Instead, Jackson and his allies found themselves head to head over the new boundaries of the Southeast.[19]

Dressed in a suit and cravat, the height of fashion at the time, an important diplomat served his country as a key negotiator of the treaty between the U.S. government and the local American Indian government. He ranked among the wealthiest planters in North America. Operating several thriving commercial enterprises, he found his personal and political interests frequently intertwined.

This description actually fits several men in this study, including Major Ridge of the Cherokee nation, Maj. Levi Colbert of the Chickasaw nation, and Gen. Andrew Jackson of the United States. Each wielded similar power in their governments, held considerable wealth, and engaged in the regional economy as planters and businessmen. As they met time and again to negotiate treaties, these men found themselves in some ways looking into a mirror, negotiating with others of comparable status in the economy of the region. These leaders played the diplomatic game in pursuit of a common prize, the lands claimed by the Chickasaws and Cherokees in what would become North Carolina, Georgia, Tennessee, Kentucky, Alabama, and Mississippi. They also sought to achieve their particular visions for their respective nations. By reflecting Anglo-American standards for success, including similar dress and accumulation of wealth in the plantation economy, these Cherokees and Chickasaws felt they came to the diplomatic negotiations on equal terms with their counterparts. However, the attitudes of U.S. officials changed drastically after that war as they found they no longer needed native allies for national security and instead set their sights on further acquisition of native lands.

Within this altered political climate, Cherokee and Chickasaw kin-based factions, including the Colberts and Ridges, as well as the Donelson family now pursued familial strategies that supported clashing visions for the economic and political future of their people. Donelson family strategies flourished because of U.S. policies encouraging western expansion and, in turn, through the career and nepotism of Andrew Jackson, reinforced the U.S. investment in expansion. The Colberts and Ridges, however, embraced familial strategies and political agendas that were not fully supported by their people. In the face of intense and growing pressure to relinquish their lands east of the Mississippi River, the Chickasaws and Cherokees remained fragmented on how to best ensure their political and territorial sovereignty. In this controversial negotiation, the Colbert, Ridge, Ward, and Donelson families employed traditional tactics that they had used for generations although modified somewhat to reflect the post-1815 shifts in intercultural power dynamics.

Rather than reiterating the familiar narrative of the era following the Creek War, this chapter highlights how the complicated relationship of the United States and its Indian allies following the drastic shifts in the balance of power following the War of 1812 was mediated by kinship networks and kin-based strategies. The tension between the possibility of "civilized" coexistence of Indians and Anglo-Americans and the pressure of western expansion on Indian lands finally came to a head in Congress and the U.S. Supreme Court in the early 1830s. The debates over Indian removal played out in all three branches of the U.S. government (within which Donelson family members held office), as some of the native families pursued legal and lobbying strategies. When those seemed hopeless, Cherokee and Chickasaw kin-based factions again determined the fate of their nations by signing treaties to trade their lands east of the Mississippi for others in Indian Territory to the west. Although the actions of kin-based factions were similar to those taken in past decades, the new centralized political systems set those families up for criticism that they had pursued the interest of their kin over that of the nation. Such allegations helped to transform traditional kin-based factions into sometimes violent kin-based rivalries.

Following the triumph of the allied forces at the Battle of Horseshoe Bend, Jackson sought a conqueror's victory, complete with the territory and abject surrender of his defeated foes. But the flexible, contested, and permeable boundaries of the Southeastern Indian nations made this sort of victory impossible. Instead Jackson's demands for land as retribution for Red Stick Creek misdeeds encompassed lands claimed as hunting grounds by all of his Indian allies. Jackson refused to believe that the lands ceded by the Creeks did not belong exclusively to the Creeks and thus by treaty exclusively to the United States. This situation is comparable to Virginia's efforts to recognize the sole ownership of the Ohio

Country by the Iroquois and therefore the land cessions in the 1768 Treaty of Fort Stanwix as superseding all rights of Cherokees, Shawnees, and others to any of that land. Jackson immediately arranged for his friend and nephew-in-law John Coffee to receive the commission to oversee the surveying of the boundary line described in the Creek treaty. Armed guards accompanied the survey party to prevent resistance, by Creeks or others, to the boundary survey. Two more of Jackson's nephews, John Hutchings and William Donelson, were among the group of surveyors accompanying Coffee, and both acted as witnesses for Coffee's payments to suppliers.[20] Allied Indians, including the Cherokees and Chickasaws, did in fact resist the proposed boundary line, not through military efforts but rather through diplomatic channels. A Cherokee delegation in particular traveled to Congress and negotiated a new treaty reifying their boundary claims, which was ratified despite Jackson's protests that it conflicted with the Creek treaty. Finding congressional lobbying strategies effective, native leaders attempted for the next several decades to use Congress to mitigate Jackson's intractable Indian policy.

Many of Jackson's allies, including a company of Chickasaws, had accompanied Jackson's troops in the Battle of New Orleans.[21] Their stunning success at New Orleans proved the only major victory for the United States in the War of 1812 and earned Jackson heroic status that would propel his political career toward the presidency. His Indian allies, however, had helped to push the British from the continent. Just a few years later the Adams-Onís Treaty of 1819 removed Spanish claims to Florida, in part thanks to Jackson's military campaign against the Seminoles, which destabilized the border between Florida and the United States, and left the United States without centralized opposition to their expansion. Tecumseh's pan-Indian armies in the Ohio Country and his Creek allies had been defeated as well. The United States no longer had need of Indian allies for defense, and those allies lost their external leverage. Nonetheless, Congress's lack of approval of the unilateral changing of native boundaries in the Southeast gave Indian leadership a counterweight to Jackson's determination.

Immediately after the signing of the Creek treaty, surveyors began running the boundary line described in the treaty, and settlers began settling upon the lands purported within the new U.S. holdings. Before the line could be run on land that Cherokees also claimed, Cherokee leaders traveled to Washington and negotiated a separate treaty reifying their claims. William Russell, a former soldier in Coffee's unit, implored that Coffee inform them of the dispute's likely outcome, "as we who have followed your fortune, in the tented field have acquired a habit of looking to you for protection and advice. [W]e solicit the favor that you would turn your attention that way and let us know if this be really the case whether there remain any prospect of our views succeeding or whether it be worthwhile to go on with Cultivating our crops of corn or not."[22] In the new treaties authorized by Congress to resolve the conflict over the Creek cession boundaries, pressure from settlers helped push native leaders to cede some lands, if not all that Jackson had hoped. Highly motivated to gain the maximum land cessions, Jackson and Coffee became treaty commissioners, along with four others, for the 1816 treaties with the Southeastern nations.

The first round of treaties in March 1816 with the Chickasaws and the Cherokees resulted in land cessions that overlapped, and each side contested the boundaries set in the treaty with the other native nation. William Barnett, one of the treaty commissioners along with Benjamin Hawkins and E. P. Gaines, reported that the gathering of the allied Creeks, Chickasaws, Cherokees, and Choctaws in June 1816 failed to produce a firm consensus on the boundaries between those nations.[23] In particular he noted, "The Chickasaws and Cherekees [sic] could come to no understanding as to their boundary."[24] Barnett found the Cherokees rude and intractable. At the end of the meeting, he decided to head home without resolving the issues, even declining to visit Coffee in person in Nashville because of his horses' sore backs and because his "head gets veary full of home." Barnett was sick of trying to straighten out the overlapping land claims.

John Coffee took over the boundary negotiation and survey in July, but the unresolved boundary between the Chickasaws and Cherokees resulted in a second round of treaties.[25] James Colbert informed Andrew Jackson that "it was determined by the chiefs then present [at a meeting to decide what to tell the commissioners] that the Chickasaw nation had no lands to sell or exchange whatever. I have also to state that the warriors of this nation have been very much dissatisfied with the chiefs ever since the treaty held with you in [March] 1816, on account of the land then sold by them."[26] The Chickasaws did, however, agree to meet again with commissioners to hear them out. This took place at Col. George Colbert's home, located where the Natchez Trace crossed the Tennessee River in the Chickasaw nation.[27] In the new treaties, U.S. commissioners resolved the conflict by compensating both the Cherokees and Chickasaws for the disputed territory. Major Ridge was among the signers of the March 1816 Cherokee treaty, but not the September Treaty. Levi

Colbert, William Colbert, George Colbert, and James Colbert signed the September 1816 Chickasaw treaty. James Colbert also served as an interpreter for the negotiations. The earlier 1816 Chickasaw treaty has not been published or located.[28] The result, according to treaty commissioners Andrew Jackson, David Meriwether, and Jesse Franklin, was that, "we have this day concluded a treaty that secures to the West a free and uninterrupted intercourse with the low country. Independent of the accession of a rich and large body of lands to the United States, the objects otherwise obtained by this treaty are of incalculable political advantage to our country."[29] Most importantly, western settlers now would have navigational rights to many of the Southeast's major rivers as "the whole southern country from Kentucky and Tennessee to Mobile has been opened by the late treaties,"[30] which "secured the affections of the population of the South and West to the present administration"[31] and, one might add, to Jackson's future administration.

The Chickasaw treaty of September 1816 withheld specific tracts from the land cession for the continued use of individual Chickasaws and their families. George and Levi Colbert, along with two other men, each received tracts of land exempted from the U.S. purchase "only so long as they shall be occupied, cultivated, or used, by the present proprietors or heirs." Another article specified that "as a particular mark of distinction and favor for his long services and faithful adherence to the United States' Government, the commissioners agree to allow to Gen. William Colbert an annuity of one hundred dollars, for and during his life."[32] The treaty also held a detailed clause limiting the trading licenses issued for trading with the Chickasaw nation, likely as a way of protecting the commercial interests of the Colbert family and other enterprising Chickasaws who had stores in the Chickasaw nation. These special articles revealed strategies on both sides of the treaty table geared toward insulating the wealth and political power of those Chickasaws who supported these treaties, including the Colberts.[33]

The following year the United States held another treaty with the Cherokee nation that included the first clauses about the exchange of lands east of the Mississippi River for acreage in what would soon become the Arkansas territory.[34] Several Chickamauga towns had relocated west to that region following the defeat of Dragging Canoe and the Chickamauga resistance movement in 1794. The remaining Lower Towns, which had retained some of the leaders from the Chickamauga movement, expressed a willingness to join those refugees in an effort to escape

continuing land speculation around Muscle Shoals, pursued not unsur-
prisingly by several members of the Donelson family network including
Andrew Jackson. The commissioners made the exchange as attractive
as possible including the promise of a rifle, ammunition, blanket, and
either a kettle or beaver trap as well as provisions for the move and provisions for the first year in the new territory.[35] They also attempted to create an allotment policy giving the remaining Cherokees a 640-acre plot
each. The latter clause was ignored, but the removal of the Lower Towns
set a precedent for treaty negotiators among the Southeastern nations,
including Andrew Jackson, whose name was the first signing the document.[36] The United States signed treaties with the Cherokee nation in
1818 and with the Chickasaw nation in 1819, each demanding more land.
The leaders of these nations, under extreme pressure from U.S. officials
to cede more and more land, looked for ways to preserve the land and
political autonomy of their nations. The following section illustrates the-
matically the mix of traditional strategies and new tactics used by these
leaders to navigate this new, challenging diplomatic environment.

The treaties following the Creek War signaled to the leading Chickasaw and Cherokee families that the rules of the game had changed significantly. No longer was it enough to be on the right side of imperial
conflicts. Native leadership now had to convince American leadership
to take them seriously without the benefit of European competition that
threatened warfare on both the North American and European conti-
nents. As in the previous decade, the Colbert, Ridge, and Ward families used the rhetoric of civilization to convince U.S. officials that they
were aligned with the present and future visions of their allies. They also
reconditioned the old tools that had served them well in past intercultural negotiation: diversifying their economy, calling upon old alliances,
and marrying outsiders to create and reinforce new alliances.

By 1815 the Colbert, Ridge, and Ward families melded aspects of plantation agricultural, animal husbandry, spinning, weaving, running river
ferries, tavern keeping, and provisioning treaties and survey crews into
their more traditional economic strategies of hunting, fishing, tanning
pelts, creating basketry and pottery, and selling horses and excess foodstuffs to travelers through the nation. These new "civilized" endeavors
augmented rather than replaced the more traditional strategies, which
was prudent as the demand and price for deerskins and other peltry
declined, the wildlife supply diminished from overhunting, and the size
of native hunting grounds contracted through sales made under duress
of pressure by U.S. officials. Although these families had maintained

diversified economic strategies for centuries, even while the slave and deerskin traders encouraged them to focus their labor strategies for the market, the economic environment of the post-1815 trans-Appalachian frontier pushed them to develop new entrepreneurial avenues while maintaining older ones.[37]

7 / Kinship Networks and Evolving Concepts of Nationhood

As pressure to have Indians remove to the West increased, Beloved Woman Nancy Ward sought to use her influence among the Cherokees and her notoriety among Americans to gain the attention and support of U.S. politicians. She drew upon her reputation as a political ally of the settlers during the Revolution as well as the personal connections she and her daughters had forged through marital alliances. In 1818, Nancy Ward, as a representative of the Cherokee Women's Council, argued that the Cherokees should remain in the East because they had become "civilized." Her words would soon be published to add heft to the growing antiremoval movement:

> Our Father the President advised us to become farmers, to manu-facture our own clothes, & to have our children instructed. To this advice we have attended in every thing as far as we were able. Now the thought of being compelled to remove the other side of the Mis-sissippi is dreadful to us, because it appears to us that we, by this removal, shall be brought to a savage state again, for we have, by the endeavor of our Father the President, become too much enlight-ened to throw aside the privileges of a civilized life.[1]

According to Ward, her people were too entrenched in the regional econ-omy to live in a "savage state." The "civilized life" provided distinct advan-tages to native people who reshaped it to reflect their societies' values. According to Ward, "Civilization" (through economic diversification) had changed her people and provided them with the economic and cultural tools to live in peace among the white people.

Ward also used familial language to call upon the young Cherokee leaders to heed their mother's wisdom and respect the mothers of the nation who knew what was best for their sons: "We have raised all of you on the land which we now have, which God gave us to inhabit and raise provisions, . . . [removal] would be like destroying your mothers."[2] Using language that would be especially moving in a matrilineal society, Ward hoped her talks would similarly move the sons of the new nation to do what was right by ending efforts to force Cherokees to remove. She expressed disappointment that many cross-cultural marriages failed in uniting the political interests of those Anglo-Americans and Indians: "There are some white men among us who have been raised in this country from their youth, are connected with us by marriage, & have considerable families, who are very active in encouraging the emigration of our nation. These ought to be our truest friends but prove our worst enemies."[3] Ward's appeal to her nation's sons might also have resonated with a new set of allies, American women, whose rhetoric of "republican motherhood" gave them a place in the political arena where they banded together to advocate for missionary efforts among Indians in the Southeast and later to fight removal. Historian Mary Hershberger argues that women's organizations were among the most powerful voices in opposition to removal and that the antiremoval movement served as the predecessor to both the abolition and women's rights movements. Women and missionaries would be the heart and soul of the moral reform movements of the Jacksonian era, and they proved the most dedicated allies to promoting "civilization" projects among the Indians and opposing encroachment on Indian rights.[4]

The diversification of strategies both described and embodied by Nancy Ward mirrored the political diversification employed by these families throughout the eighteenth century which evolved into new political strategies in the nineteenth century. Oconostota had desired that the children of intermarried traders would become a bridge between the red and white peoples, helping both to understand one another better. The Colbert family sought to use American education to facilitate that understanding. Jeffersonian rhetoric of "civilization" was channeled by native leaders into educational opportunities to learn the oratorical and debate skills that would support them in their verbal defense of sovereignty. Levi Colbert also made a point to send all of his children, male and female, to a nearby mission school.[5] The Colberts sought to use that knowledge to their advantage. As a treaty commissioner in 1818, Andrew Jackson complained to Isaac Shelby: "[The] Colberts say, they will part with their lands for the price the u. states gets for theirs. These are high toned sentiments and they must be taught to know that they do not Possess sovereignity [sic], with the right of domain."[6] Although they successfully negotiated the legal world of the Anglo-Americans and took on many of their trappings, the Colberts maintained several markers of Chickasaw identity. They continued to speak Chickasaw in addition to English and remained dedicated to using their education to reinforce Chickasaw political autonomy. Jackson, however, saw the Colberts' influence and "civilization" as evidence of "designing half-breeds" who had apparently inherited their greed and cunning from their Anglo-American ancestors and were at odds with "true Indians, the natives of the forest."[7]

Although Major Ridge was considered a "full blooded" Cherokee, his son and nephews attended the local Moravian mission school and then New England schools to learn, among other things, Anglo-American rhetorical and legal philosophies. His grandson John Rollin Ridge, who would go on to be among the first published American Indian poets and novelists, wrote about his perceptions of America and his own native heritage.[8] Another grandson, Cornelius Boudinot, the son of Elias Boudinot, became the editor and publisher of the *Arkansian* newspaper in Fayetteville, Arkansas.[9]

Anglo-style education enabled the Ridge family to forge new alliances, as their association with New England clergymen and teachers could now be added to older military and diplomatic relationships. Northeasterners, particularly missionary organizations and women's aid societies, became active allies on behalf of southern native peoples, supporting their right to political sovereignty, especially because of their willingness to become "civilized Christians." Elias Boudinot and John Ridge presented themselves as evidence of Indian "civilization" on the northeastern lecture circuit.[10]

As Nancy Ward and her daughters had cemented their ties to traders through intercultural marriage, John Ridge and Elias Boudinot (who adopted the name of the aging Continental Congress representative and American Bible Society president) sought to marry Anglo-American girls they had met while away at school. This strategy backfired as writers lambasted the marriages as racially repugnant and an angry crowd burned effigies of Elias Boudinot and his bride, Harriott Gold, on the town green in Cornwall, Connecticut. Even among the seemingly supportive northeastern mission societies, the rhetoric of "civilization" contrasted against a rhetoric of innate savagery, which meant that to some degree recognition of "civilization" implied that "civilized" Indians had been savage prior to their adoption of white ways. Clothes, careful diction, religious piety, and logical arguments could not overcome their racist perceptions of Boudinot. Intercultural marriage was a tactic that lost some of its effectiveness in the aftermath of the Creek War. No longer able to link peoples diplomatically through ties of kinship as the Betsy Ward/Joseph Martin marriage had in 1777, the Ridge network marriages nonetheless endured, and the couples moved back to the Cherokee nation to continue their campaign for "civilized" sovereignty in publications for Cherokee and white audiences.[11]

H. S. Gold, Boudinot's brother-in-law, wrote a journal of his travels in Cherokee country, which he sent as a letter to his uncle-in-law, Gen. D. B. Brinsmade in May 1830. Gold recorded details about the structure, cleanliness, and furnishings of the houses, a piano concert performed by chief David Vann's wife (noting that both Vann and his wife were "descendants of Cherokees"), and the spinning, weaving, and cotton plantations that signified "civilization." Gold also noted in careful detail the familial connections among those he visited. For Gold, like his Cherokee in-laws, family connections seemed to indicate valuable connections that helped him better understand the people and places he encountered.[12]

Elias Boudinot edited the *Cherokee Phoenix* from 1828 through 1834.[13] The *Phoenix* described a "civilized Cherokee" identity both similar to the lifestyles of their elite southern neighbors, and distinctly Cherokee. The *Phoenix*, for example, advocated literacy in both English and the Cherokee syllabary. The Cherokee syllabary was an alphabet completed by Sequoyah in 1821 with eighty-five symbols to represent the sounds in the Cherokee language in written form.[14] While instructing Cherokees how to be good Christians, they cultivated alliances with missionaries who voiced their support in their organizational newsletters, northern newspapers, and before the U.S. Supreme Court.[15] Producing the *Cherokee Phoenix* newspaper was an outgrowth of Ridge family efforts to reinforce their political position within the Cherokee nation through creating alliances outside it and through obtaining critical skills that aided in U.S./Cherokee diplomacy. Boudinot published pamphlets to sway Christians to the cause of Cherokee sovereignty. He wrote "An Address to the Whites Delivered in the First Presbyterian Church on the 26th of May, 1826," in which he posed the rhetorical question, "What is an Indian?" He replied, "You here behold an Indian, my kindred are Indians and my fathers sleeping in the wilderness grave—they too were Indians."[16] He presented to them the example of an educated, sophisticated man in order to have Indians seen as people worthy of respect and support. Boudinot also wrote articles for Christian newspapers throughout the country, detailing the "civilization" and political plights of Southeastern Indians to a significant number of subscribers.[17] The Ridge family network's use of newspapers was a new take on old strategies; whereas native leaders in the eighteenth century relied upon treaty talks and personal relationships to sway their allies, by the nineteenth century they augmented those talks and relationships with additional forms of written persuasion, convincing those allies (in this case, northern Christians) that supporting native sovereignty was in both of their best interests.

Chickasaws and Cherokees augmented old strategies like economic diversification, calling on established allies, creating new allies through marriage, and persuasive writing with the trappings and rhetoric of "civilization" from plantation agriculture to newspapers to make these strategies more effective in the nineteenth century. They did not use other strategies, such as kin-based military resistance and trade negotiation, because they no longer seemed tactically sound as the Creek War and subsequent land grabs illustrated. Without a tangible threat from European powers in the Southeast, native leaders used personal and kinship relationships to lobby for their continued political presence in the region. These strategies encountered the stiffening obstacles of unchecked U.S. power, rampant land speculation, and virulent racism. Native families' most effective defense against removal now proved to be a language condemning its immorality and injustice, which did gain Southeastern Indians important political allies in both the Congress and the Supreme Court.[18]

Like the leading Indian families during this period, the Donelson family network strategies exhibited continuities with those pursued by previous generations of Donelsons, including treaty negotiation, land speculation, and kin-based military connections. The network operated as a web of individuals who relayed valuable information, pursued similar economic goals (often by investing together), and backed one another in political and military conflicts. The coterie of Andrew Jackson's in-laws and nephews that had aided him in the Creek War continued to be instrumental to the function of his New Orleans and Florida campaigns.

The Donelson family network included land speculators who benefited from the large tracts of land obtained through the post–Creek

War treaties of 1816 and 1818. John Donelson Jr. was a founder of the Pensacola Land Company in 1817.[19] John Coffee, Andrew Jackson, and James Jackson, among others, founded the Cypress Land Company that bought the land on the Tennessee River that would become the town of Florence, Alabama.

As in early Donelson land speculation, surveying provided extra income and connections that served the familial network. Andrew Jackson secured the office of state surveyor of Alabama for John Coffee in 1816, which provided Coffee and his relations with valuable information on choice lands in the state, especially around Muscle Shoals. John Donelson Jr. told Coffee, Donelson's son-in-law, that he planned to buy two tracts of land, selling one to pay for the other. Donelson quipped, "This is my way of speculation."[20] Coffee's brother-in-law Lemuel Donelson also informed him that he would like "to have a finger in the [land speculation] pie."[21] When the Cypress Land Company documents were lost in a fire at the Alabama land office nearly a decade after the formation of the company, Jackson wrote to Coffee that "your survayors business will occasion the Government (not you) some expense. . . . [Y]our attention must be draw[n] to the duties of your office as survayor & to close the business of the Cypress land company."[22] Coffee's position as state surveyor brought him and his family significant income through survey fees and land speculation activities.

Donelson network members also continued to conduct business with one another. A covenant between Andrew Jackson and William Donelson dated July 19, 1820, reveals the ongoing intertwined economic relationships of the network:

> I, William Donelson, bind myself &c to convey unto Andrew Jackson when called on for undivided half of the 640 acres of land originally granted by the State of North Carolina to Hugh Hays, lying on the south side of Cumberland adjoining the land on the north whereon said Andrew now lives and known by the name of Hugh Hays Preemption which said tract of 640 acres was bought by me and Samuel Donelson in his lifetime from said Hugh Hays. This 11 Dec 1806. Test: Jno. Coffee. July Term 1820.[23]

Brothers William and Samuel Donelson had bought the tract from neighbor Hugh Hays, also a distant relative, and promised Jackson he could have the land when he wanted it. When the time came for Jackson to claim the land, his friend and nephew-in-law Coffee signed as witness.

A letter from Andrew Jackson to John Coffee in 1825 reflects earlier patterns of familial legal activities: "I shall write you by Major Green a relation of yours & McLamores from NoCarolina [sic] who will be with you some next week & send you powers of atto. [attorney] from Mrs. [Catherine Donelson] Hutchings & Mrs. [Jane Donelson] Hays to Locate their share of the grant separately." Jackson requested in the same missive that Capt. Jack Donelson take inventory of Jackson's slaves and livestock.[24] The family network continued to utilize power of attorney to stake land claims for one another.

Much like Jackson having taken on his nephews as wards upon the deaths of his brothers-in-law, raising young family members and administering their estates continued to be a responsibility shared by multiple family members. The death of Jackson's nephew John Hutchings resulted in Andrew Jackson gaining guardianship over his grandnephew Andrew Jackson Hutchings. Jackson and Coffee, who owned the neighboring tract, acted as executors of the estate and together managed the plantation and upbringing of the young Hutchings.[25] In 1826 Jackson bought a horse from Capt. Jack Donelson for Andrew Jackson Hutchings's plantation that was forwarded on to Coffee, who managed the plantation for Hutchings. Jackson wrote to his nephew William Donelson that their charge (Hutchings) had "been suspended from College, & is now at the Hermitage Idle. This intelligence is a sore grief to me, and one from his pledge to me, of good behaviour . . . and I must adopt such measures, such as will yet preserve him from ruin, & myself from disgrace."[26] He asked Donelson to enroll Hutchings in school with Mr. Otey of Franklin, Tennessee, "as I find it useless to attempt to make him a good classic scholar; and all I now hope for is, to give him an education to fit him for a farmer."[27] Jackson, Coffee, and Donelson together took financial and social responsibility for Andrew Jackson Hutchings, balancing the management of the boy's plantation and education alongside their other business, political, and familial responsibilities.

The Donelson family network, like the Colbert, Ridge, and Ward families, practiced continuity in their political and economic strategies by drawing heavily upon their kinship connections to one another. However, the Donelsons in the years following the Creek War had little need to adjust those strategies to the new political and economic environment of the trans-Appalachian frontier. Instead, their strategies functioned effectively unchanged from their early speculative ventures of the Revolutionary period. New generations of Donelsons got rich from land speculation, surveying, legal connections, and plantation agriculture just as previous ones had.

The U.S. government had been encouraging Indians to leave their homes east of the Mississippi since early in Jefferson's presidency. The Georgia state government was so sure of this inevitability that when they ceded their rights to their western territories (which would become Alabama and Mississippi) to the U.S. government in 1802, the agreement included a clause that required the federal government to remove all Indian land claims from Georgia. After the Cherokee nation ratified its own constitutional government based on the U.S. Constitution, the Georgia state government recognized that the Cherokees were officially denying the right of Georgia to enforce its laws within Cherokee territory and on Cherokee citizens. The ratification provoked Georgians to further step up their efforts to force Cherokees to remove through legislation and physical intimidation as Anglo-Americans set up homesteads in Cherokee territory that were subsequently legitimized through surveys and deeds by Georgia. "Civilization" strategies, intended to support political sovereignty, created a backlash from Georgians determined to assert their dominion over Cherokee territory to the north. They sent the militia to enforce Georgia law, they settled on Cherokee land, they imprisoned principal chief John Ross, and they seized the *Cherokee Phoenix*.[28]

By 1828 the leadership of the Choctaws and Chickasaws were seriously considering U.S. offers of land west of the Mississippi. A group of chiefs, including Levi Colbert and his nephew Charles Colbert, U.S. Army personnel, and missionaries set out together to inspect the lands proposed to them. In the course of the journey the chiefs reaffirmed peaceful relations with several tribes along the way, including the Shawnees, Osages, and western Cherokees. Peter Pitchlynn, one of the Choctaw chiefs, kept a journal of the trip, noting the deceptive efforts of the Anglo-Americans who traveled with them. He recalled: "The country between the Osages and Kanzas [sic] is all Prairie, no game of any kind whatever, and the soil of the lands by no means good. But notwithstanding that these are facts to me and all of the Choctaws and Chickasaws in company, the whites who are with us, some of them have been presumtious enough to tell us that it is a fine country, and even have said that it is the best in the world."[29] Pitchlynn and his Choctaw and Chickasaw associates undertook reconnaissance of Indian Country to determine if removal might be to the advantage of their people. They followed traditional protocols of smoking the calumet and making or reinforcing alliances along the way. While the Anglo-Americans attempted to delude the delegation into taking the least desirable territory, the delegation was well aware of the productive potential of the lands they examined and chose a section that remained fertile enough for agriculture and that retained game. Both of these attributes would support the diversified economic strategies they embraced.

The Cherokees were especially divided over how "civilization" could be used to support the sovereignty of their people. Several authors have investigated how this issue caused the family networks of Major Ridge and John Ross to square off politically against one another. The two groups agreed that the adoption of slavery and plantation agriculture made Cherokee leaders more competitive in the Anglo-dominated economic markets and lent prestige to their diplomatic negotiations with U.S. planter elites.[30] Following the passage of the Indian Removal Act in 1830 by a vote of 102 to 97, the Ridge family network began to feel that their efforts to convince America of the value of "civilized" Indians would not prevent those most determined to have their land from taking it. John Ross and his supporters continued to lobby Congress for support against the onslaught until federal troops had rounded up the Cherokee nation into holding pens until they could be transported west against their will.

The Indian Removal Act "provide[d] for an exchange of lands with the Indians residing in any of the states or territories, and for their removal west of the river Mississippi." It promised payment for improvements, "aid and assistance . . . to enable them to remove," and funding for their subsistence in the first year of residency in the new Indian territory. Most importantly, it allocated five hundred thousand dollars "for the purpose of giving effect to the provisions of this act." This sum, as it would turn out, was insufficient for funding the removals themselves and would not provide any of the first-year support promised in the Indian Removal Act. The act did not authorize Jackson or anyone else to seize land or force Indians to remove but only to make voluntary treaties. Americans, especially Georgians, used the authorization to make treaties to make living east of the Mississippi unbearable. They physically moved onto Indian lands and pushed native people out of their homes. By refusing to enforce native boundaries and sovereignty as mandated by the Marshall Supreme Court, Jackson tacitly encouraged Anglo-Americans to settle on native lands.[31]

When the Indian Removal Act threatened Chickasaw lands and government, the Colberts negotiated to minimize the cost in lives and financial assets by determining the terms for Chickasaw removal. The Colberts illustrate how Chickasaws could so thoroughly adopt pieces of "Western culture" while retaining an Indian identity that privileged Chickasaw political sovereignty. The Colberts' most important diplomatic role in the nineteenth century was their participation in the negotiations of the terms of Chickasaw removal west of the Mississippi in 1835. Levi Colbert was effective as the lead negotiator, getting the U.S. government to pay market value for Chickasaw lands and ensuring the payments were made to the Chickasaw government rather than funneled through corrupt government contractors.[32] The nation's new lands in Indian Territory were to be bought at a fair price and chosen by an expedition of tribal leaders and U.S. officials who evaluated potential territories on-site. The remaining funds were then used by the Chickasaw government, rather than the U.S. government, to provide adequate transportation on the journey to Indian Territory. Prior to the treaty, some of the Colberts had toured their potential future territory alongside Choctaw leaders and found the territory lacking. By 1835, they had still not found a suitable territory. Signing the treaty forced the Chickasaws to purchase territory already claimed by the Choctaws in Indian Territory, and Martin Colbert, Pitman Colbert, and Thomas Colbert were among the negotiators for that territory.[33] While the removal treaty still forced the tribe to exchange their homeland for less desirable territory west of the Mississippi, the efforts of Colbert and others ensured that the Chickasaw nation did not suffer the same degree of loss in lives and resources as other southern tribes.

The process of removal was easier for the Chickasaws, who migrated semi-voluntarily rather than at the points of federal bayonets. Still, they suffered significant losses in lives and property. An estimated five hundred to six hundred Chickasaws died of a smallpox epidemic related to the move. They lost so many horses and oxen along the way that they had to abandon much of their baggage.[34] Their losses, however, paled in comparison with those suffered by the Cherokees.

Levi Colbert oversaw the preparations for the removal process for the Chickasaws but died prior to the actual move. The Colberts remained important political leaders after removal. Benjamin Franklin Colbert built a new Colbert's Ferry on the Red River. Winston Colbert and Holmes Colbert, nephews of George Colbert, were instrumental in developing the Chickasaw Constitution in Indian Territory during the 1850s.[35] Winchester Colbert, Levi Colbert's nephew and ward, later served as governor of the Chickasaw nation from 1858 to 1860 and from 1862 to 1866. Their commitment to slaveholding and their physical proximity to Confederate Texas meant that the Chickasaw nation fought alongside the Confederates in the Civil War.[36]

The Cherokees by 1835, however, were divided over the question of removal. The Ridge family network, in particular, had been directly affected by Anglo-American racism in spite of their obvious "civilization." Their marriages had been harangued, their printing press seized, and their property had been assaulted by white Georgians. U.S. officials continually presented Cherokee leaders with new, slightly revised treaties that were rejected again and again. Finally, in 1835, Major Ridge, his son John Ridge, and his nephews Elias Boudinot and Stand Watie, along with several other Cherokee leaders, signed the Treaty of New Echota exchanging the eastern Cherokee nation for land in Indian Territory and $4.5 million in payment for improvements and to fund removal.[37] According to the treaty, the Cherokees had until 1838 to evacuate their lands.

Because only about 2,000 Cherokees had actually removed by the 1838 deadline, President Martin Van Buren authorized Gen. Winfield Scott to enforce the removal militarily.[38] The process of rounding up those who had not yet emigrated and marching them to Indian Territory took a total of around ten months. Between 4,000 and 8,000 Cherokees out of a population of 21,500 died on the 2,200 mile trek that became known as the "Trail of Tears."[39] The surviving Cherokees in Indian Territory suffered the aftershocks of removal, which included a kin-based feud between the Ross and Ridge factions.

While decentralized political power had commonly operated in the colonial period, the Cherokee Constitution of 1828 declared that signing a treaty without an affirmative vote of the national council was punishable by death.[40] This sentence was carried out by John Ross's political and kinship networks although Ross himself denied sanctioning the attacks. By 1839, Major Ridge, John Ridge, and Elias Boudinot, as well as several other signers, were dead. In June of that year, John Ross related to Brevet Brig. Gen. Matthew Arbuckle at Fort Gibson in Indian Territory that he would be arriving for their meeting with an armed guard because "an additional number of my friends have assembled at this place for the purpose of repelling an attack upon me, as was reasonably anticipated from the violent threats of personal revenge."[41] A month later, U.S. Capt. Benjamin Bonneville reported on the standoff:

> A delegation of the treaty party of Cherokees—about 750 men, women & children have fled beyond the limits of the Nation for

safety. Murders are still continued. Light horse or police companies are assigned to each district three companies. [A]re certainly very summary dealers in justice. . . . Stand Wattie has collected around him 120 Cherokees & he is determined not to leave the nation. Says he will not act on the offensive. [O]r on the defensive & leaves the decision of their present condition to the Presdt. U.S.[42]

The Cherokee nation was again fragmented into kin-based factions pursuing different agendas, but this time with deep animosity that threatened to overturn the centralized government that had grown out of the "civilization" movement. These factions remained at opposition through the Civil War. The Cherokees began the war as allies of the Confederates, but after the Union army invaded the nation and captured the capital, Ross's administration declared their allegiance to the Union. Stand Watie, the last of the Ridge contingent of the treaty party still living in the Indian Territory, became a Confederate general, leading Cherokee troops against the Ross party in the Cherokee nation. Watie's nephews John Rollin Ridge and Cornelius Boudinot were also staunch Confederates.[43]

The era following the Creek War produced drastic changes in the Chickasaw and Cherokee nations, but the centrality of kinship remained, even becoming more prominent in these times of crisis. The Colbert family was instrumental in negotiating the best deal possible once removal became unavoidable. The Ridge family lost their reputation and several family members in the controversy surrounding removal. Both family networks, however, continued to draw upon their kin for political and, in the Ridge family's case, military support.

Jackson first ran for president of the United States in 1824 and was elected to that office in 1828 and 1832. During and after his presidency, family remained central to his political and economic strategies. Gen. John Coffee remained a treaty negotiator and was the U.S. Indian agent to the Chickasaws. Jackson chose his nephew Andrew Jackson Donelson as his private secretary and asked his niece-in-law, Emily, to be the White House hostess upon the death of his wife, Rachel.[44] The Donelson family network, as in the years before the presidency, created a family-based political framework for President Jackson. As in years past, Jackson played an influential role in shaping the network itself through guiding his nephews to suitable marriages and negotiating the conflicts that arose when business deals between multiple family members went awry.

Although social standing was clearly one of many factors that shaped the Donelson family network, it was not the central factor. Prior allegiances or valuable skills could overwhelm the impulse to encourage matches between prominent families. The tension within the Donelson family network over differences of opinion on the purpose and function of the institution of marriage became clear in a disagreement between Andrew Jackson and his niece and nephew over the White House scandal known as the "Eaton Affair." When Jackson's friend, cabinet member, and later biographer John Eaton married Peggy O'Neil, a local innkeeper's daughter and occasional barmaid, Washington society was appalled. Jackson himself had no objections to the marriage and had even encouraged it. The other wives of Jackson's cabinet members, including Jackson's niece Emily, refused to associate with Mrs. Eaton. Jackson ordered the women to end their ostracizing of Mrs. Eaton, but his demand had no effect on their actions. This rebellion sowed strife within the cabinet itself. The tension within the family over the conflict lasted from January 1829 through July 1831. Remini claims that Emily's refusal was because of "her husband's admitted indignation over Eaton's influence with his uncle."[45]

Jackson, however, proved his allegiance to the matching of prominent families by mitigating the marriage opportunities of his nephew in 1832. He wrote to Eliza Fauquier, mother of the bride-to-be, extolling the virtues of his nephew and the Donelson family more generally,

> Thomas was reared by an amiable & pious mother having lost his father when very young—his moral character as well as all his family is without a stain. [H]is fortune tho small, is competent with industry & economy to live independantly—he is clear of debt, of amicable disposition, free from all kind of . . . intemperate habits, from all which, I have no doubt he is well calculated to make your daughter happy. [H]e possesses a good tract of land and ten negroes with stock on his farm, adjoining me.[46]

Eliza Fauquier was the aunt of Sarah York, who had married Andrew Jackson Jr. just a year earlier. Andrew Jackson continued the kinship strategy of tying together prominent families into the Donelson family network. The marriage of Thomas J. Donelson to Emma Fauquier created another bond between the two families.[47]

The intertwined economic activities of Jackson's son and nephews gave him some trouble in 1843, when one nephew, Stockley Donelson, defaulted on a contract that he bought from Andrew Jackson Jr. The complicated mess threatened to derail Andrew Jr.'s financial stability and the honor of the family itself. Jackson relayed the situation as follows:

> Shortly after the purchase of the negroes by Major A J. Donelson, & A. Jackson jnr the latter desposed [sic] of his interest in that purchase to Stockly Donelson, who became liable for all sums of mony on said contract that A. Jackson jnr was liable for having stepped into the shoes of the said J. Jnr. It has been owing to the default of Stockly Donelson in not complying punctually with his engagement that any delay in payment has happened to compell S. Donelson to secure the payment of his part of this debt, . . . Mr. A. Jackson jur [sic] has been badly treated by Stockly Donelson, who bought his interest in the negroes, and expected great punctuality in Stockly Donelson, but has been much injured by his failure to comply.[48]

Former president Andrew Jackson was forced to bring a suit against his nephew to ensure that neither he nor his son would be liable for Stockley Donelson's failure to pay the debt. As in generations past, members of the Donelson family network engaged in business ventures together, and, as in the past, not all of those deals came off without damaging the finances and the relationships of those investors.

After Jackson's death in 1845, Donelson family members continued to be politically active. Andrew Jackson Donelson ran for vice president of the United States in 1856 alongside Millard Fillmore as representatives of the Know-Nothing Party. The Know-Nothing Party, or American Party, appealed to middle-class Protestants who feared losing their jobs and influence to Catholic immigrants. He was also the United States' foreign minister to Texas, Prussia, and Germany.[49] Donelson's political career marked the last vestiges of the Donelson family network's presence on the national stage. The family's status, financial gains, and land speculation proved longer-lasting than their time in the national spotlight.

Although Cherokee and Chickasaw leaders dressed and spoke like gentlemen, ran plantations and owned slaves, and even adopted U.S.-style centralized governments, Lewis Cass, deemed by his contemporaries one of the "highly thoughtful experts . . . on United States Indian policy and the histories and cultures of the tribes," declared in 1830 that efforts to civilize the Indians had failed. He argued that "such a wish [to incorporate Indians into Anglo-American society] is in vain. A barbarous people, depending for subsistence upon the scanty and precarious supplies furnished by the chase, cannot live in contact with a civilized community."[50] Cass's "expert opinion" revealed that native "civilization" strategies could only accomplish so much. While they could persuade religious and women's groups, individuals with a vested interest in Indian removal, including western politicians and land speculators (often individuals were both), believed what they wanted about the "civilization" or "hunter lifestyle" of Indians. Southern Indians had engaged in farming and other activities in a mixed economy since first contact with Europeans. Europeans and Americans, furthermore, included hunting as part of their own culture for sport or subsistence. U.S. proponents of westward expansion argued that "barbarous people" should not exist in close proximity to Anglo-American communities. "Civilizationists" attempted to remove that excuse and worked to convince old and new allies that they had indeed done so. That Cass's comments came after more than three decades of "civilizing" and despite the best efforts of leaders, such as Major Ridge and Levi Colbert, proved the native opponents of "civilization" correct in their assertion that adopting elements of Anglo-American "civilization" would not stop westward expansion.

The political and economic strategies of both Indian and Anglo-American leaders reflected the continued role of kinship and familial strategies in nineteenth-century intercultural negotiation and conflict. The Colbert, Ward, and Ridge family networks continued to diversify their economic strategies, to call upon old alliances forged through military and diplomatic association, to use familial language persuasively, and to cement new allies to their interests through marriage. They adapted to the changing economic and political environment by tapping into extensive communication avenues to increase their rhetorical effectiveness through newspapers and lecture circuits. They reached beyond traditional alliances to engage religious and women's society networks throughout the United States on their behalf. Meanwhile, the Donelsons also employed strategies that had worked for them in the past in order to capitalize on the new political and economic environment. Their kinship network reaped political and economic benefits as western politicians who gained power in Washington embraced western expansion, which enabled family members to continue to profit from land speculation.

Kinship and familial strategies in the 1830s resembled those employed by leading families in the colonial era but also displayed the ingenuity and flexibility of those using them as they adapted to the opportunities and challenges unique to the period. Although the native families had some success with their efforts to retain political sovereignty with the help of their allies, the Donelson family was significantly more effective at translating their generations-old strategies into nineteenth-century profits thanks to the federal government's embrace of western expansion ideals.

Conclusion: Piecing Together a New Society from the Remnants of the Old

Sitting at a table in the library and archives of the Chickasaw nation, elder and librarian Glenda Galvan patiently explained to a young graduate student how Chickasaws at the beginning of the twenty-first century defined family and kinship: "Everything, family means every-thing to us."[1] Kinship, she explained, shaped individuals' relationships and responsibilities but also how those relationships guided decisions about marriage partners, where one lived, occupations, and even politi-cal debates, including those over the Native American Graves Protec-tion and Repatriation Act (NAGPRA). While patriarchal naming and inheritance practices had become commonplace, family was defined expansively to include those ancestors long buried. In essence, she had described how family gained its definitions, including membership, and how those definitions drove strategies of individuals and kin groups to support the needs, guide the ambitions, and protect the heritage of fam-ily members past and present. Our discussion helped to ensure that this account would be about continuity as well as change.

The discussion quickly turned to the ways the Chickasaw nation in Oklahoma sought to use NAGPRA to protect the native burial sites in the state. The graves they sought to protect were those of people she referred to as "our ancestors," whose burial sites, according to archae-ologists, long predated the 1830s, when Chickasaws were relocated into the area from east of the Mississippi River. She seemed to embrace a modern pan-Indian identity that defined people of the Mississippian era as ancestors of all of the formerly Southeastern tribes, or perhaps she was basing the definition of kinship on a more ancient definition derived from the Chickasaw origin story that told of their travels from far west to what would become their homelands east of the Mississippi River. Galvan noted that NAGPRA had given native people much more control over their ancestors' graves, physical remains, and burial goods. Corporations, she argued, often willfully disregarded the federal law or sought loopholes to build on valuable land either on top of burial sites or by hastily removing remains. These efforts were continual insults to the families and clans of those who had been put to rest in sacred ceremonies. Family, she noted, even those members whose direct genealogical lineages can no longer be found, must still be honored and protected. Kinship responsibilities still resonated strongly in the Chickasaw nation and provided the motivation for actively pursuing strict adherence to the NAGPRA regulations.[2]

Transitioning from regional politics to individual families, Galvan explained that failing to heed the advice of elders on kinship could also result in disaster for young couples. She used as evidence the many failed marriages of Chickasaw youth who had sought to marry native people outside of the tribe. As if it had been scripted, a Chickasaw man in his early thirties entered the library. His example would work to illustrate what the elder had said. He was recently divorced as a result of his marrying a non-Chickasaw woman. The cultures could not mesh, Galvan explained, and the marriage had been doomed from the beginning. His fate was representative, she said, of the trend of young people to ignore the centrality of Chickasaw culture to their identities and therefore to their choice of spouse. At the individual level, family responsibilities were part of that culture and could not be translated into a pan-Indian culture. Chickasaws who married American Indians from other tribes were sure to struggle to make their marriages work. Chickasaw culture was unique and was embedded in the identity of tribal members. To assume that cultural difference did not matter was to be surprised later by the degree to which it informed one's decisions, relationships, and actions. Definitions of family and familial responsibilities, among other cultural traits, were specific to the culture. All cultures seem to believe that familial relationships are important, but how exactly those relationships are defined and how they work is culturally dependent in ways that are significant to the parties involved.

The conversation resonated with me as I saw a strong correlation between the stories told to me and the patterns of behavior evident in the sources I had been reading from the trans-Appalachian region in the eighteenth and early nineteenth centuries. Rather than inspiring me to read these relationships backward in time, the conversation confirmed that I was asking the right questions about how the connections between kinship and leaders' decision making shaped intercultural interactions in early America. It also signaled that such commonalities between issues of the past and the present revealed a story that was as much about continuity as it was about historical change. To ignore that family was "everything" in the early twenty-first century with concrete influence on lives and decisions would be to deny the importance of one of the primary tools of individual and collective agency that had functioned for generations, albeit in ways that responded to the particular circumstances of the times in which people lived.

While the larger story emphasizes continuity of the power of kinship to shape lives through the centuries, the specific circumstances of particular eras had significant impacts on the effectiveness of kinship strategies in the short term. The consequences, for example, of removing Cherokees and Chickasaws, along with many other native peoples, from the Southeast were devastating. The huge loss in lives resulted in tribes creating orphanages to support the many children left without parents. Losing up to 25 percent of their tribal population, the clans no longer held the same connectedness and ability to care for the children in need. Institutions were set up to take over the jobs that clans had previously held responsibility for, such as child care, education, and elder care. The clan system appeared to be severely damaged by the death toll and the displacement brought about by removal.[3]

The American government worked toward dismantling distinct native cultures by forcing native children into boarding schools where they would become "civilized," assimilating into an "American" culture. In boarding schools children were isolated from their families, forbidden to speak their native languages, and stripped of their native dress, including hairstyles. Whereas native parents of the early nineteenth century, such as Levi Colbert, had sought out missionary-run boarding schools as a means to securing knowledge that could help their children navigate between native and American societies, after removal these places increasingly became a tool for purging native culture from the children. The mantra "Kill the Indian, Save the Man" was invoked as epitomizing the mission of boarding schools to drive out, often by force, the cultural attributes distinctive to native cultures and raise up children instead to be a "man" who would recognize the "superiority" of the American culture over Indian cultures. American political policies of allotment, reorganization, and termination likewise sought to divest Indians of their lands, sovereignty, and distinctive cultures. The process of cultural divestiture would be an ongoing project for America.[4]

The horrors of the journey and the loss of family and friends meant that native people were forced to deal with the scraps of their former world as they worked to create a new one. They named new towns after the ones they had left. Families, like the Colberts, who had run ferries back east built new ferries on new rivers. The loss of so many lives, and with them the ability to provide clan support to those in need, stripped away many of the primary functions of clans. While many of the jobs of clans were taken over by government, tribal or federal, the affection, loyalty, and obligations associated with kin remained. Families took on new identities based on tribe and family name, even as clan identity faded. The definitions and functions of family and kinship changed. Clans lost the place they had held as central institutions in town and regional politics, but extended kin groups remained important in the life of families. Grandparents continued to care for small children, and children looked after aging relatives. Patrilineal descent took the place of matrilineal clans, but knowing "who your people are" remained central to defining one's identity. The definitions of family and the use of relationships within kinship networks were expanded and reshaped over time to accommodate the needs of the family during each particular historical climate and their current needs to achieve changing familial goals.

Kinship networks proved useful means to shared familial ends continuously from the colonial era through the Civil War and beyond. Regardless of families' cultural affiliation, the goals families sought to reach, as well as the ways they utilized their networks, changed significantly over a period of 150 years. The families of James Logan Colbert of the Chickasaws, of Little Carpenter, Dragging Canoe, and the Ridge of the Cherokees, and of John Donelson of the United States included several influential political leaders and soldiers who served their people at crucial moments. The actions of members of these families illustrate how deeply intertwined the institution of family, the use of kinship networks, and the operation of government were in the colonial and early republic eras. Intergovernment negotiations directly shaped the fates of these leading families and vice versa.

Anthropologist Charles Hudson stated: "Kinship was a kind of mentality that pervaded many areas of life. . . . One can scarcely overemphasize the importance of kinship in the social life of the Southeastern Indians."[5]

Family relationships and kinship networks played as significant a role in the politics of Anglo-Americans as it did in American Indian politics. Rather than contrasting kinship-based native governments against that of a modern democratic nation state (the United States) defined by rugged individualism, leaders of these three cultural groups all utilized their familial relationships to gain and maintain political positions and to pursue familial economic goals. The flexibility of kinship networks enabled these families to endure as important forces in regional politics well into the nineteenth century.

While each of these groups defined specific kinship obligations differently, kinship was crucial to forging effective political strategies for the families in all three of these societies. This fact provided a common ground upon which diplomats attempted to build relationships between their governments using the language of kinship in treaties. The differences between them, however, undermined the effectiveness of that language and the treaties themselves. All of the families embraced strategic marriages to further their economic goals, whether related to trade, as in the case of the native families, or investments, like the land speculation ventures of the Donelsons. Military service remained an essential element of familial strategies, and each group drew upon kinship networks to form their military units. Familial language continued to invoke culturally specific family obligations and was used by both native and Anglo-American treaty negotiators. Finally, the families all drew political support from their kinship network, which at times formed factions that sometimes limited or increased the effectiveness of their governments through fragmented political policy. These strategies were consistent through both centuries and across cultural boundaries. The families' political and economic goals, however, changed over time.

Cherokee leaders, such as Little Carpenter, sought to forge firm trade alliances that would yield quality goods in a quantity and at a price that help to make the family, clan, and town prominent in regional politics among Cherokees, but also in relationship to the growing influence of the British colonies in the Southeast. Little Carpenter and his matrilineal descendants primarily sought to secure trade connections that could provide the Cherokees, especially his town of Chota, with an abundant supply of quality goods. Their neutral stance during the American Revolution reflected their commitment to this goal, as well as their physical proximity to Anglo-American settlements. This strategy was handed down from generation to generation in opposition to the strategies of other kin groups. Rivals sought to gain similar prominence for their own families and towns. Others, like Dragging Canoe, pursued an entirely different warfare-based strategy to gain regional influence by driving those who expanded into their territory. Dragging Canoe and his matrilineal kin and other followers preferred to protect their territorial integrity through kin-based war parties.

In the nineteenth century, the Ridge family network increased their wealth and political position within the tribe through their military alliance with the United States. Leading kinship-based war parties, The Ridge received a field promotion in the Creek War to major. He and others attempted to translate those military alliances into political alliances with key congressmen to fight Anglo-American efforts to remove the Cherokees from their lands east of the Mississippi. Eventually, members of the Ridge kinship network decided that holding out against U.S. pressure to remove was futile. Signing the Treaty of New Echota in 1835 without the authorization and support of the National Council resulted in the network being labeled the "Treaty Party" and deemed traitors to their people.[6] While fragmented political policy led by different kin-based factions had worked in the eighteenth century, similar actions in 1835 by the Ridge family network spurred decades of warfare between the factions. The goals of these Cherokee families had gone from seeking secure trade to working to preserve political and territorial sovereignty. Even as the goals changed, kinship networks remained central to their strategies employed to reach each of those goals.

The Colbert family history had a similar trajectory. James Logan Colbert married into a prominent clan to secure trade access to the Chickasaws and giving trade access to his wife's, later wives', clan and town. As the Chickasaws had been at war with the French for decades before Colbert's arrival, kin-based warfare was central to the family's political and economic strategies throughout the eighteenth century. Colbert, his sons, and his nephews fought for Chickasaw interests but also served in ways that cemented the family's alliance with the British. His sons would later lead kin-based war parties in Anthony Wayne and Arthur St. Clair's campaign against a confederation of northern and southern Indians as well as against the Creeks in the Creek War. These military alliances helped to bolster the family's reputation in the Chickasaw nation and among U.S. officials even as rivals discredited the family as unrepresentative of the Chickasaws. The Colberts used their military alliances, political and economic position in the Chickasaw nation, and reputation as political allies with the United States to achieve their goals. Like the Cherokee families, their goals changed from securing trade and military allies in the early eighteenth century to familial political and economic prosperity to retention of political sovereignty in the mid-nineteenth century. When Chickasaw efforts to avoid removal failed, the Colberts were instrumental in using their kinship network and mission school educations to negotiate for removal terms that would best benefit the Chickasaws.

The Donelson family network maintained consistent goals throughout this period, pursuing elite status through the acquisition of wealth, land, and prestige. Early on members of this network, including John Donelson, Andrew Jackson, and Samuel Donelson, employed economic strategies that diversified their investments in ironworks, plantation agriculture, general stores, and land speculation. By the mid-nineteenth century the network was still engaging in land speculation, performing surveys, and serving as lawyers and judges, but their interests in stores and iron had given way to more concentrated focus on slave-based plantation agriculture. To achieve their personal and collective economic goals, the Donelson family network utilized their connections to one another to gain the best information on land speculation opportunities, to defend those claims in court, and to ensure the family's offspring were raised properly, especially if a member died. The strength of kin obligations increased through the generations as branches of the family intermarried and network members accumulated decades of experience making business deals with one another.

The Donelson family network continued to reinforce its power through strategic, influential marriages through Andrew Jackson's lifetime. While native economic strategies hinged upon inclusion and diversification, the strategies of the Anglo-American Donelson family truncated into cotton-based plantation agriculture that suffered with the market fluctuations in the antebellum era. Still, their investments in plantations and land speculation ensured they were among the region's elite families. Although they had seen the zenith of their place in the national scene with Jackson's presidency, the family remained politically connected and retained substantial wealth.[7]

These case studies illustrate the importance of familial relationships. Those relationships provided motivation and strategy for family members as they dealt with the extremely volatile, dangerous, and exciting times of the colonial and early republic eras. They also provided structure and an economic and social safety net to the lives of their members. The events of those eras, from wartime alliances and strategies to approaches to Indian removal, were fundamentally shaped by familial ties. Those relationships made it possible for men, like Andrew Jackson, Attakullakulla, and Levi Colbert, to become politically and economically powerful. Women continually played central roles in the forging and functionality of these kinship ties. Their roles, however, were often relegated to historical silences within the treaties and official communications that governed the officially recorded intercultural relationships between Cherokees, Chickasaws, and Anglo-Americans. How women specifically shaped this interaction needs additional focus and study. The roles of family and kinship in the lives and strategies of Cherokee, Chickasaw, and Anglo-American men, however, comes through clearly in the treaties, official correspondence, and legacy of the negotiation that constructed the colonial and early republic political economy.

Familial relationships provided the foundation for the decisions that determined who would be most prominent in the historical events of the time and how those events would play out. Without his adoptive brother Attakullakulla's help, John Stuart would have been left dead on the road alongside the other soldiers outside of Fort Loudon. Without her marriage to Bryan Ward, Nan-ye-hi's actions and speeches might never have been recorded and her influence within the tribe would have remained one of history's silences. Without the military support of his sons and nephews, James Logan Colbert might have failed in his efforts to prevent control of the Mississippi River falling to the Americans, and Fort Jefferson would have survived to be a stronghold in the American Revolution. Without extended kinship networks, neither Dragging Canoe's Chickamauga Cherokee Indians nor the pan-Indian alliance to the north could have defeated the armies of General St. Clair or the Tennessee militia over and over through the decade after the 1783 Treaty of Paris was signed. Without his marriage into, and the support of, the Donelson family, Andrew Jackson might have been just another settler pushing into Indian lands in western North Carolina. Without the kinship relationships and family-based strategies of these families, the history of Indian relations within North America would have been drastically different and American history would be a collection of an entirely different set of stories.

Notes

Introduction

1. Richard Beard, *Brief Biographical Sketches of Some of the Early Ministers of the Cumberland Presbyterian Church*, 2d ser. (Nashville: Cumberland Presbyterian Board of Publication, 1874), 217–18.

2. J. G. M Ramsey, *The Annals of Tennessee to the End of the Eighteenth Century* (Johnson City, TN: Overmountain Press, 1999), 514. For another version of this captivity narrative and analysis of these narratives, see Duane H. King, ed., "Captivity Narrative: Joseph Brown" and "Lessons in Cherokee Ethnology from the Captivity of Joseph Brown, 1788–1789," *Journal of Cherokee Studies* 2, no. 2 (Spring 1977): 208–29.

3. Ramsey, *Annals of Tennessee*, 508–15.

4. I use the terms "American Indian," "Indian," and "native" interchangeably. These terms reflect the discussions at the 2010 annual meeting of the Native American and Indigenous Studies Association and their use by recent historians. "Anglo-Americans" here refers to people who were born in, or descended from those born in, the British Empire, including Scotland.

5. Francois Furstenberg, "The Significance of the Trans-Appalachian Frontier in Atlantic History," *American Historical Review* 113, no. 3 (June 2008): 647–77.

6. This work is part of a broader historiography of borderland and frontier interaction. Jeremy Adelman and Stephen Aron's 1999 article "From Borderlands to Borders" redefined both frontiers and borderlands as productive historical terms: frontier as "a meeting place of peoples in which geographic and cultural borders were not clearly defined . . . [where] intercultural relations produced mixing and accommodation as opposed to unambiguous triumph" and borderlands as "the contested boundaries between colonial domains." This book adopts these definitions of "frontier" and "borderland," referring specifically to the spaces of intercultural negotiation and border contests that shaped the political, economic, and social strategies on both sides of the contested borders on the southern trans-Appalachian frontier (Adelman and Aron,

"From Borderlands to Borders: Empires, Nation-States, and the Peoples in between in North American History," *American Historical Review* 103, no. 3 [June 1999]: 814–41, quote on 815–16).

7. Lorri Glover, *All Our Relations: Blood Ties and Emotional Bonds among the Early South Carolina Gentry* (Baltimore: Johns Hopkins University Press, 2000); Carolyn Earle Billingsley, *Communities of Kinship: Antebellum Families and the Settlement of the Cotton Frontier* (Athens: University of Georgia Press, 2004); Craig Thompson Friend, ed., *The Buzzel about Kentuck: Settling the Promised Land* (Lexington: University of Kentucky Press, 1981); Elizabeth Fox-Genovese, *Within the Plantation Household: Black and White Women of the Old South* (Chapel Hill: University of North Carolina Press, 1988); Thad Tate, ed., *Race and Family in the Colonial South* (Jackson: University of Mississippi Press, 1986).

8. Theda Perdue, *Cherokee Women: Gender and Culture Change, 1700–1835* (Lincoln: University of Nebraska Press, 1998), 44–45; Theda Perdue, *"Mixed Blood" Indians: Racial Construction in the Early South* (Athens: University of Georgia Press, 2003); Andrew Frank, *Creeks and Southerners: Biculturalism on the Early American Frontier* (Lincoln: University of Nebraska Press, 2005); Cynthia Cumfer, *Separate Peoples, One Land: The Minds of Cherokees, Blacks, and Whites on the Tennessee Frontier* (Chapel Hill: University of North Carolina Press, 2007); Michelle LeMaster, "'Thorough-paced girls' and 'cowardly bad men': Gender and Family in Indian-White Relations in the Colonial Southeast, 1660–1783" (PhD diss., Johns Hopkins University, 2001); Michelle LeMaster, *Brothers of One Mother: British-Native American Relations in the Colonial Southeast* (Charlottesville: University of Virginia Press, 2012); John Phillip Reid, *A Law of Blood: The Primitive Law of the Cherokee Nation* (New York: New York University Press, 1970), 35–48; Raymond Eugene Craig, "The Colberts in Chickasaw History, 1783–1818: A Study of Internal Tribal Dynamics" (PhD diss., University of New Mexico, 1998); Charles Hudson, *The Southeastern Indians* (Knoxville: University of Tennessee Press, 1976), 185–95; Tiya Miles, *Ties That Bind: The Story of an Afro-Cherokee Family in Slavery and Freedom* (Berkeley: University of California Press, 2005).

9. Ann Laura Stoler, *Carnal Knowledge and Imperial Power: Race and the Intimate in Colonial Rule* (Berkeley: University of California Press, 2002); Anne F. Hyde, *Empires, Nations, and Families: A New History of the North American West 1800–1860* (New York: HarperCollins, 2011); Richard C. Trexler, *Sex and Conquest: Gendered Violence, Political Order, and the European Conquest of the Americas* (Ithaca, NY: Cornell University Press, 1995).

10. The very definitions of "family" and "kinship networks" invoke a rich historiography dating from the 1970s. Thanks to the work of Steven Ozment, Alan Macfarlane, Peter Laslett, and Lawrence Stone, the term "family" conjures up images of the European or Euro-American nuclear units of parents and children rather than extended networks and patrilineal rather than matrilineal descent (Peter Laslett, *Family Life and Illicit Love in Earlier Generations, Essays in Historical Sociology* [Cambridge: Cambridge University Press, 1977]; Steven Ozment, *Ancestors: The Loving Family in Old Europe* [Cambridge: Harvard University Press, 2001]; Alan Macfarlane, *The Origins of English Individualism: The Family, Property and Social Transition* [Oxford: Basil Blackwell, 1978]; Lawrence Stone, *The Family, Sex and Marriage in England, 1500–1800* [New York: Harper and Row, 1977]).

11. Naomi Tadmor, *Family and Friends in Eighteenth-Century England: Household, Kinship, and Patronage* (Cambridge: Cambridge University Press, 2001).

12. Joseph M. Hawes and Elizabeth I. Nybakken, eds., *Family and Society in American History* (Urbana: University of Illinois Press, 2001), 37–38.

13. The specific intertwining of strands of these families through the generations mirror those described by David Sabean in his account of the networking strategies within the community of Neckarhausen in early modern Germany (Sabean, *Kinship in Neckarhausen, 1700–1870*, Cambridge Studies in Social and Cultural Anthropology Series [Cambridge: Cambridge University Press, 1998]). American Indian kinship systems have been the subject of sociological, anthropological, and historical study from the 1770s onward. One example of this is James Adair's *History of the American Indians*, published in 1775 (see Kathryn E. Holland-Braund, ed., *The History of the American Indians, by James Adair* [Tuscaloosa: University of Alabama Press, 2005]). For a recent account of social network analysis, see Christina Prell, *Social Network Analysis: History, Theory, and Methodology* (London: Sage, 2012), 19–58.

14. John Reed Swanton, *Chickasaw Society and Religion* (Lincoln: University of Nebraska Press, 2006). For a similar analysis of Cherokee political systems, see Raymond Fogelson, "Cherokee Notions of Power," in *The Anthropology of Power: Ethnographic Studies from Asia, Oceania, and the New World* (New York: Academic Press, 1977), 185–95. Perdue, *Cherokee Women*, 44–45; Reid, *A Law of Blood*, 35–48; Hudson, *The Southeastern Indians*, 185–95.

15. James Adair, *Adair's History of the American Indians*, ed. Samuel Cole Williams (New York: Promontory Press, 1930), 459–60.

16. Perdue, *"Mixed Blood" Indians*, 41.

17. Hudson, *The Southeastern Indians*, 191–92. Hudson provided the example: "Thus the Bear clan consisted of all the people who belonged to Bear lineages; a member of a particular Bear lineage could trace his relationships to all other members of his lineage, but he might not be able to trace his relationship to a member of a Bear lineage from a distant village. Still they were of the Bear clan, and kinship terms were extended to all members of the clan" (192).

18. Incunnomar referred to a familial grouping within the Chickasaw nation and would become a name, first name and/or surname, associated with the Colbert and Love families in the 1780s and beyond.

19. Gordon Wood, *The Radicalism of the American Revolution* (New York: Knopf, 1992), 129.

1 / Founding Networks, 1740–1765

1. Little Carpenter, "The Little Carpenter's Speech to Captain Raymond Demere," July 13, 1756, in *The Colonial Records of South Carolina, Series II, Documents Relating to Indian Affairs, 1754–1763*, vol. 3, ed. William L. McDowel Jr. (Columbia: University of South Carolina Press, 1970), 138.

2. Reid, *A Law of Blood* 1–35.

3. Adair, *Adair's History of the American Indians*, ed. Williams, 460.

4. Kathryn Braund, *Deerskins and Duffles: The Creek Indian Trade with Anglo-America, 1685–1815* (Lincoln: University of Nebraska Press, 1996), 81–83.

5. Ibid.; Perdue, *Cherokee Women*, 80–82.

6. William L. Ramsey, *The Yamasee War: A Study of Culture, Economy, and Conflict in the Colonial South* (Lincoln: University of Nebraska Press, 2008); Robbie Ethridge and Charles Hudson, eds., *The Transformation of the Southeastern Indians, 1540–1760* (Jackson: University Press of Mississippi, 2002).

7. On Little Carpenter's visit to England, see Alden T. Vaughan, *Transatlantic Encounters: American Indians in Britain, 1500–1776* (Cambridge: Cambridge University Press, 2006), 137–64.

8. Tom Hatley, *The Dividing Paths: Cherokees and South Carolinians through the Era of Revolution* (New York: Oxford University Press, 1993), 94, 109.

9. Lt. Henry Timberlake, *The Memoirs of Lt. Henry Timberlake: The Story of a Soldier, Adventurer, and Emissary to the Cherokees, 1756–1765*, ed. Duane King (Cherokee, NC: Museum of the Cherokee Indian Press, 2007), 37.

10. For the competition and relationships between towns and regions among the Cherokee, see Tyler Boulware's *Deconstructing the Cherokee Nation: Town, Region, and Nation among Eighteenth-Century Cherokees* (Gainesville: University Press of Florida, 2011).

11. Excellent works on Cherokee diplomatic efforts prior to the Seven Years' War and their consequences during that war are David H. Corkran, *The Cherokee Frontier: Conflict and Survival, 1740–1762* (Norman: University of Oklahoma Press, 1962); and Hatley, *The Dividing Paths*. Corkran and Hatley both point out that these "gifts" were really payment for service and that by denying Cherokees the gifts they sought, the colonies of Virginia and South Carolina were pressing their allies to fight the French and French-allied Indians for free.

12. Alan Taylor, *American Colonies: The Settling of North America* (New York: Penguin, 2002), 421–37.

13. Ibid., 428–29.

14. For more on the origins, progression, and aftermath of the Seven Years' War, see Fred Anderson, *Crucible of War: The Seven Years' War and the Fate of Empire in British North America, 1754–1766* (New York: Knopf, 2000).

15. Corkran, *Cherokee Frontier*, 115. Corkran notes that in 1757, "250 or more Cherokees were among the 400 Indians who defended the Virginia frontier."

16. Ibid., 75–101; Hatley, *Dividing Paths*, 95–98.

17. The roles of kinship in intercultural treaty negotiations have been explored in detail by Richard White, Nathaniel Sheidley, Wendy St. Jean, Cynthia Cumfer, Michelle LeMaster, and others. My analysis builds upon their work (Nathaniel J. Sheidley, "Unruly Men: Indians, Settlers, and the Ethos of Frontier Patriarchy in the Upper Tennessee Watershed, 1763–1815" [PhD diss., University of Princeton, 1999]; Richard White, *The Middle Ground: Indians, Empires, and Republics in the Great Lakes Region, 1650–1815* [Cambridge: Cambridge University Press, 1991]; Wendy St. Jean, "Trading Paths: Chickasaw Diplomacy in the Greater Southeast, 1690s–1790s" [PhD diss., University of Connecticut, 2004]; Cynthia Cumfer, *Separate Peoples, One Land*; and LeMaster, *Brothers of One Mother*).

18. See the introduction of this volume for definitions of family and kinship and how cultural definitions of particular kinship obligations differed between Chickasaws, Cherokees, and Anglo-Americans.

19. U.S. Government, "Treaty held with the Catawba and Cherokee Indians," 23rd December, 1755 to 12th April, 1756, Case FG 801.56 no. 222, p. vi, Newberry Library, Chicago.

20. Hudson, *The Southeastern Indians*, 185–92.

21. Ibid., 14, emphasis added.

22. Ibid., 15.

23. Ibid., 20–22.

24. Hatley, *Dividing Paths*, 206.

25. Corkran, *Cherokee Frontier*, 66–84.

26. Hatley, *Dividing Paths*, 114–27; Anne F. Rogers and Barbara R. Duncan, eds., *Culture, Crisis, and Conflict: Cherokee British Relations 1756–1765* (Cherokee: Museum of the Cherokee Indian Press, 2009), 8–9; Timberlake, *Memoirs*, xix.

27. James Mooney, *History, Myths, and Sacred Formulas of the Cherokees* (repr., Asheville, NC: Bright Mountain Books, 1992), 44.

28. For more on the Anglo-Cherokee War, see John Oliphant, *Peace and War on the Anglo-Cherokee Frontier, 1756–63* (Hampshire, England: Palgrave, 2001); Hatley, *Dividing Paths*, 113–78; Anderson, *Crucible of War*, 457–71; and Corkran, *Cherokee Frontier*, 178–272.

29. Corkran, *Cherokee Frontier*, 254.

30. Timberlake, *Memoirs*, xxiv–xxv.

31. Ibid., 19.

32. Ibid., 20–21.

33. Rogers and Duncan, eds., *Culture, Crisis, and Conflict*, 26.

34. Timberlake, *Memoirs*, xxvi–xxx.

35. Daniel H. Usner Jr., *Indians, Settlers, and Slaves in a Frontier Exchange Economy: The Lower Mississippi Valley before 1783* (Chapel Hill: University of North Carolina Press, 1992); Braund, *Deerskins and Duffels*; Claudio Saunt, *A New Order of Things: Property, Power and the Transformation of the Creek Indians, 1733–1816* (Cambridge: Cambridge University Press, 1999; Joseph M. Hall Jr., *Zamumo's Gifts: Indian-European Exchange in the Colonial Southeast* (Philadelphia: University of Pennsylvania Press, 2009); Michael P. Morris, *The Bringing of Wonder: Trade and the Indians of the Southeast, 1700–1783* (Westport, CT: Greenwood Press, 1999). On trading and exchange patterns outside the Southeast, see James Brooks, *Captives and Cousins*; Susan Sleeper-Smith, *Rethinking the Fur Trade*; and Richard White, *The Middle Ground*.

36. Clara Sue Kidwell, "Indian Women as Cultural Mediators," in *Native Women's History in Eastern North America before 1900: A Guide to Research and Writing*, ed. Rebecca Kugel and Lucy Eldersveld Murphy (Lincoln: University of Nebraska Press, 2007), 53–64; Cynthia Cumfer, "Nan-ye-hi (Nancy Ward) Diplomatic Mother," in *Tennessee Women: Their Lives and Times*, ed. Sarah Wilkerson Freeman and Beverly Greene, vol. 1 (Athens: University of Georgia Press, 2009), 1–22. Nan-ye-hi's husband is alternately referenced in sources as either Bryan Ward or Bryan Ward. Ward's eldest daughter, Katy, married two traders in succession, John Walker and Ellis Harlan. Her youngest daughter, Betsy, married Virginia's Indian agent Joseph Martin in 1770.

37. Robbie Ethridge and Sheri M. Shuck-Hall, eds., *Mapping the Mississippian Shatter Zone: The Colonial Indian Slave Trade and Regional Instability in the American South* (Lincoln: University of Nebraska Press, 2009), 339.

38. Galloway, "Colonial Period Transformations," 233.

39. The terms "genesis" and "coalescent societies" are taken from Patricia Galloway, *Choctaw Genesis, 1500–1700* (Lincoln: University of Nebraska Press, 1998).

40. Joan E. Cashin, *A Family Venture: Men and Women on the Southern Frontier* (Baltimore: Johns Hopkins University Press, 1991), 19–50.

41. Craig, "The Colberts," 112–19.

42. Ibid., 88.

43. James R. Atkinson, *Splendid Land, Splendid People: The Chickasaw Indians to Removal* (Tuscaloosa: University of Alabama Press, 2004), 88.

44. Ethridge and Shuck-Hall, eds., *Mapping the Mississippian Shatter Zone*, 339.

45. Qtd. in Atkinson, *Splendid Land, Splendid People*, 99.

46. For more on plantation culture among southern tribes, see Tiya Miles, *The House on Diamond Hill: A Cherokee Plantation Story* (Chapel Hill: University of North Carolina Press, 2010).

47. United States, *Journal of the Congress of the Four Southern Governors, and the Superintendent of That District, with the Five Nations of Indians, at Augusta, 1763* (Charles Town, SC: Peter Timothy, 1764), 14.

48. Ibid. This was not entirely true as the resulting treaty included large land cessions by the Creeks.

49. Ibid., 19–23.

50. Ibid., 22–23.

51. Ibid., 23.

52. Ibid., 26.

53. Ibid., 29–30.

54. Ibid., 38. Two other Cherokee chiefs, Young Warrior and Tistowih, held friendly talks with Creek chiefs Mustisicah and Fool-Harry, also giving them "beads."

55. For more on this congress, see Colin G. Calloway, *The Scratch of a Pen: 1763 and the Transformation of North America* (New York: Oxford University Press, 2006, 100–111.

56. For more on colonial intercultural interaction in the Southeast prior to 1754, see Lynda Norene Shaffer, *Native Americans before 1492: The Moundbuilding Centers of the Eastern Woodlands* (Armonk, NY: M. E. Sharpe, 1992); Patricia B. Kwachka, ed., *Perspectives on the Southeast: Linguistics, Archaeology, and Ethnohistory*, Southern Anthropological Society Proceedings, No. 27 (Athens: University of Georgia Press, 1994); Robbie Ethridge and Charles Hudson, eds., *The Transformation of the Southeastern Indians, 1540–1760* (Jackson: University of Mississippi Press, 2002); and Ethridge and Shuck-Hall, eds., *Mapping the Mississippian Shatter Zone*.

57. Calloway, *Scratch of a Pen*, 111.

58. James Adair, "A List of Traders and Packhorsemen in the Chickasaw Nation January 22d. 1766," transcribed by Grant Foreman, Oklahoma Historical Society, www.chickasawhistory.com/Chick_Traders.html.

59. United States, *Journal of the Congress of the Four Southern Governors*, 26.

60. Corkran, *Cherokee Frontier*, 85–101.

2 / Militant Families

1. Thomas Perkins Abernethy, *From Frontier to Plantation in Tennessee: A Study in Frontier Democracy* (University: University of Alabama Press, 1967); 347; John P. Brown, *Old Frontiers: The Story of the Cherokee Indians from Earliest Times to the Date of their Removal to the West, 1838* (Kingsport, TN: Southern Publishers, 1938), 127–33.

2. A recent swell of historiography suggests that scholars have moved beyond traditional narratives of Revolution to shed light on the conflicts in the West. Eric Hinderaker, for example, has illustrated how intricately linked expansion was to creating a patriot movement and a new American "empire of liberty." Colin Calloway, Alan Taylor, and Gregory Dowd have depicted the Revolution as part of a wave of Indian resistance to encroachment and dissolution of regional power. Francois Furstenberg contends that "the Appalachian Mountains were responsible for the great problem of North American, and perhaps even Atlantic, history from 1754 to 1815: the fate of the trans-Appalachian West." He suggests that the Seven Years' War "in fact continued with only brief interruptions to 1815—in the form of the American Revolution of the 1770s, the Indian Wars of the 1780s and 1790s, and the War of 1812." Over this period, he points to what he calls animating questions for Indians, European imperial interests, and American settlers: Would trans-Appalachia "become a permanent Native American country? Would it fall to some distant European power? Or, perhaps the most unlikely scenario of all, would it join with the United States?" (Furstenberg, "Significance of the Trans-Appalachian Frontier," 650). See also Eric Hinderaker, *Elusive Empires: Constructing Colonialism in the Ohio Valley, 1763–1800* (Cambridge: Cambridge University Press, 1999); Colin G. Calloway, *The American Revolution in Indian Country: Crisis and Diversity in Native American Communities* (Cambridge: Cambridge University Press, 1995); Gregory Evans Dowd, *A Spirited Resistance: The North American Indian Struggle for Unity, 1745–1815* (Baltimore: Johns Hopkins Univeristy Press, 1992); Patrick Griffin, *American Leviathan: Empire, Nation, and Revolutionary Frontier* (New York: Hill and Wang, 2007); Woody Holton, *Forced Founders: Indians, Debtors, Slaves, and the Making of the American Revolution in Virginia* (Chapel Hill: University of North Carolina Press, 1999); Wayne E. Lee, *Crowds and Soldiers in Revolutionary North Carolina* (Gainesville: University Press of Florida, 2001); John Buchanan, *The Road to Guilford Court House: The American Revolution in the Carolinas* (New York: Wiley Press, 1999); John Resch and Walter Sargent, eds., *War and Society in the American Revolution: Mobilization and Home Fronts* (DeKalb: Northern Illinois University Press, 2007); Alan Taylor, *The Divided Ground: Indians, Settlers, and the Northern Borderland of the American Revolution* (New York: Knopf, 2006); Alfred F. Young, *The Shoemaker and the Tea Party: Memory and the American Revolution* (Boston: Beacon Press, 1999); Peter Silver, *Our Savage Neighbors: How Indian War Transformed Early America* (New York: Norton, 2008); and Kristofer Ray, "New Directions in Early Tennessee History," *Tennessee Historical Quarterly* 69 (Fall 2010): 204–23.

3. For simplicity's sake, I refer to those colonists who adhered to the British government of the colonies as "loyalists," to regular troops from or directed by British officers as "British," and to those who broke from British colonial leadership as "Americans." "Anglo-Americans" refers to people of British, Scottish, or Scots-Irish origin or ancestry before, during, and after the American Revolution. Indigenous people in this chapter are referred to as "American Indian," "Indian," "native," or by their tribal identifications of "Chickasaw," "Cherokee," "Chickamauga," or "Chickamauga-Cherokee."

4. Griffin, *American Leviathan*, 19–45.

5. George III, King of Great Britain, "By the King, A Proclamation, London, 1763," broadside, Document GLC05214, Gilder Lehrman Collection; Calloway, *Scratch of a Pen*, 10–18.

6. Abernethy, *From Frontier to Plantation in Tennessee*; Eric Hinderaker, *Elusive Empires: Constructing Colonialism in the Ohio Valley, 1673–1800* (Cambridge: Cambridge University Press, 1997), 164–83; Warren R. Hofstra, *The Planting of New Virginia: Settlement and Landscape in the Shenandoah Valley* (Baltimore: Johns Hopkins University Press, 2004), 241–42; Archibald Henderson, *The Conquest of the Old Southwest* (1920; repr., Dodo Press, 2010), 87–101.

7. William Johnson, "Proceedings of Sir William Johnson with the Indians at Fort Stanwix to Settle a Boundary Line," Ratified treaty #7: Treaty of Fort Stanwix, or The Grant from the Six Nations to the King and Agreement of Boundary—Six Nations, Shawnee, Delaware, Mingoes of Ohio, 1768, *Documents Relative to the Colonial History of the State of New York*, ed. E. B. O'Callaghan, vol. 8 (Albany, NY: Weed, Parsons, and Co., 1857), 118. Digitized on http://earlytreaties.unl.edu/treaty.00007.html.

8. John Haywood, *The Civil and Political History of Tennessee of the State of Tennessee: From Its Earliest Settlement up to the Year 1796, Including the Boundaries of the State* (Nashville: Overmountain Press, 1891), 29.

9. For more on Iroquois claims to the region, see Jon Parmenter, *Edge of the Woods: Iroquoia, 1534–1701* (East Lansing: Michigan State University Press, 2010).

10. "Proceedings of Sir William Johnson," 123.

11. Patrick Griffin describes the British purpose and function for the Proclamation Line as well as discusses the revolution as a result of tampering with that boundary (Griffin, *American Leviathan*, 19–96).

12. Louis De Vorsey, *The Indian Boundary in the Southern Colonies, 1763–1775* (Chapel Hill: University of North Carolina Press 1966), 85–88.

13. Reuben Gold Thwaites, and Louise Phelps Kellogg, eds., *Documentary History of Dunmore's War 1774, Compiled from the Draper Manuscripts in the Library of the Wisconsin Historical Society and Published at the Charge of the Wisconsin Society of the Sons of the American Revolution* (Madison: Wisconsin Historical Society, 1905), 44.

14. Clarence Monroe Burton, *John Connolly: A Tory of the Revolution* (Worchester, MA: Davis Press, 1909), 8–15.

15. Thwaites and Kellogg, eds., *Documentary History of Dunmore's War*, 48; Cameron B. Strang, "Michael Cresap and the Promulgation of Settler Land-Claiming Methods in the Backcountry, 1765–1774," *Virginia Magazine of History and Biography* 118 (2010): 107–36.

16. Holton, *Forced Founders*, 152–63.

17. Griffin, *American Leviathan*, 97–123; Hinderaker, *Elusive Empires*, 185–225.

18. Many of the same frontier settlers who allied themselves as Americans during the Revolution would threaten to secede, taking that newly gained territory under the banner of the Spanish if the American government could not protect them and their economic interests in the 1780s (see Griffin, *American Leviathan*; and Hinderaker, *Elusive Empires*, for more on how the imperative to acquire land became intertwined with the Revolutionary mission for Americans).

19. Many of the earliest settlers had been members of the failed Regulator movement that had challenged the legitimacy of the North Carolina colonial government in 1769. Although the movement was quickly defeated, some of the members escaped east of the Appalachian Mountains to the Watauga settlements. (Ramsey, *Annals of Tennessee*, 92–111).

20. The families of these three men over time became linked by marriage. This kinship network would become famous for settling the territory, for Indian fighting, and for serving in the region's early government. The political influence of kinship networks like this one would be instrumental in making the acquisition of Indian lands central to the overall motives of the American Revolution.

21. Abernethy, *From Frontier to Plantation in Tennessee*, 347; Brown, *Old Frontiers*, 127–33.

22. Hinderaker, *Elusive Empires*, 176–83.

23. Haywood, *Civil and Political History*, 58–59.

24. Brown, *Old Frontiers*, 3. Peter H. Wood compares the revolutionary leadership of Dragging Canoe to that of George Washington in his chapter "George Washington, Dragging Canoe, and Southern Indian Resistance," in *George Washington's South*, ed. Tamara Harvey and Greg O'Brien (Gainesville: University Press of Florida, 2004), 259–77.

25. Tyler Boulware, *Deconstructing the Cherokee Nation: Town, Region, and Nation among Eighteenth-Century Cherokees* (Gainesville: University Press of Florida, 2011), 152–77.

26. Perdue, *"Mixed Blood" Indians*. 35.

27. Brown, *Old Frontiers*, 249.

28. Tyler Boulware convincingly argued that the Chickamaugas created new towns and a new region for the Cherokees rather than creating a separate tribe (Boulware, *Deconstructing the Cherokee Nation*, 152–77). Dowd, *A Spirited Resistance*, 47–64.

29. Josiah Martin, *North Carolina, by his Excellency Josiah Martin, Esq. Captain-General, Governor, and Commander in Chief, in and over the said Province. A Proclamation*, Newbern, NC, February 10, 1775, emphasis in original.

30. Hinderaker, *Elusive Empires*, 267.

31. William Christian, "Fincastle Town, to William Preston Smithfield, June 8, 1776," Folder 410, A/B937c, Bullitt Family Papers Collection, Filson Historical Society, Louisville, KY.

32. Brown, *Old Frontiers*, 156.

33. Cumfer, *Separate Peoples, One Land*, 27. See also Perdue, *Cherokee Women*.

34. Pat Alderman, *Nancy Ward Cherokee Chieftainess; Dragging Canoe: Cherokee-Chickamauga War Chief* (Johnson City, TN: Overmountain Press, 1978), 4.

35. Brown, *Old Frontiers*, 148–51; Ramsey, *Annals of Tennessee*, 151; David Ray Smith, "Nancy Ward, 1738–1822," *Tennessee Encyclopedia of History and Culture* (Knoxville: University of Tennessee Press, 2002); Clara Sue Kidwell, "Indian Women as Cultural Mediators," *Ethnohistory* 39, no. 2 (Spring 1992): 97–107; Alderman, *Nancy Ward*.

36. Judge John Haywood, writing in 1823, dubbed her "the Cherokee Pocahontas," as did future historians who cited his work (Haywood, *Civil and Political History*, 60). This comparison continued as historians such as J. G. M. Ramsey used the same terminology in 1853 in his *Annals of Tennessee* (144). In the 1880s, John P. Brown and W. W. Clayton would also use Haywood's account as the basis for their own histories of the Cherokee frontier and Davidson County respectively.

37. Calloway, *American Revolution in Indian Country*, 200.

38. Ramsey, *Annals of Tennessee*, 134–38, 197–202; Maud Carter Clement, *History of Pittsylvania County*, (Baltimore: Regional, 1987), 153; Haywood, *Civil and Political History*, 93–107.

39. Elizabeth Perkins, *Border Life: Experience and Memory in the Revolutionary Ohio Valley* (Chapel Hill: University of North Carolina Press, 1998), 115.

40. Vine Deloria Jr. and Raymond J. DeMallie, eds., *Documents of American Indian Diplomacy: Treaties, Agreements, and Conventions, 1775–1979*, vol. 1. (Norman: University of Oklahoma Press, 1999), 70–78, quotation on 72.

41. Lawrence Fleenor, "General Joseph Martin," *Appalachian Quarterly* 6 (2001): 59–62; Cynthia Cumfer, "Nan-ye-hi (Nancy Ward)," 12; Joseph Martin to Henry Knox, January 15, 1789, in *American State Papers: Indian Affairs*, Class II (Washington, DC: Gales and Seaton, 1832), 46–47; Sheidley, "Unruly Men."

42. The Chickamauga Cherokees relationship to the Cherokee nation is comparable to that of the Irish Republican Army (IRA) to Ireland. They are not sanctioned by the Irish government, but they claim to serve the Irish people through military resistance to political control.

43. Calloway, *American Revolution in Indian Country*, 200–201.

44. Furstenberg, "Significance of the Trans-Appalachian Frontier," 235–50; Dowd, *A Spirited Resistance*, 47–64.

45. James Paul Pate, "The Chickamauga: A Forgotten Segment of Indian Resistance on the Southern Frontier" (PhD diss., Mississippi State University, 1969), 181.

46. State Historical Society of Wisconsin, *Calendar of the Tennessee and King's Mountain Papers of the Draper Collection of Manuscripts*, vol. 3 (Madison, 1929), 1xx28, 11.

47. Boulware, *Deconstructing the Cherokee Nation*, 172.

48. These specific familial relationships are inconclusive because different sources list the individuals and their affiliations differently.

49. Indian agent Joseph Martin and Josiah Martin, the colonial governor of North Carolina, were to my knowledge unrelated.

50. Alderman, *Nancy Ward*, 57.

51. Dowd, *A Spirited Resistance*, 65–66.

52. Peter Silver, Eric Hinderaker, and Wayne Lee describe intercultural violence on the frontier as an increasingly important motivator for American forces in the backcountry over the course of the Revolutionary War (Silver, *Our Savage Neighbors*, 227–60; Griffin, *American Leviathan*, 152–80; Wayne E. Lee, *Crowds and Soldiers in Revolutionary North Carolina: The Culture of Violence in Riot and War* [Gainesville: University Press of Florida, 2001], 176–211).

53. John Caughey, *McGillivray of the Creeks* (Norman: University of Oklahoma Press, 1938); R. Michael Pryor, *Alexander McGillivray and the Creek Confederacy: The Struggle for the Southern Backcountry* (Chicago: Pryolino Press, 2010). Following the Revolution, Spain, which had been an ally of the Americans, turned into a competitor for land and resources. McGillivray and other Indian resistance leaders following the Revolution would receive support from Spain in the form of arms and trade goods to support Indian campaigns to keep settlers out of the trans-Appalachian region.

54. Atkinson, *Splendid Land, Splendid People*, 125; D. C. Corbitt, "James Colbert and the Spanish Claims to the East Bank of the Mississippi," *Mississippi Valley Historical Review* 24, no. 4 (March 1938): 461; Arrel Gibson, *The Chickasaws* (Norman: University of Oklahoma Press, 1971), 72.

55. Haywood, *Civil and Political History*, 20–21.

56. Donelson's Journal mentions eighty-two people, but the context hints that there were many more whom he failed to mention (Tennessee Historical Commission, *Three*

Pioneer Tennessee Documents: Donelson's Journal, Cumberland Compact, and Minutes of Cumberland Court [Nashville, 1964], 1–10).

57. Ibid., 10.

58. Gibson, *The Chickasaws*, 72.

59. John Floyd to George Rogers Clark, August 10, 1781, in *George Rogers Clark Papers*, ed. James Alton James, vol. 8 (Springfield: Trustees of the Illinois State Historical Library, 1912), 584, Collection of the Illinois State Historical Library.

60. George Rogers Clark to Thomas Nelson, October 1, 1781, in *George Rogers Clark Papers*, 605–6.

61. Kathleen DuVal, *Independence Lost: Lives on the Edge of the American Revolution* (New York: Random House, 2016), 238–43; Atkinson, *Splendid Land, Splendid People*, 125; Corbitt, "James Colbert and the Spanish Claims to the East Bank of the Mississippi," 461.

62. Corbitt, "James Colbert and the Spanish Claims to the East Bank of the Mississippi," 466.

63. Colbert would likely not have had any English nephews to draw upon in battle. Rather he would have been more likely to have had Chickasaw nephews by being adopted into a clan. It is possible that Colbert had both marital and adoptive ties, but this is not evident in the historical record.

64. Joseph Martin and John Donelson to Governor Benjamin Harrison, December 16, 1783, Library of Virginia, Richmond, manuscript letter signed, online resources, http://lvaimage.lib.va.us/GLR/04973, Document Image.

65. Deloria and Demaille, eds., *Documents of American Indian Diplomacy*, 125–27.

66. Hinderaker, *Elusive Empires*, 226–70; Griffin, *American Leviathan*, 152–82; Dowd, *A Spirited Resistance*, 90–122; Furstenberg, "Significance of the Trans-Appalachian Frontier," 238–50; Calloway, *American Revolution in Indian Country*, 182–212; Gordon S. Wood, *Empire of Liberty: A History of the Early Republic, 1789–1815* (Oxford: Oxford University Press, 2011).

3 / Ongoing Warfare

1. Cumfer, "Nan-ye-hi (Nancy Ward)," 13.

2. Ibid.

3. Ramsey, *Annals of Tennessee*, 416–425.

4. James Emerick Nagy, "Biographical Sketch of Brigadier-General Joseph Martin" (master's thesis, Vanderbilt University, 1932), 6.

5. Cumfer, "Nan-ye-hi (Nancy Ward)," 13.

6. Nagy, "Biographical Sketch of Brigadier-General Joseph Martin,"186.

7. Joseph Martin and John Donelson to Governor Benjamin Harrison, December 16, 1783, Library of Virginia, Richmond, Virginia, manuscript letter signed, online resources, http://lvaimage.lib.va.us/GLR/04973, Document Image.

8. Brown, *Old Frontiers*, 249. See also Brent Alan Yanusdi Cox, *Heart of the Eagle: Dragging Canoe and the Emergence of the Chickamauga Confederacy* (Milan, TN: Chenanee, 1999), 34–39.

9. Brown, *Old Frontiers*, 250.

10. Ibid., 251. A copy of this treaty is available in Commissioner of Indian Affairs, *Treaties between the United States of America, and the Several Indian Tribes from 1778 to 1837*, new ed. (1837; repr., Millwood, NY: Kraus Reprint Co., 1975), 8–11.

11. Commissioner of Indian Affairs, *Treaties between the United States of America, and the Several Indian Tribes*, 15–17.

12. Deloria and DeMallie, eds., *Documents of American Indian Diplomacy*, 125–27.

13. Cynthia Cumfer describes the couple as having two homes in the Cherokee nation, one at Long Island on the Holston and another at Citico (Cumfer, *Separate Peoples, One Land*, 35).

14. Perdue, *"Mixed Blood" Indians*, 9–13.

15. Brown, *Old Frontiers*, 245.

16. Ibid.

17. The State of Franklin received much historiographical coverage but has been addressed infrequently in recent years. For more on the movement, resistance, and resolution, see Noel B. Gerson, *Franklin: America's "Lost State"* (New York: Crowell-Collier Press, 1968); Thomas Perkins Abernethy, "The State of Franklin," in *From Frontier to Plantation in Tennessee*, 64–90; Kristofer Ray, *Middle Tennessee 1775–1825: Progress and Popular Democracy on the Southwestern Frontier* (Knoxville: University of Tennessee Press, 2008), 9; Malcolm Rohrbough, *Trans-Appalachian Frontier: People, Societies, and Institutions, 1775–1850*, 3rd ed. (Bloomington: Indiana University Press, 2008), 29–30; and Kevin Barksdale, *The Lost State of Franklin: America's First Secession* (Lexington: University Press of Kentucky, 2008).

18. Ramsey, *Annals of Tennessee*, 266–76, 417. The dynamics of this relationship have received at most a line or two in the histories of Cherokee-U.S. diplomacy. For more on the complexities of intercultural marriages in this period, see Theda Perdue, "'A Sprightly Lover Is the Most Prevailing Missionary': Intermarriage between Europeans and Indians in the Eighteenth-Century South," in *Light on the Path: The Anthropology and History of the Southeastern Indians*, ed. Thomas J. Pluckhahn and Robbie Ethridge (Tuscaloosa: University of Alabama Press, 2006), 165–78.

19. Leonna Taylor Aiken, *Donelson, Tennessee: Its History and Landmarks* (self-published, 1968), 309–10. Aiken notes that the two young men who were traveling with Donelson were suspects in his death because the deceased's saddlebags disappeared with him. They were cleared when both the body and the saddlebags were found. Indians were then blamed for Donelson's death (Ramsey, *Annals of Tennessee*, 345).

20. Perdue, *Slavery and the Evolution of Cherokee Society*, xi–49; Alan Gallay, *The Indian Slave Trade: The Rise of the English Empire in the American South, 1670–1717* (New Haven: Yale University Press, 2002). For a different geographical context, see James Brooks, *Captives and Cousins: Slavery, Kinship, and Community in the Southwest Borderlands* (Chapel Hill: University of North Carolina Press, 2002).

21. Perdue, *Slavery and the Evolution of Cherokee Society*, 46; Halliburton, *Red over Black*, 139–40; Hatley, *The Dividing Paths*, 225. Hatley argues that Chickamauga Indians had no need to please Anglo-American diplomats and thus were willing to incorporate runaway slaves into the Chickamauga towns and the resistance movement.

22. "William Blount, Governor in and over the territory of the United States of America, south of the river Ohio, and Superintendent of Indian Affairs, for the Southern district, to Doublehead, and the other Chiefs and Warriors of the Lower Cherokees," in *American State Papers, Indian Affairs*, vol. 1 (Washington, DC: Government Printing Office, 1816), 534.

23. "John Sevier to Chiefs and Warriors of the Cherokee Nation, Knoxville, 7th July 1796," "Letters of Tennessee Governors—John Sevier," Microfilm GP-2, Roll 1, Folder 2.81, Box 1, Tennessee State Library and Archives, Nashville.

24. "John Sevier to The Little Turkey, Knoxville 25th August, 1796," "Letters of Tennessee Governors—John Sevier," Microfilm GP-2, Roll 1, Folder 2, Box 1, Tennessee State Library and Archives, Nashville.

25. Louis-Phillippe, *Diary of My Travels in America: Louis-Phillippe, King of France, 1830–1848*, trans. Stephen Becker (New York: Delacorte Press, 1977), 96.

26. The Creek allies of the Chickamauga also participated heavily in abduction of slaves (see *American State Papers, Indian Affairs*, 1:77–81, 546; and Saunt, *A New Order of Things*, 111–39, 273–90).

27. Conversation: Governor Blount, Hanging Maw, and Colonel Watts, November 8, 1794, in *American State Papers, Indian Affairs*, 1:537.

28. Dowd, *A Spirited Resistance*, 48–54.

29. Cherokee Nation to Richard Winn, "A Talk from the Head Men at Ustinale," 20 Nov, 1788, Vault Oversize Ayer MS 167, Ayer Collection, Newberry Library, Chicago.

30. Piamingo to Samuel Johnson, "A Talk (Delivered Genl Joseph Martin) by Piamingo Chief Warrior [*sic*] of the Chickasaw Nation the 23rd of Sept 1789 for his Excellency Samuel Johnson Esqr. Governor of the State of North Carolina," 23 September, 1789, Vault Box Ayer MS 722, Newberry Library, Chicago.

31. Deloria and DeMaille, eds., *Documents of American Indian Diplomacy*, 106–7, quotation on 126.

32. Ibid., 15–17.

33. William Blount, "A Return of Persons Killed, Wounded and Taken Prisoners, from Miro District, since the 1st of January, 1791," *American State Papers Indian Affairs*, 1:329.

34. Ibid.

35. "The Breath and Charles to William Blount," Lookout Mountain, September 15, 1792, *American State Papers Indian Affairs*, 1:293.

36. "Reports by Richard Finnelson and Joseph Deraque to William Blount," *American State Papers Indian Affairs*, 1:288–92.

37. William Blount, "Information by Governor Blount, respecting the Cherokee Chiefs whose names are mentioned in the narrative given by Richard Finnelson," Knoxville, September 26, 1792, *American State Papers, Indian Affairs*, 1:291.

38. William Blount, "Blount, William 1749–1800 (Miscellaneous Letters)," James Carey's Account, November 3, 1792, Collection Mss C B Doc. 3, Filson Historical Society, Louisville, KY.

39. Benjamin Hawkins, "Journal of the Commissioner of the United States," Vault Ayer MS 3180, p. 6, Newberry Library, Chicago.

40. William Blount to Henry Knox, Knoxville, October 10, 1792, *American State Papers, Indian Affairs* 1:294–95.

41. Ibid.

42. Ibid., 1:294.

43. William Blount to Henry Knox, Knoxville, November 5, 1792, *American State Papers, Indian Affairs*, 1:331.

44. Governor Blount to the Secretary of War, Knoxville, November 8, 1792, *American State Papers, Indian Affairs*, 1:325.

45. John R. Finger, *Tennessee Frontiers: Three Regions in Transition* (Bloomington: Indiana University Press, 2001), 123–49; Susan Gaunt Sterns, "Spanish Conspiracy?" The Quest for Safety and Trade amongst Western Elites," in "Streams of Interest: The

Mississippi River and the Political Economy of the Early Republic, 1783–1803" (PhD diss., University of Chicago, 2011), 126–76.

46. Anthony Wayne, Greeneville, to Arthur St. Clair, August 19, 1795, manuscript letter, Folder 3, Vault Box Ayers MS 966, Anthony Wayne Letters, Newberry Library, Chicago.

47. Ibid.

48. United States, War Department, "Letters [manuscript] 1795–1798," Timothy Pickering to David Campbell, War Office, August 28, 1795, Vault Box Ayer MS 926, Newberry Library, Chicago.

49. Timothy Pickering, "Letters from the War Department," Timothy Pickering to Colonel Henley, August 26, 1795, Vault Box Ayer MS 926, Newberry Library, Chicago.

50. James Paul Pate, "The Chickamauga: A Forgotten Segment of Indian Resistance on the Southern Frontier" (PhD diss., Mississippi State University), 247–50; Brown, *Old Frontiers*, 450–53; Finger, *Tennessee Frontiers*, 146–47, 208; Abernethy, *From Frontier to Plantation in Tennessee*, 197–207; Celia Barnes, *Native American Power in the United States, 1783–1795* (London: Associated University Presses, 2003).

51. Silas Dinsmore to Gov. John Sevier, Knoxville, March 11, 1797, "Letters of Tennessee Governors—John Sevier," MF GP-2, Reel 3, 432–37, Tennessee State Library and Archives, Nashville.

4 / The Donelsons

1. This number is based upon the genealogical information in Sam B. Smith and Harriet Chappell Owsley, eds., *The Papers of Andrew Jackson*, vol. 1, *1770–1803* (Knoxville: University of Tennessee Press, 1988), 416–22, and upon letters found in this volume from Jackson addressed to his Nashville family including Robert Hays, John Caffree, William Donelson, and John Donelson in 1797 (132, 135, 161, and 167). The birth, death, and marriage dates are corroborated by references to military and civil appointments in and around Nashville noted in William Blount, *The Blount Journal, 1790–1796: The Proceedings of Government over the Territory of the United States of America, South of the River Ohio, William Blount, Esquire, in his Executive Department as governor* (Nashville: Tennessee Historical Commission, 1955), 127–34. John Wooldridge, ed., *History of Nashville, Tennessee* (Nashville: Barbee & Smith, 1890), 95–103.

2. Robert Remini, *Andrew Jackson* (New York: Harper-Perennial, 1999), 16. Many accounts have been written on the most famous Donelson family member, Andrew Jackson, but few look closely at his relationships with his in-laws. Mark Cheathem's books *Andrew Jackson, Southerner* and *Old Hickory's Nephew: The Political and Private Struggles of Andrew Jackson Donelson* provide the most comprehensive kinship analysis in the historiography to date, illustrating the role of kinship in regional and national political success for Jackson and his kin. In Virginia Reardon's thesis "The Family and Home Life of Andrew Jackson," she examines Jackson's relationships with his wife, his adopted son, and two of his wards (Andrew Jackson Donelson and Andrew Jackson Hutchings). Robert Beeler Satterfield wrote about Jackson's relationship with Andrew Jackson Donelson, but only after Jackson's election to the presidency. Leona Taylor Aiken wrote a short history of the family in 1968 that depicts Col. John Donelson's trip on the flatboat he named the *Adventure* and then skims over his sons to discuss Jackson, John Donelson Jr., and Andrew Jackson Donelson with few

interconnections. None thoroughly explores the legal, political, and economic aspects of the early relationships between the Donelson brothers and brothers-in-law, including Jackson, during the extremely dynamic period of the first Anglo-American settlements in the Cumberland region.

3. Clayton, *History of Davidson County*, 148–49.

4. Mark R. Cheathem, *Andrew Jackson, Southerner* (Baton Rouge: Louisiana State University Press, 2013); Mark R. Cheathem, *Old Hickory's Nephew: The Political and Private Struggles of Andrew Jackson Donelson* (Baton Rouge: Louisiana State Press, 2007); Virginia Reardon, "The Family and Home Life of Andrew Jackson" (master's thesis, Vanderbilt University, 1934); R. Beeler Satterfield, *Andrew Jackson Donelson: Jackson's Confidant and Political Heir* (Bowling Green, KY: Hickory Tales, 2000); and R. Beeler Satterfield, "The Early Public Career of Andrew Jackson Donelson, 1799–1846" (master's thesis, Vanderbilt University, 1948); Leona Taylor Aiken, *Donelson, Tennessee: Its History and Landmarks* (Kingsport, TN: Kingsport Press, 1968).

5. Abernethy, *From Frontier to Plantation in Tennessee*, 40–41; Finger, *Tennessee Frontiers*, 103. These historians argue that the frontier was not the bastion of democracy and of the common man, as was touted in earlier hagiographic frontier histories, but rather that the economic and political development of such regions were largely controlled by moneyed elites who speculated heavily in western lands.

6. Ray, "Land Speculation," 6.

7. Timothy R. Marsh and Helen C. Marsh, eds., *Land Deed Genealogy of Davidson County Tennessee, 1793–1797*, 3 vols. (Greenville, SC: Southern Historical Press, 1992), 2:88–89; *Davidson County Deed Index, (A-K)*, microfilm roll A, slides c-340, c-341, and c-494, Tennessee State Library and Archives, Nashville.

8. Abernethy, *From Frontier to Plantation in Tennessee*; Friend, ed., *The Buzzel about Kentuck.*

9. Ray, "Land Speculation," 180.

10. Ibid., 168–80.

11. The histories of the development of economic and legal infrastructures in new cultural and political borderlands, like the Cumberland region, illuminate the ways in which these institutions were utilized and transformed in the process of re-forming societies in the face of cultural competition. Most works on these topics assume interplay of economy and law as people attempted to re-create the societies from which they came. Few, however, make the relationship explicit in ways that help explain how the interplay of law and economy yielded profitable relationships like those of the Donelson family. Deborah Rosen's book *Courts and Commerce: Gender, Law, and the Market Economy in Colonial New York* describes the discourse between law and economy as the colony evolved into a primarily commercial center. However, much of her work disputes that of Allan Kulikoff by engaging definitions of market and arguing that the economic interactions in the British-American colonies were not characterized by romantic communitarian values but rather by impersonal commercial interaction. Similarly, Kulikoff describes mutually exclusive "households and markets" as better representations of early American commerce than a chronological periodization of market interaction. His strict definition of "market" creates problems when applied to the trans-Appalachian frontier environment (Rosen, *Courts and Commerce: Gender, Law and the Market Economy in Colonial New York* [Columbus: Ohio State University Press, 1997]; Kulikoff, "Households and Markets: Toward a

New Synthesis of American Agrarian History," *William and Mary Quarterly* 50, no. 2 [April 1993]: 342–55). For a definition of "markets" that better fits the model of the Cumberland settlements, see Walter S. Dunn Jr., *Opening New Markets: The British Army and the Old Northwest* (London: Praeger, 2002).

12. Anita Goodstein, "Leadership on the Nashville Frontier, 1780–1800," *Tennessee Historical Quarterly* 35, no. 2 (1976): 175–98, quotation on 197.

13. Byron and Barbara Sistler, *Index to Early Tennessee Tax Lists* (Evanston, IL: Byron Sistler, 1977), 55, 90, 102, 104.

14. Mary Elizabeth Young, *Redskins, Ruffleshirts and Rednecks: Indian Allotments in Alabama and Mississippi, 1830–1860* (Norman: University of Oklahoma Press, 1961); Nina Leftwich, *Two Hundred Years at Muscle Shoals, Being an Authentic History of Colbert County, 1700–1900, With Special Emphasis on the Stirring Events of the Early Times* (Tuscumbia, AL: 1935); Clayton's *History of Davidson County*, 135.

15. Jerry K. Price, *Tennessee History of Survey and Land Law* (Kingsport, TN: Kingsport Press, 1976), 186–87. Price's book ends with the telling comment: "When I die and if I should be reincarnated, let me return as a surveyor: a worthy, fulfilling profession" (198).

16. See Marsh and Marsh, eds., *Land Deed Genealogy of Davidson County Tennessee, 1797–1803*, 3 vols.

17. Aiken, *Donelson, Tennessee*, 306; Robert E. Corlew, *Tennessee: A Short History*, 2nd ed. (Knoxville: University of Tennessee Press, 1993), 75. While familial networks were not the only social networks that knit together frontier elites, they were among the most effective and durable of those networks.

18. Marsh and Marsh, eds., *Land Deed Genealogy of Davidson County Tennessee, 1797–1803*, 3:11, emphasis added.

19. Ibid., 31, emphasis added.

20. Corlew, *Tennessee: A Short History*, 133–34; "Stockley Donelson to Andrew Jackson," ibid., 160–61.

21. Corlew, *Tennessee: A Short History*, 133–34.

22. "Andrew Jackson to Elizabeth Glasgow Donelson, June 28, 1801," in Smith and Owsley, eds., *The Papers of Andrew Jackson*, 247–48.

23. "Donelson File," Tennessee State Library and Archives, Nashville, includes newspaper articles on Stockley Donelson's plantation and the Hermitage. "Hutchings v. Mayberry, Jackson, and Miller," Superior Courts of Law and Equity for the State of Tennessee, Hamilton District, Manuscript case pleadings (Knoxville: Supreme Court Building, transcribed by Dr. Judy Cornett, 2001), Adjudicated March Term 1805, Abstracted Book 1, 13–32; "Miller v. Hutchings and Donalson," Superior Courts of Law and Equity for the State of Tennessee, Hamilton District, Manuscript case pleadings (Knoxville: Supreme Court Building, transcribed by Dr. Judy Cornett, 2001), Adjudicated September Term 1806. Abstracted Book 1, 33–35.

24. Aron, *How the West Was Lost*, 82.

25. Smith and Owsley, eds., *The Papers of Andrew Jackson*, 36–37, spelling and punctuation as in original.

26. Ibid., 38.

27. Ibid., 417.

28. "Power of Attorney to Robert Hays, December 12, 1794," in Smith and Owsley, eds., *The Papers of Andrew Jackson*, 52.

29. "Samuel Donelson to Andrew Jackson, June 29, 1795," in Smith and Owsley, eds., *The Papers of Andrew Jackson*, 62–63.

30. Clayton, *History of Davidson County*, 95–97.

31. Blount, *Blount Journal*, 41, 46, 66.

32. Ibid., 41.

33. On Stockley Donelson, see Corlew, *Tennessee: A Short History*, 93; Blount, *Journal*, 37, 99; and Aiken, *Donelson, Tennessee*, 303.

34. Remini, *Andrew Jackson*, 33.

35. Ely, *Legal Papers of Andrew Jackson*. For Donelson family members' positions with the various state and county courts, see Clayton, *History of Davidson County*, 88–93. See also Clayton, *History of Davidson County*, 95; and Smith and Owsley, eds., *The Papers of Andrew Jackson*, 414.

36. Elizabeth Perkins, *Border Life: Experience and Memory in the Revolutionary Ohio Valley* (Chapel Hill: University of North Carolina Press, 1998), 148–49.

37. Clement, *History of Pittsylvania County*, 153.

38. Corlew, *Tennessee: A Short History* 93; Blount, *Journal*, 37, 41, 99, 102; Aiken, *Donelson, Tennessee*, 303, 307.

39. Ray, "Land Speculation," 7–8, 19–21; Sheidley, "Unruly Men," 25–33, 54–57, 155–56; Blount, *Journal*, 37, 42, 46, 50–53, 56, 102; Ramsey, *Annals of Tennessee*, 365; Clayton, *History of Davidson County*, 77–83; Glover, *Southern Sons*, 152–57; Harry S. Laver, "Refuge of Manhood: Masculinity and the Militia Experience in Kentucky," in *Southern Manhood: Perspectives on Masculinity in the Old South*, ed. Craig Thompson Friend and Lorri Glover (Athens: University of Georgia Press, 2004).

40. For Col. John Donelson's role in the 1783 treaties with the Southeastern nations, see Clayton, *History of Davidson County*, 39, 42. For the roles of Andrew Jackson, John Coffee, and Daniel Smith, see Commissioner of Indian Affairs, *Treaties between the United States of America, and the Several Indian Tribes*, 108–9, 124–25, 199–201, 204–5, 208–15, 261–64, 513–27.

41. Mercantile ventures were secondary to land speculation in the Donelson family economic strategies (Smith and Owsley, eds., *The Papers of Andrew Jackson*, 34, 54, 58, 62, 92–94).

42. See "Andrew Jackson to Robert Hays, November 2, 1797," in Smith and Owsley, eds., *Papers of Andrew Jackson*, 151; and "Andrew Jackson to Robert Hays, January 12, 1798," ibid., 165–66.

43. Aiken, *Donelson, Tennessee*, 78–79.

44. Smith and Owsley, eds., *The Papers of Andrew Jackson*, 331–32n.

45. Cheathem, *Andrew Jackson, Southerner*; Cheathem, *Andrew Jackson Donelson*; Reardon, "The Family and Home Life of Andrew Jackson"; Satterfield, *Andrew Jackson Donelson*.

5 / Family Strategies and "Civilization"

1. Historians have recently given significant attention to the effects of these transitions of territorial claims and the impact that had on the peoples that lived in the Gulf coastal, lower Mississippi Valley, and trans-Mississippian regions, especially regarding self-definitions of identity and political alliances (see Gene Allen Smith and Sylvia L. Hilton, eds., *Nexus of Empire: Negotiating Loyalty and Identity in the Revolutionary Borderlands, 1760s-1820s* [Gainesville: University Press of Florida, 2010]; Jon Kukla,

A Wilderness So Immense: The Louisiana Purchase and the Destiny of America [New York: Knopf, 2003]; and Richmond F. Brown, *Coastal Encounters: The Transformation of the Gulf South in the Eighteenth Century* [Lincoln: University of Nebraska Press, 2007]). For works that extend this analysis to the American Southwest, see Patrick G. Williams, S. Charles Bolton, and Jeannie M. Whayne, eds., *A Whole Country in Commotion: The Louisiana Purchase and the American Southwest* (Fayetteville: University of Arkansas Press, 2005); and Jesús F. de la Teja and Ross Frank, eds., *Choice, Persuasion, and Coercion: Social Control on Spain's North American Frontiers* (Albuquerque: University of New Mexico Press, 2005).

2. See Paul E. Hoffman, *Florida's Frontiers* (Bloomington: Indiana University Press, 2002); and Jane Landers, *Black Society in Spanish Florida* (Urbana: University of Illinois Press, 1999).

3. Craig, "The Colberts in Chickasaw History," 112–6l; "Oral History: Malcolm McGee, Chickasaw Interpreter," *Journal of Chickasaw History* 4, no. 4 (1998): 6. The historical record presents overwhelming evidence that the Colberts played an important role in diplomacy for the Chickasaw nation with the United States, from negotiating treaties to serving among those Chickasaws charged with choosing the location of the lands the Chickasaws would accept in Indian Territory. Still, the extant sources were mostly written from the perspective of American observers and participants. McGee's source hints at the different perspective that other sources might have corroborated if other voices had been recorded.

4. William P. Anderson, "Letter [manuscript]: Nashville, [Tenn.], to George W. Campbell, Washington City, 1809 Jan. 9," Vault Box Ayer MS 20, Newberry Library, Chicago, spelling, grammar, and punctuation as in original.

5. Samuel Mitchell to Henry Dearborn, August 26, 1802, Doc. 106, Box 89, Series 488, Mississippi Department of Archives and History, Jackson.

6. Samuel Mitchell to William Claiborne, January 23, 1803, Doc. 138, Box 166818, Series 488, Mississippi Department of Archives and History .

7. Ibid.

8. Samuel Mitchell to William Claiborne, May 28, 1803, Doc. 164, Box 100, Series 488, Mississippi Department of Archives and History .

9. William McLoughlin, *Cherokee Renascence in the New Republic* (Princeton: Princeton University Press, 1986), 109.

10. Ibid., 109–10.

11. Robert A. Myers, "Cherokee Pioneers in Arkansas: The St. Francis Years, 1785–1813," *Arkansas Historical Quarterly* 56 (Summer 1997): 127–57.

12. David Andrew Nichols, *Red Gentlemen and White Savages: Indians, Federalists, and the Search for Order on the American Frontier* (Charlottesville: University of Virginia Press, 2008); Reginald Horsman, "The Indian Policy of an 'Empire of Liberty,'" in *Native Americans and the Early Republic*, ed. Frederick E. Hoxie, Ronald Hoffman, and Peter J. Albert (Charlottesville: University Press of Virginia, 1999), 37–61.

13. Robert Troup to Peter Van Schaack, May 2, 1800, qtd. in Nobel E. Cunningham Jr., *Jefferson vs. Hamilton: Confrontations That Shaped a Nation* (Baltimore: Bedford/St. Martin's Press, 2000), 127.

14. Roger G. Kennedy, *Mr. Jefferson's Lost Cause: Land, Farmers, Slavery, and the Louisiana Purchase* (New York: Oxford University Press, 2003).

15. Thomas Jefferson to Benjamin Hawkins, March 14, 1800, in *Thomas Jefferson Papers*, Library of Congress Online. Jefferson's fascination with Indian cultures also led him to encourage Meriwether Lewis and William Clark to keep detailed accounts of their meetings with trans-Mississippi Indians on their exploration of the Louisiana Purchase.

16. Roger G. Kennedy, *Mr. Jefferson's Lost Cause: Land, Farmers, Slavery, and the Louisiana Purchase* (New York: Oxford University Press, 2003); John Freeman, *A Guide to the Manuscripts Relating to the American Indian in the Library of the American Philosophical Society* (Philadelphia: American Philosophical Society, 1966); Daythal Kendall, *A Supplement to A Guide to the Manuscripts Relating to the American Indian in the Library of the American Philosophical Society* (Philadelphia: American Philosophical Society, 1982).

17. Thomas Jefferson to Congress, January 18, 1803, in *Thomas Jefferson Papers*, Library of Congress Online.

18. Calloway, *American Revolution in Indian Country*; Braund, *Deerskins and Duffels*; Saunt, *A New Order of Things*.

19. Deloria and DeMallie, eds., *Documents of American Indian Diplomacy*, 34–38.

20. Benjamin Hawkins, "Journal of the Commissioner of the United States," Vault Ayer MS 3180, p. 74, Newberry Library, Chicago.

21. Tisshamastubbe, "A Talk from the King Chiefs and Warriors of the Chickasaw Nation to the Secretary of War, delivered by Tisshamastubbe, Speaker for the Chickasaws," Doc. 123, Box 89, Series 488, Mississippi Department of Archives and History, Jackson.

22. S. Mitchell, Chickasaw Agency, to Henry Dearborn, [August] 26, 1802, Doc. 106, Box 89, Series 488, Mississippi Department of Archives and History, Jackson.

23. Thomas McKenney qtd. in Wilkins, *Cherokee Tragedy*, 33.

24. Andrew K. Frank, *Creeks and Southerners: Biculturalism on the Early American Frontier* (Lincoln: University of Nebraska Press, 2005); Barbara Krauthamer, *Black Slaves, Indian Masters: Slavery, Emancipation, and Citizenship in the Native American South* (Chapel Hill: University of North Carolina Press, 2013); Tiya Miles, *The House on Diamond Hill: A Cherokee Plantation Story* (Chapel Hill: University of North Carolina Press, 2010); Tiya Miles, *Ties That Bind: The Story of an Afro-Cherokee Family in Slavery and Freedom* (Berkeley: University of California Press, 2005).

25. Sheidley, "Unruly Men"; Daniel Barr, *The Boundaries Between Us: Natives and Newcomers along the Boundaries of the Frontier of the Old Northwest Territory, 1750–1850* (Kent, OH: Kent State University Press, 2006); Perdue, *"Mixed Blood" Indians*.

26. Sheidley, "Unruly Men." See also Christina Snyder, *Slavery in Indian Country: The Changing Face of Captivity in America* (Cambridge: Harvard University Press, 2010).

27. Alan Gallay, *Indian Slavery*; Perdue, *Cherokee Women*; Saunt, *A New Order of Things*.

28. Commissioner of Indian Affairs, *Treaties between the United States of America, and the Several Indian Tribes*, 83–84, 116–18, 201–4.

29. Deloria and DeMallie, eds., *Documents of American Indian Diplomacy*, 116.

30. Ibid.

31. Benjamin Hawkins, "Journal of the Commissioner of the United States," Vault Box Ayers MS 3180, pp. 15–16, Newberry Library, Chicago.

32. Richard White, "The Fictions of Patriarchy: Indians and Whites in the Early Republic," in *Native Americans and the Early Republic*, ed. Frederick E. Hoxie, Ronald Hoffman, and Peter J. Albert (Charlottesville: University Press of Virginia, 1999), 62–84. White disputes Michael Paul Rogin's uncomplicated definition of patriarchal language in *Fathers and Children: Andrew Jackson and the Subjugation of the American Indian* (New York: Knopf, 1975). White argued that Rogin failed to take into account native usages of that same language (White, "Fictions of Patriarchy," 67). See Sheidley, "Unruly Men."

33. Cynthia Cumfer argues that during this period Cherokees intentionally weakened their diplomatic kinship ties by referring to officials as "friends and brothers" (Cumfer, *Separate Peoples, One Land*, 89). However, these Cherokee and Chickasaw families appeared to make concerted efforts to strengthen their ties to the United States while maintaining the maximum possible autonomy.

34. John Sevier to Return J. Meigs, "Permit for Adam Peck to buy provisions for his party cutting the road," November 2, 1804, UTK MS 368, University of Tennessee Special Collections.

35. United States Senate, "A Treaty of Reciprocal Advantages and mutual convenience between the United States of America and the Chickasaws," December 29, 1801, *American State Papers*, online; Samuel Mitchell to William Claiborne, August 15, 1803, Doc. 176, Box 16618, Series 488, Mississippi Department of Archives and History, spelling as in original.

36. William Meadows, "Enclosure: Report of William Meadows," April 18, 1808, in *Andrew Jackson Papers*, 2:193–94.

37. George Lavender, "Certificate in Relation to the Value of Major Ridge's Ferry," Jan. 23, 1837, MS 2033, Box 1, Folder 147, Penelope Allen Papers, University of Tennessee Special Collections. This document also estimates that John Ross's Ferry at the junction of Hightown and Eustinale brought a similar income.

38. George Graham to Andrew Jackson, August 5, 1816, in "A Century of Lawmaking for a New Nation: US Congressional Documents and Debates," Library of Congress Online.

39. James Colbert and Turner Brashears to The Commissioners of the Chickasaw and Choctaw Nations, appointed by the President of the United States to Treat with the Said Nations, October 18, 1816, in "A Century of Lawmaking for a New Nation: US Congressional Documents and Debates," Library of Congress Online.

40. On American Indian strategies of economic diversification strategies, see Dan Usner, "Iroquois Livelihood and Jeffersonian Agrarianism: Reaching behind the Models and Metaphors," in *Native Americans and the Early Republic*, ed. Frederick E. Hoxie, Ronald Hoffman, and Peter J. Albert (Charlottesville: University Press of Virginia, 1999), 200–225.

41. See Elise Marienstras, "The Common Man's Indian: The Image of the Indian as a Promoter of National Identity in the Early National Era," in *Native Americans and the Early Republic*, ed. Frederick E. Hoxie, Ronald Hoffman, and Peter J. Albert (Charlottesville: University Press of Virginia, 1999), 261–96.

6 / Creek War Family Networks

1. Alan Taylor, *The Civil War of 1812: American Citizens, British Subjects, Irish Rebels, and Indian Allies* (New York: Vintage, 2011); Donald R. Hickey, *The War of 1812:*

A Forgotten Conflict (Chicago: University of Illinois Press, 2012); Kathryn E. Holland Braund, *Tohopeka: Rethinking the Creek War and the War of 1812* (Auburn, AL: Pebble Hill, 2012); Tom Kanon, *Tennesseans at War, 1812–1815: Andrew Jackson, the Creek War, and the Battle of New Orleans* (Tuscaloosa: University of Alabama Press, 2014); and Robert V. Haynes, *The Mississippi Territory and the Southwest Frontier, 1795–1817* (Lexington: University Press of Kentucky, 2010).

2. Return J. Meigs, "From R. J. Meigs, Cherokee Agent," Hiwasee, May 8th, 1812, in "A Century of Lawmaking for a New Nation: US Congressional Documents and Debates," Library of Congress Online, *American State Papers, Indian Affairs*, 1:809; Susan M. Abram, "'To Keep Bright the Bonds of Friendship': The Making of a Cherokee-American Alliance during the Creek War," *Tennessee Historical Quarterly* 71, no. 3 (Fall 2012): 228–57, quotation on 236.

3. Robert Remini, *The Battle of New Orleans* (New York: Viking, 1999); Colonel David Fitz-Enz, *Redcoats' Revenge: An Alternate History of the War of 1812* (Washington: Potomac Books, 2008); Eugene M. Wait, *America and the War of 1812* (Commack, NY: Kroshka Books, 1999); David S. Heidler and Jeanne T. Heidler, *Old Hickory's War: Andrew Jackson and the Quest for Empire* (Baton Rouge: Louisiana State University Press, 2003); Robert P. Wettemann Jr., *Privilege vs. Equality: Civil-Military Relations in in the Jacksonian Era, 1815–1845* (Santa Barbara, CA: Praeger, 2009); Robert V. Remini, *Andrew Jackson and His Indian Wars* (New York: Viking, 2001). For printed primary accounts of the War of 1812, see Nathaniel Herbert Claiborne, *Notes on the War in the South; With Biographical Sketches of the Lives of Montgomery, Jackson, Sevier, the Late Gov. Claiborne, and Others* (Richmond: William Ramsay, 1819); and Arsène Lacarrière Latour, *Historical Memoir of the War in West Florida and Louisiana in 1814–15, With an Atlas*, expanded ed., ed. Gene A. Smith (Gainesville: University Press of Florida, 1999). John Reid and John Henry Eaton first published *The Life of Andrew Jackson* in 1817, which provided both an authorized biography of Jackson and an account of the war that made him famous (Reid and Eaton, *The Life of Andrew Jackson, Major General in the service of the United States Comprising a History of the War in the South, From the Commencement of the Creek Campaign, to the Termination of Hostilities Before New Orleans*, ed. Frank L. Owsley Jr. [University: University of Alabama Press, 1974]).

4. Michael A. Bellesiles, "Experiencing the War of 1812," in *Britain and America Go to War: The Impact of War & Warfare in Anglo-America, 1754–1815*, ed. Julie Flavell and Stephen Conway (Gainesville: University Press of Florida, 2004), 227.

5. Halbert and Ball, *Creek War*, 41; McLoughlin, *Cherokee Renaissance*, 187. For more on Tecumseh, see John Sugden, *Tecumseh's Last Stand* (Norman: University of Oklahoma Press, 1985); Gregory A. Waselkov, *A Conquering Spirit: Fort Mims and the Redstick War of 1813–1814* (Tuscaloosa: University of Alabama Press, 2006); H. S. Halbert and T. H. Ball, *The Creek War of 1813 and 1814*, ed. Frank L. Owsley Jr. (University: University of Alabama Press, 1969); and George Cary Eggleston, *Red Eagle and the Wars with the Creek Indians of Alabama* (1878; repr., New York: Dodd, Mead, 1980).

6. Atkinson, *Splendid Land, Splendid People*, 201–3.

7. McLoughlin, *Cherokee Renaissance*, 191–92.

8. Penelope Johnson Allen Papers, Folders 9–10, Box 1, UTKMS 2033.

9. *Andrew Jackson Papers*, 3:8.

10. Reid, *Life of Andrew Jackson*, 128.

11. *Andrew Jackson Papers*, 2:379.

12. Ibid., 2:459.

13. Ibid., 2:444.

14. Ibid., 2:397.

15. Ibid., 3:45.

16. Ephraim Foster to George Graham, April 8, 1814, Document GLC2804, Gilder Lehrman Collection.

17. *Andrew Jackson Papers*, 3:54.

18. Remini, *Battle of New Orleans*, 97.

19. Atkinson, *Splendid Land, Splendid People*, 201–3. Historian Arrell Gibson argues that following the Creek War the Colberts' diplomatic negotiations were key to the loss of Chickasaw lands: "General Jackson accepted Colbert family power as the most strategic element in Chickasaw negotiations and bragged that he knew how to manage them. His formula was 'touching their interest, and feeding their avarice'" (Gibson, *Chickasaws*, 100). While historians agree that the Colberts played an important role in the diplomatic relationship between the Chickasaws and the United States before and after the War of 1812, they disagree over whether that role ultimately produced more positive or negative outcomes for the Chickasaws.

20. William Barnett, Benjamin Hawkins, and Edmund P. Gaines, Survey Commission of John Coffee, Fort Hawkins, February 9, 1816, Folder 1, Box 1, Dyas Collection of the John Coffee Papers, Heard Library, Vanderbilt University, Microfilm 3113; Edmund P. Gaines to John Coffee, November 28, 1815, Folder 1, Box 1, ibid.; Receipt of payment to George Black for provisioning survey crew, January 27, 1816, and Receipt of Samuel Gordon, March 16, 1816, Folder 2, Box 1, ibid.

21. Heidel, *Old Hickory's War*, 45–48.

22. William Russell to John Coffee, May 8, 1816, Folder 2, Box 1, Dyas Collection of the John Coffee Papers, Heard Library, Vanderbilt University, Microfilm 3113.

23. Charles C. Royce, *The Cherokee Nation*, ed. Richard Mack Bettis (Washington, DC: Native American Library, 2007), 79.

24. William Barnett to John Coffee, June 7, 1816, Folder 2, Box 1, Dyas Collection of the John Coffee Papers, Heard Library, Vanderbilt University, Microfilm 3113.

25. John Coffee to the Secretary of War, July 25, 1816, Folder 2, Box 1, Dyas Collection of the John Coffee Papers, Vanderbilt University, Microfilm 3113.

26. James Colbert to Andrew Jackson, July 17, 1816, in "A Century of Lawmaking for a New Nation: US Congressional Documents and Debates," Library of Congress Online.

27. William Cocke to John Coffee, July 20, 1816, Folder 2, Box 1, Dyas Collection of the John Coffee Papers, Heard Library, Vanderbilt University, Microfilm 3113.

28. Commissioner of Indian Affairs, *Treaties between the United States of America and the Several Indian Tribes*, 185–204.

29. Andrew Jackson, D. Meriwether, and J. Franklin to William H. Crawford, September 20, 1816, in "A Century of Lawmaking for a New Nation: US Congressional Documents and Debates," Library of Congress Online.

30. Andrew Jackson to William H. Crawford, November 12, 1816, in "A Century of Lawmaking for a New Nation: US Congressional Documents and Debates," Library of Congress Online.

31. Andrew Jackson, D. Meriwether, and J. Franklin to William H. Crawford, September 20, 1816, in "A Century of Lawmaking for a New Nation: US Congressional Documents and Debates," Library of Congress Online.

32. Commissioner of Indian Affairs, *Treaties between the United States of America and the Several Indian Tribes*, 202–3.

33. Ibid., 201–4; Gibson, *The Chickasaws*, 76–162.

34. Commissioner of Indian Affairs, *Treaties between the United States of America and the Several Indian Tribes*, 209–15.

35. Ibid.

36. Ibid., 215; S. Charles Bolton, "Jeffersonian Indian Removal and the Emergence of Arkansas Territory," *Arkansas Historical Quarterly* 62, no. 3 (Autumn 2003): 253–71; Stephen Bragaw, "Thomas Jefferson and the American Indian Nations: Native American Sovereignty and the Marshall Court," *Journal of Supreme Court History* 31, no. 2 (2006): 155–80.

37. Daniel H. Usner Jr., *American Indians in the Lower Mississippi Valley: Social and Economic Histories* (Lincoln: University of Nebraska Press, 1998), 73–110.

7 / Kinship Networks and Evolving Concepts of Nationhood

1. Nancy Ward, "Petition of Cherokee Women," June 30, 1818, reproduced in Perdue and Green, *Cherokee Removal*, 133; Sturgis, *Trail of Tears*, 96–97, spelling, grammar, and punctuation as in original.

2. Nancy Ward, Petition of Cherokee Women, May 2, 1817, qtd. in Perdue, *Cherokee Removal*, 131–32.

3. Nancy Ward, Petition of Cherokee Women, June 30, 1818, qtd. in Perdue, *Cherokee Removal*, 133.

4. Tiya Miles, "'Circular Reasoning': Recentering Cherokee Women in the Anti-Removal Campaigns," *American Quarterly* 61, no. 2 (June 2009): 221–43; Mary Hershberger, "Mobilizing Women, Anticipating Abolition: The Struggle against Indian Removal in the 1830s," *Journal of American History* 86, no. 1 (June 1999): 15–40.

5. Carolyn Thomas Foreman, "Charity Hall: An Early Chickasaw School," *Chronicles of Oklahoma* 11, no. 3 (September 1933): 912–26; S. J. Carr, "Bloomfield Academy and Its Founder," *Chronicles of Oklahoma* 2:4 (December 1924): 366–79.

6. Andrew Jackson to Isaac Shelby, August 11, 1818, in *Andrew Jackson Papers*, 4:234–35,

7. Remini, *Andrew Jackson and His Indian Wars*, 56; Rogin, *Fathers and Children*, 113–250.

8. James W. Parins, *John Rollin Ridge: His Life and Works* (Lincoln: University of Nebraska Press, 1991); Cheryl Walker, *Indian Nation: Native American Literature and Nineteenth-Century Nationalisms* (Durham: Duke University Press, 1997), 111–38.

9. James W. Parins, *Elias Cornelius Boudinot: A Life on the Cherokee Border* (Lincoln: University of Nebraska Press, 2006), 22–23.

10. Ibid., 32; Bernard Feder, "The Ridge Family and the Death of a Nation," *American West* 15, no. 5 (October 1978): 28–31, 61–63.

11. Theda Perdue, ed., *Cherokee Editor: The Writings of Elias Boudinot* (Knoxville: University of Tennessee Press, 1983); Ralph Henry Gabriel, *Elias Boudinot Cherokee & His America* (Norman: University of Oklahoma Press, 1941); Theresa Strouth Gaul, *To Marry an Indian: The Marriage of Harriett Gold & Elias Boudinot in Letters, 1823–1839*

(Chapel Hill: University of North Carolina Press, 2005); Edward Everett Dale and Gaston Litton, *Cherokee Cavaliers: Forty Years of Cherokee History as Told in the Correspondence of the Ridge-Watie-Boudinot Family* (Norman: University of Oklahoma Press, 1939).

12. H. S. Gold to General D. B. Brinsmade, May 22, 1830, MS 2033, Folder 19, Box 2, Penelope Johnson Allen Papers, Special Collection Library, University of Tennessee, Knoxville.

13. Reproductions of the *Cherokee Phoenix* are available online at www.wcu.edu/library/CherokeePhoenix/. The paper has also been reincarnated by the Cherokee Nation of Oklahoma; recent editions are available in print and online at www.cherokeephoenix.org/.

14. Margaret Bender, *Signs of Cherokee Culture: Sequoyah's syllabary and Eastern Cherokee Life* (Chapel Hill: University of North Carolina Press, 2002); Grant Foreman, *Sequoyah* (1938; Norman: University of Oklahoma Press, 1973); Maureen Konkle, "Sequoyah, Cherokee Antiquarians, and Progress," in *Writing Indian Nations: Native Intellectuals and the Politics of Historiography, 1827-1863* (Chapel Hill: University of North Carolina Press, 2004), 78–96.

15. Bragaw, "Thomas Jefferson," 155–80.

16. Elias Boudinott, *An Address to the Whites Delivered in the First Presbyterian Church on the 26th of May, 1826* (Philadelphia: William F. Geddes, 1826), quotation on 3, Folder 1679, Box 586.2-2329.1, Phillips Pamphlet Collection, Western History Collection, University of Oklahoma.

17. Hershberger, "Mobilizing Women," 18.

18. Grant Foreman, *Indian Removal: The Emigration of the Five Civilized Tribes of Indians*, new ed. (Norman: University of Oklahoma, 1953); Brown, *Old Frontiers*; Paula Mitchell Marks, *In a Barren Land: American Indian Dispossession and Survival* (New York: William Morrow, 1998); Remini, *Andrew Jackson and His Indian Wars*; Perdue, *The Cherokee Removal*; Amy H. Sturgis, *The Trail of Tears and Indian Removal* (Westport, CT: Greenwood Press, 2007); Claudia B. Haake, *The State, Removal, and Indigenous Peoples in the United States and Mexico, 1620-2000* (New York: Routledge, 2007); Jason Meyers, "No Idle Past: Uses of History in the 1830 Indian Removal Debates," *Historian* (2001): 53–65.

19. *Andrew Jackson Papers*, 4:284–85, 285n4.

20. Rogin, *Fathers and Children*, 175.

21. Ibid.

22. Andrew Jackson to John Coffee, December 22, 1827, in *Andrew Jackson Papers*, 6:405–6.

23. Helen C. and Timothy R. Marsh, *Davidson County Tennessee Wills and Inventories*, vol. 2: *1816-1830* (Greenville, SC: Southern Historical Press, 1989), 74.

24. Andrew Jackson to John Coffee, October 12, 1825, in *Andrew Jackson Papers*, 6:107.

25. Andrew Jackson to John Coffee, January 5, 1825, in *Andrew Jackson Papers*, 6:5–6.

26. Andrew Jackson to William Donelson, March 22, 1829, in *Andrew Jackson Papers*, 7:109–10.

27. Ibid.

28. "Memorial of a Delegation from the Cherokee Indians, January 18, 1831, Folder 7311, Box 7282-7311, Phillips Pamphlet Collection, Western History Collection, University of Oklahoma, Norman.

29. Peter P. Pitchlynn, Journal, November 28, 1828, Box 5, Peter P. Pitchlynn Collection, Western History Collection, University of Oklahoma, Norman.

30. Theda Perdue and Michael Greene, *The Cherokee Removal: A Brief History with Documents*, 2nd ed. (Boston: Bedford/St. Martin's Press, 2005); Edward Everett Dale and Gaston Litton, *Cherokee Cavaliers: Forty Years of Cherokee History as Told in the Correspondence of the Ridge-Watie-Boudinot Family* (Norman: University of Oklahoma Press, 1995); Thurman Wilkins, *Cherokee Tragedy: The Ridge Family and the Decimation of a People*, 2nd ed. (Norman: University of Oklahoma Press, 1986).

31. United States Congress, "Indian Removal Act," May 28, 1830, published in Perdue, *Cherokee Removal*, 123; Alfred A. Cave, "Abuse of Power: Andrew Jackson and the Indian Removal Act of 1830," *Historian* 65, no. 6 (2003): 1330–53; Anthony F. C. Wallace, *The Long Bitter Trail: Andrew Jackson and the Indians* (New York: Hill and Wang, 1993), 50–72.

32. Young, *Redskins, Ruffleshirts and Rednecks*.

33. Foreman, *Indian Removal*, 202.

34. Ibid., 221–23.

35. Jesse Burt and Bob Ferguson, *Indians in the Southeast: Then and Now* (New York: Abingdon Press, 1973), 147–50.

36. Gibson, *Chickasaws*, 226, 249–80; John Bartlett Meserve, "Governor Daugherty (Winchester) Colbert," *Chronicles of Oklahoma* 18, no. 4 (December 1940): 348–56.

37. Commissioner of Indian Affairs, *Treaties between the United States of America and the Several Indian Tribes*, 633–45.

38. Perdue, *Cherokee Removal*, 167.

39. Sturgis, *Trail of Tears*, 2, 60. The population and mortality statistics vary according to which historian one cites. Sturgis is among the most recent historians to cover Indian Removal and has the most recent data on the subject.

40. Cherokee National Council, "Constitution of the Cherokee Nation: Formed by a Convention of Delegates from the Several Districts at New Echota, July 1827," printed in *Laws of the Cherokee Nation* (1852; repr., New York: Gryphon Editions, 1995), 118–30.

41. John Ross to Matthew Arbuckle, June 24, 1839, Document GLC06741.01, Gilder Lehrman Collection, New York.

42. Benjamin L. Bonneville to unknown recipient, July 22, 1839, Document GLC01233.06, Gilder Lehrman Collection, New York.

43. Clarissa Confer, *The Cherokee Nation in the Civil War* (Norman: University of Oklahoma Press, 2007); Fay A. Yarbrough, *Race and the Cherokee Nation: Sovereignty in the Nineteenth Century* (Philadelphia: University of Pennsylvania Press, 2008); Dale and Litton, *Cherokee Cavaliers*, 98–228; Frank Cunningham, *General Stand Watie's Confederate Indians* (Norman: University of Oklahoma Press, 1998); Mabel Washburn Anderson, *Life of General Stand Watie: The Only Indian Brigadier General of the Confederate Army and the Last General to Surrender* (Pryor, OK: Mayes County Republican, 1915).

44. Pauline Wilcox Burke, *Emily Donelson of Tennessee*, ed. Jonathan M. Atkins (Knoxville: University of Tennessee Press, 2001).

45. Robert Remini, *Andrew Jackson*, 124–32, quotation on 126; John Marszalek, *The Petticoat Affair: Manners, Mutiny, and Sex in Andrew Jackson's White House* (New York: Free Press, 1997); Cheathem, *Old Hickory's Nephew*, 60–120.

46. Andrew Jackson to Eliza Fauquier, August 28, 1832, Philadelphia, Autographed Letter Signed, Document GLC07464, Gilder Lehrman Collection, spelling, punctuation, and grammar as in original.

47. Ibid.; Smith and Owsley, eds., *Papers of Andrew Jackson*, 421.

48. Andrew Jackson to R. W. Latham, December 28, 1843, Document GLC03423, Gilder Lehrman Collection, New York.

49. Cheathem, *Old Hickory's Nephew*, 299; Anna Ella Carroll, *The Great American Battle: or The Contest between Christianity and Political Romanism* (New York: Miller, Orton, & Mulligan, 1856).

50. Theda Perdue and Michael D. Green, *The Cherokee Removal: A Brief History with Documents* (New York: Bedford/St. Martin's Press, 2005), 115–16.

Conclusion

1. Informal Interview with Glenda Galvan, Chickasaw Tribal Library, Ada, OK, July 20, 2005.

2. Ibid. Definition courtesy of the United States National Park Service at www.nps.gov/nagpra.

3. Amanda L. Paige, Fuller L. Bumpers, Daniel F. Littlefield, Jr., *Chickasaw Removal* (Ada, OK: Chickasaw Press, 2010); Julie L. Reed, "Family and Nation: Cherokee Orphan Care, 1835–1903," *American Indian Quarterly* 34, no. 3 (Summer 2010); Wendy St. Jean, *Remaining Chickasaw in Indian Territory, 1830s to 1907* (Tuscaloosa: University of Alabama Press, 2011); Carolyn Ross Johnston, *Cherokee Women in Crisis: Trail of Tears, Civil War, and Allotment, 1838–1907* (Birmingham: University of Alabama Press, 2003).

4. Brenda J. Child, *Boarding School Seasons: American Indian Families, 1900–1940* (Lincoln: University of Nebraska Press, 1988); Cathleen D. Cahill, *Federal Fathers and Mothers: A Social History of the United States Indian Service, 1869–1933* (Chapel Hill: University of North Carolina Press, 2011); Fay A. Yarbrough, *Race and the Cherokee Nation: Sovereignty in the Nineteenth Century* (Philadelphia: University of Pennsylvania Press, 2008); Rose Stremlau, *Sustaining the Cherokee Family: Kinship and the Allotment of an Indigenous Nation* (Chapel Hill: University of North Carolina Press, 2011).

5. Hudson, *The Southeastern Indians*.

6. Thurman Wilkins, *Cherokee Tragedy: The Ridge Family and the Decimation of a People*, 2nd ed. (Norman: University of Oklahoma Press, 1986).

7. John Donelson III's obituary is available at www.legacy.com/obituaries/tennessean/obituary.aspx?n=john-donelson&pid=139305061. For the article on the Dickenson reburial, see www.newschannel5.com/global/story.asp?s=12713217. For more on Jackson VI, see www.knoxnews.com/news/2010/mar/21/andrew-jackson-vi-has-fun-with-famous-name/.

Index

EARLY AMERICAN PLACES

On Slavery's Border: Missouri's Small Slaveholding Households, 1815–1865
by Diane Mutti Burke

Sounding America: Identity and the Music Culture of the Lower Mississippi River Valley, 1800–1860
by Ann Ostendorf

The Year of the Lash: Free People of Color in Cuba and the Nineteenth-Century Atlantic World
by Michele Reid-Vazquez

Ordinary Lives in the Early Caribbean: Religion, Colonial Competition, and the Politics of Profit
by Kirsten Block

Creolization and Contraband: Curaçao in the Early Modern Atlantic World
by Linda M. Rupert

An Empire of Small Places: Mapping the Southeastern Anglo-Indian Trade, 1732–1795
by Robert Paulett

Everyday Life and the Construction of Difference in the Early English Caribbean
by Jenny Shaw

Natchez Country: Indians, Colonists, and the Landscapes of Race in French Louisiana
by George Edward Milne

Slavery, Childhood, and Abolition in Jamaica, 1788–1838
by Colleen A. Vasconcellos

Privateers of the Americas: Spanish American Privateering from the United States in the Early Republic
by David Head

Charleston and the Emergence of Middle-Class Culture in the Revolutionary Era
by Jennifer L. Goloboy

Anglo-Native Virginia: Trade, Conversion, and Indian Slavery in the Old Dominion, 1646–1722
by Kristalyn Marie Shefveland

Slavery on the Periphery: The Kansas-Missouri Border in the Antebellum and Civil War Eras
by Kristen Epps

In the Shadow of Dred Scott: *St. Louis Freedom Suits and the Legal Culture of Slavery in Antebellum America*
by Kelly M. Kennington

Brothers and Friends: Kinship in Early America
by Natalie R. Inman

George Washington's Washington: Visions for the National Capital in the Early American Republic
by Adam Costanzo

Borderless Empire: Dutch Guiana in the Atlantic World, 1750–1800
by Brian Hoonhout

CPSIA information can be obtained
at www.ICGtesting.com
Printed in the USA
LVHW090349280220
648294LV00004BA/487